Multimedia
Concepts
Illustrated Introductory

James E. Shuman

**COURSE
TECHNOLOGY** ™

THOMSON LEARNING

Australia • Canada • Mexico • Singapore • Spain • United Kingdom • United States

COURSE TECHNOLOGY
THOMSON LEARNING

**Multimedia Concepts—
Illustrated Introductory**

by James E. Shuman

Managing Editor:
Nicole Jones Pinard

Development Editor:
Pam Conrad

Product Manager:
Rebecca Berardy

Associate Product Manager:
Emeline Elliot

Editorial Assistant:
Danielle Roy

Production Editor:
Elena Montillo

Marketing Manager:
Sean Teare

Manufacturing Coordinator:
Alec Schall

QA Manuscript Reviewer:
Jeff Schwartz, Ashlee Welz

Text Designer:
Joseph Lee, Black Fish Design

Cover Designer:
Doug Goodman, Doug Goodman
Designs

Composition House:
GEX Publishing Services

COPYRIGHT © 2001 Course Technology, a division of Thomson Learning, Inc. Thomson Learning™ is a trademark used herein under license.

Printed in the United States of America

2 3 4 5 6 7 8 9 BM 04 03 02 01

For more information, contact Course Technology, 25 Thomson Place, Boston, Massachusetts, 02210.

Or find us on the World Wide Web at: www.course.com

ALL RIGHTS RESERVED. No part of this work covered by the copyright hereon may be reproduced or used in any form or by any means—graphic, electronic, or mechanical, including photocopying, recording, taping, Web distribution, or information storage and retrieval systems—without the written permission of the publisher.

For permission to use material from this text or product, contact us by
Tel (800) 730-2214
Fax (800) 730-2215
www.thomsonrights.com

Disclaimer
Course Technology reserves the right to revise this publication and make changes from time to time in its content without notice.

RealNetworks and RealAudio are trademarks or registered trademarks of RealNetworks.

Macromedia Authorware, Director, Flash, Lingo, and Shockwave are registered trademarks of Macromedia, Inc., 600 Townsend Street, San Francisco, CA, 94103, USA. All rights reserved.

WebCT is a trademark of WebCT, Inc. Freddi Fish and Putt-Putt are trademarks of Humongous Entertainment, Inc.

Figure C-18: Courtesy of WebCT, Inc.

Figure E-3: Freddi Fish—Courtesy of Humongous Entertainment, Inc.

Figure E-4: Thaddeus Pole—Courtesy of Microsoft Corp.

Figure E-13: Courtesy of Sue Willoughby

Figure E-14: Courtesy of Corbis, Inc.

Figure F-1: Putt-Putt—Courtesy of Humongous Entertainment, Inc.

Figure F-1: Musical Instruments—Courtesy of Microsoft Corp.

ISBN 0-619-01765-1

Exciting New Products

Master Microsoft Office 2000

Multimedia tools teach students how to create text, graphics, video, animations, and sound, all of which can be incorporated for use in printed materials, Web pages, CD-ROMs, and multimedia presentations.

New Titles
- ▶ Adobe Photoshop 5.5—Illustrated Introductory (0-7600-6337-0)
- ▶ Adobe Photoshop 6.0—Illustrated Introductory (0-619-04595-7)
- ▶ Adobe Illustrator 9.0—Illustrated Introductory (0-619-01750-3)
- ▶ Macromedia Director 8 Shockwave Studio—Illustrated Introductory (0-619-01772-4)
- ▶ Macromedia Director 8 Shockwave Studio—Illustrated Complete (0-619-05658-4)
- ▶ Macromedia Shockwave 8—Illustrated Essentials (0-619-05656-8)
- ▶ Macromedia Fireworks 4—Illustrated Essentials (0-619-05657-6)

Check out E-Commerce Concepts—Illustrated Introductory

E-commerce Concepts—Illustrated Introductory, by Carol M. Cram, the quick and visual way to learn today's cutting-edge e-commerce topics. Designed to teach students to explore and evaluate e-commerce technologies, sites, and issues, E-Commerce Concepts combines concepts with exploratory exercises. The goal of the text is to encourage students to develop critical thinking skills and to tailor their exploration of e-commerce to suit their individual interests. In addition, a continually updated Student Online Companion allows students to explore relevant sites and articles, ensuring a complete and current learning experience.

Enhance any Illustrated Text with these Exciting Products

Course Technology offers a continuum of solutions to meet your online learning needs. Three Distance Learning solutions enhance your classroom experience: MyCourse.com (hosted by Course Technology), Blackboard, and WebCT.

MyCourse.com is an easily customizable online syllabus and course enhancement tool. This tool adds value to your class by offering brand new content designed to reinforce what you are already teaching. MyCourse.com even allows you to add your own content, hyperlinks, and assignments.

WebCT and Blackboard are course management tools that deliver online content for eighty-five Course Technology titles. This growing list of titles enables instructors to edit and add to any content made available through WebCT and Blackboard. In addition, you can choose what students access. The site is hosted on your school campus, allowing complete control over the information. WebCT and Blackboard offer their own internal communication system, including internal e-mail, Bulletin Boards, and Chat rooms. For more information please contact your Course Technology sales representative.

Create Your Ideal Course Package with CourseKits™

If one book doesn't offer all the coverage you need, create a course package that does. With Course Technology's CourseKits—our mix-and-match approach to selecting texts—you have the freedom to combine products from more than one series. When you choose any two or more Course Technology products for one course, we'll discount the price and package them together so your students can pick up one convenient bundle at the bookstore.

Preface

Welcome to *Multimedia Concepts—Illustrated Introductory*. This highly visual book offers a comprehensive introduction to the key elements of multimedia as well as the design principles and management skills needed to develop dynamic, interactive multimedia products. This book is appropriate for a full semester or quarter course, and its modular structure allows great flexibility—you can cover the units in any order you choose.

Organization and Coverage

This book teaches students the principles of multimedia in a unique approach with six conceptual units and two hands-on units. In the first six units, students learn the various categories of multimedia and the hardware components needed to develop and view multimedia titles; the elements of multimedia, such as sounds, animation, video, text, and graphics; and the software authoring programs and management issues that are used in the development of multimedia titles.

The two hands-on units give students step-by-step instructions, which cover incorporating multimedia into a Web site and creating an interactive application with Macromedia® Director® 8. This text assumes no prior knowledge of multimedia, but by the end of the book, students will be creating their own animated Director movies and will be learning about Director's scripting language, Lingo. A Web focus throughout the book helps students explore the most popular vehicle for delivering multimedia today!

About this Approach

What makes the Illustrated approach so effective? It's quite simple. Each concept is presented on two facing pages, with the concepts or step-by-step instructions on the left page, and large screen illustrations on the right page. Students can focus on a single concept without having to turn the page. This unique design makes information extremely

---

Details provide key information on the main concept.

Exploring multimedia on the Web

The **Internet** is a vast communications system linking computers around the world, as shown in Figure A-3. First developed several decades ago by the U.S. government and research institutions, the Internet became widely popular after the development of **browsers**. A browser is a visual interface that interprets Web documents and allows for the display of graphics. Browsers, such as Netscape Navigator and Internet Explorer, enable graphics, sound, movies, and animation to be delivered to the user. The development of browsers helped spawn the **World Wide Web**, which supports delivery of multimedia, and provides for hyperlinking of content over the Internet. Together, browsers and the Web give the Internet multimedia capabilities. This lesson looks at multimedia on the Web.

DETAILS

▶ The fastest-growing area for multimedia delivery is online, including delivery via telecommunications and the Internet. Telecommunications involving phone line, satellite, wireless, and cable transmission is being used by educational institutions to deliver multimedia courseware to rural areas and by companies for teleconferencing and training. The use of the Internet is growing exponentially. Many companies are developing home pages for the Web that allow customers to access product data including video demonstrations, to purchase products, and even to subscribe to news services.

▶ One of the most compelling features of the Web is its immediacy. Events such as rock concerts, baseball games, and conference keynote speeches can be **Webcast**—that is, broadcast, in real time over the Web, as shown in Figure A-4. All Webcasts are audio and some include video.

▶ Animations, as simple as rotating text or as sophisticated as 3-D settings, are an exciting part of multimedia on the Web. They have proved especially useful for attracting attention and creating virtual learning environments. Animations can be created using simple HTML tags, animation software such as Macromedia Flash, or programming languages such as Virtual Reality Modeling Language (VRML).

▶ The "coding language" for Web documents is called **HyperText Markup Language** (HTML). Multimedia developers know that as long as their programs are written using HTML, the user should be able to run the application on the Web. Unfortunately, no standard hardware configuration exists for computers linked to the Internet. For example, the user's computer may or may not include a sound card. If it lacks a sound card, then the user cannot hear sound used in the multimedia application.

▶ HTML allows Web page developers to include **hyperlinks**, which consist of text or graphics that are coded to "jump" to another location. Hyperlinks give users the ability to "navigate" from place to place in a document or across documents.

▶ HTML uses **HTML tags** to mark text. For example, *Welcome!* would be coded as <i>Welcome!</i> in HTML. The HTML tags <i> and </i> display all text contained within the tags in italic.

▶ While HTML is used to create basic Web pages, other programming languages and development software are more appropriate for creating multimedia events. **Programming languages**, like Java, are used to produce sophisticated features such as animations and database searches. **Applets** are Java programs that are developed for a specific purpose and can be used in more than one application. For example, an applet might track stock prices and periodically display them on a Web page. Java applets are run within the browser on the user's computer and are downloaded from the Web when the browser opens a Web page that supports them. A person with programming knowledge can create applets. Applets are also available from commercial developers such as Sun Microsystems as well as third-party developers. Some are available free of charge and can be downloaded from the Web.

accessible and easy to absorb, and provides a great reference for after the course is over. This hands-on approach is ideal for both self-paced or instructor-led classes.

Additional Features

The two-page lesson format featured in this book provides students with a powerful learning experience. Additionally, this book contains the following features:

• Student Online Companion

The Student Online Companion contains a wide array of links for students to explore when completing the Web Works exercises in the end-of-unit material. This innovative online companion enhances and augments the printed page by bringing students to the Web for a dynamic and continually updated learning experience.

• Distance Learning

Distance Learning options are available with this book. Content has been created for MyCourse, WebCT, and Blackboard. Check out course.com for more information.

• Trial Software

Included in the companion CD-ROM at the back of this book, you will find a CD containing a trial version of Macromedia® Director® 8 for both Macintosh and Window operating systems. Students can use this software to work through Unit H, Case Study: Using Macromedia Director. Note: The trial software will cease operating after 30 days. Check the Read Me on the CD for more information.

• Dual Platform

Unit H, Case Study: Using Macromedia Director, can be completed on either a Macintosh or Windows operating system.

• Outstanding Assessment and Reinforcement

Every unit concludes with a wide variety of assessment exercises to test students' understanding and reinforce the material covered. Units A-F end with an *Issue* section, which explores current topics in multimedia. *Study Tips*, *Select the Best Answer*, and *Fill in the Best Answer* give students further assessment and reinforcement of the concepts presented in the unit. *Independent Challenges* ask students to explore topics in multimedia, which encourage critical thinking and research.

Units G and H, the two hands-on units, also include a variety of assessment and reinforcement to actively engage students and further enhance their skills. The end-of-unit material for these units includes a *Concepts and Skills Review* section, *Independent Challenges*, and a *Visual Workshop*. In each *Visual Workshop*, students are given an at-a-glance view of a multimedia environment. They are then asked to further research and analyze this environment by answering questions based on its design as well as further identifying its critical multimedia components.

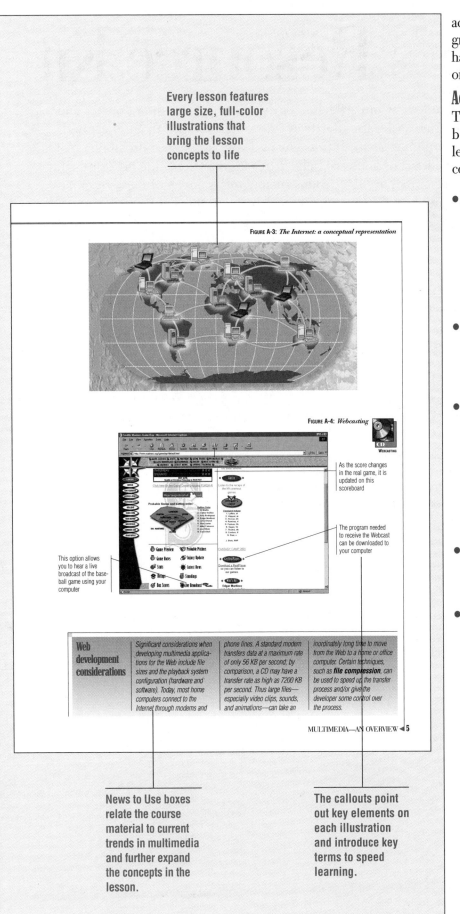

Every lesson features large size, full-color illustrations that bring the lesson concepts to life

FIGURE A-3: *The Internet: a conceptual representation*

FIGURE A-4: *Webcasting*

As the score changes in the real game, it is updated on this scoreboard

The program needed to receive the Webcast can be downloaded to your computer

This option allows you to hear a live broadcast of the baseball game using your computer

Web development considerations — Significant considerations when developing multimedia applications for the Web include file sizes and the playback system configuration (hardware and software). Today, most home computers connect to the Internet through modems and phone lines. A standard modem transfers data at a maximum rate of only 56 KB per second; by comparison, a CD may have a transfer rate as high as 7200 KB per second. Thus large files—especially video clips, sounds, and animations—can take an inordinately long time to move from the Web to a home or office computer. Certain techniques, such as **file compression**, can be used to speed up the transfer process and/or give the developer some control over the process.

MULTIMEDIA—AN OVERVIEW ◄ 5

News to Use boxes relate the course material to current trends in multimedia and further expand the concepts in the lesson.

The callouts point out key elements on each illustration and introduce key terms to speed learning.

Instructor's Resource Kit

The Instructor's Resource Kit is Course Technology's way of putting the resources and information needed to teach and learn effectively into your hands. With an integrated array of teaching and learning tools that offers you and your students a broad range of technology-based instructional options, we believe this kit represents the highest quality and most cutting edge resources available to instructors today. Many of these resources are available at www.course.com. The resources available with this book are:

▶ **ExamView**—This textbook is accompanied by ExamView, a powerful testing software package that allows instructors to create and administer printed, computer (LAN-based), and Internet exams. ExamView includes hundreds of questions that correspond to the topics covered in this text, enabling students to generate detailed study guides that include page references for further review. The computer-based and Internet testing components allow students to take exams at their computers, and also save the instructor time by grading each exam automatically.

▶ **Instructor's Manual**—Available as an electronic file, the Instructor's Manual is quality-assurance tested and includes unit overviews, detailed lecture topics for each unit with teaching tips, an Upgrader's Guide, solutions to all lessons and end-of-unit material, and extra Independent Challenges. The Instructor's Manual is available on the Instructor's Resource Kit CD-ROM or you can download it from **www.course.com**.

▶ **Course Faculty Online Companion**—You can browse this textbook's password-protected site to obtain the Instructor's Manual, Solution Files, Project Files, and any updates to the text. Contact your Customer Service Representative for the site address and password.

▶ **Project Files**—Project Files contain all of the data that students will use to complete the lessons and end-of-unit material. A Readme file includes instructions for using the files. Adopters of this text are granted the right to install the Project Files on any standalone computer or network. The Project Files are available on the Instructor's Resource Kit CD-ROM, the Review Pack, and can also be downloaded from **www.course.com**.

▶ **Solution Files**—Solution Files contain every file students are asked to create or modify in the lessons and end of-unit material. A Help file on the Instructor's Resource Kit includes information for using the Solution Files.

▶ **Figure Files**—The figures in the text are provided on the Instructor's Resourse Kit CD to help you illustrate key topics or concepts. You can create traditional overhead transparencies by printing the figure files. Or you can create electronic slide shows by using the figures in a presentation program such as PowerPoint.

▶ **Student Online Companion**—This book features its own Online Companion where students can go to access Web sites that will help them complete the Web Work Independent Challenges. Because the Web is constantly changing, the Student Online Companion will provide the reader with current updates regarding links referenced in the book.

Author's Vision

Teaching about multimedia can be extremely rewarding—it is for me. Helping students learn what multimedia is and how it is changing our lives; helping them understand the technologies—current and forecasted; and working with them in the design and development of multimedia titles has been very satisfying. It also has been quite challenging. How do I cover all of the material? How do I keep current in such a dynamic field? How can I use the technology to teach the technology? These were some of the questions that helped shape the vision for *Multimedia Concepts*. As I set out to write this book my goals were to develop a textbook that:

► is appropriate for a beginning student

► provides a way to keep the material current

► focuses on the emerging technologies especially related to multimedia on the Web

► allows students to acquire skills in developing multimedia applications using an authoring program

This textbook provides a comprehensive yet manageable introduction to multimedia, a companion Web site that keeps the content current, and the Macromedia Director authoring program that provides a hands-on application for students. *Multimedia Concepts* is more than a textbook—it is a teaching package for the instructor and a learning experience for the student.

ACKNOWLEDGMENTS

As in any multimedia project, this book was a team effort. I am indebted to many people for making this textbook a reality. In particular, I would like to thank the reviewers, Colleen Case and David Curtis, for their critiques and extremely helpful suggestions. A special thank you to Asha Nelson, Micro Insights, for her programming expertise and development of several figures; and to Sara Chapman for her graphic design skills. My heartfelt thanks to Pam Conrad, whose patience and encouragement helped me get over the hurdles and whose editorial expertise contributed so much to the book; to the Illustrated Team, especially Rebecca Berardy who guided us through the process, was extremely supportive of me, and who provided a great deal of creative problem-solving; and to Nicole Pinard, who provided the vision for this project and the management expertise to make it all happen.

James E. Shuman

Brief Contents

Contents

UNIT B   Multimedia Elements—Text and Graphics   25

UNIT E — Development and Design of Multimedia Titles   97

UNIT F **Management and Distribution of Multimedia Titles** **121**

UNIT G Case Study: Incorporating Multimedia into a Web Site   145

Read This Before You Begin

Project Files

To complete the lessons and end-of-unit material in this book, students need to obtain the necessary project files. Please refer to the instructions on the front inside cover for various methods of getting these files. Once obtained, the user selects where to store the files, such as to the hard disk drive, network server, or Zip disk. Depending on where you store the files, you might need to relink any external files, such as a video clip, associated with a Director project file. When you open a project file, Director will ask you the location of the external file.

Director for Windows and Macintosh

Unit H is written for the Windows version and the Macintosh version of Macromedia® Director® 8 Shockwave Studio. Both versions of the software are virtually the same, but there are a few platform differences. Differences between the two versions of the software have been indicated in the steps.

Free Trial Software

Included on a CD with this book is the Macromedia® Director® 8 Shockwave Studio and Macromedia® Fireworks® 4 Trial Software. Students should not use the trial software until Unit H, *Case Study: Using Macromedia Director*, because it will expire after 30 days. Please check the CD for more information.

Installation instructions for the CD-ROM are included below.

Windows: Insert the CD in the CD-ROM drive, open Windows Explorer, select the CD-ROM drive, double-click director8trial.exe or fireworks4-TBYB.exe in the right pane of Windows Explorer, then follow the on-screen instructions to complete installation.

Macintosh: Insert the CD in the CD-ROM drive, double-click the CD icon titled Director 8 Tryout, double-click the VISE™ Fireworks 4 Trial Installer or the StuffIt™ Install D8Trial.sea icon, then follow the on-screen instructions to complete the installation.

Multimedia— An Overview

Unit A

OBJECTIVES

Define multimedia

Explore multimedia on the Web

Study the growth of multimedia

Examine educational applications

Examine entertainment applications

Examine business applications

Understand multimedia computer playback systems

Understand multimedia computer development systems

In this unit you will be introduced to the concept of multimedia. You will learn what multimedia is and why it has become so pervasive. You will learn about the elements that make up multimedia and how interactivity is a necessary part of multimedia. You will learn how easy and fun it is to use multimedia. You will discover that multimedia is freeform and that it is limited only by the reader's imagination. In addition, you will see examples of multimedia in a variety of settings and using various delivery modes. The unit also presents a study of the computer systems used in the playback and development of multimedia applications. Finally, the unit addresses the issues of privacy and development standards.

Defining multimedia

In a generic sense, multimedia is simply the use of many media. Thus a speaker making a presentation using a slide projector and VCR is giving a multimedia presentation. Today, however, the word "multimedia" is generally meant to apply to a broad spectrum of computer-related products and processes. You have encountered multimedia if you have visited music stores on the Web where you can listen to a music clip and then make a purchase or if you have played interactive games on the Web. Likewise, you have encountered multimedia if you have used CD-ROM and DVD titles, computer-generated games, interactive kiosks, CBT (Computer-Based Training) materials, instructional courseware, and online services. But what exactly is multimedia? For the purpose of discussion in this book, **multimedia** is defined as a computer-based, interactive experience that incorporates text, graphics, sound, animation, video, and virtual reality. This lesson provides an overview of multimedia.

DETAILS

▶ **Multimedia elements** include text, graphics, sound, video, animation, and virtual reality. These elements are broad categories that can be subdivided further. For example, the graphics multimedia element includes drawings and photos; the animation multimedia element includes 2-D as well as 3-D. In most cases, a combination of two or more multimedia elements provides the best results when developing multimedia. For instance, using sound narration with a video clip may be more effective in helping someone learn a new concept than using sound or video alone.

▶ A fundamental feature of multimedia is **interactivity**—that is, the ability of the user to interact with an application. Multimedia allows the content to be presented in a nonlinear way, which allows the user to be active rather than passive. The user determines what content is delivered, when it is delivered, and how it is delivered. User interactivity comes in many forms, including keyboard input, mouse point-and-click, mouse rollovers, voice activation, and touch screens. Figure A-1 shows some of the interactivity that a user might encounter when accessing an online encyclopedia.

▶ Fundamental to the development and delivery of multimedia is a computer system capable of incorporating multimedia elements such as sound and animation. It also must support an environment in which the user can interact with the program. Figure A-2 shows a typical **computer playback system** capable of delivering multimedia. Today most computer systems are equipped with the hardware and software needed to deliver multimedia. The typical configuration includes CD-ROM or DVD drives, audio cards, graphics cards, speakers, and sufficient speed and processing power to deliver multimedia. Most multimedia computer playback systems include an Internet connection, a browser, and a modem that allows the user to access multimedia applications from the Web.

▶ **Multimedia applications** is a broad term that covers all uses of multimedia. Examples of multimedia include an online college course Web site that uses 3-D animation to explain how earthquakes occur or an e-commerce Web site that shows video clip demonstrations of its products. **Multimedia titles** refer to specific products, including CD-ROM-based games like Flight Simulator and educational CDs such as Grandma and Me.

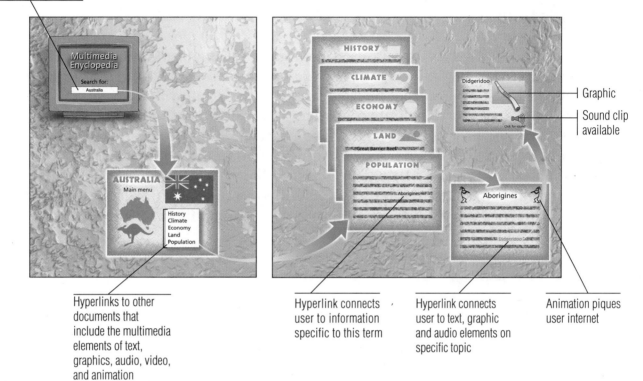

User controls content to be viewed by typing key search term

Graphic

Sound clip available

Hyperlinks to other documents that include the multimedia elements of text, graphics, audio, video, and animation

Hyperlink connects user to information specific to this term

Hyperlink connects user to text, graphic and audio elements on specific topic

Animation piques user internet

FIGURE A-2: *Typical multimedia computer playback system*

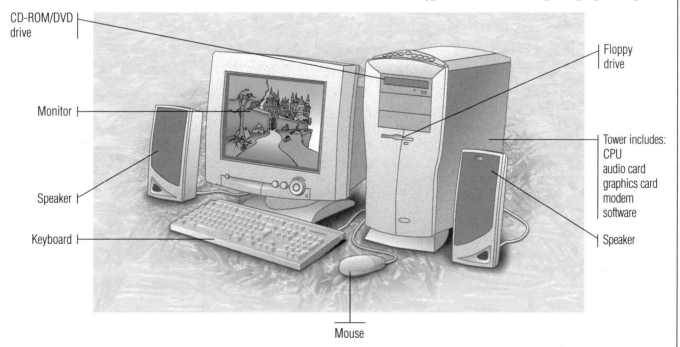

CD-ROM/DVD drive

Floppy drive

Monitor

Tower includes:
CPU
audio card
graphics card
modem
software

Speaker

Speaker

Keyboard

Mouse

Exploring multimedia on the Web

The **Internet** is a vast communications system linking computers around the world, as shown in Figure A-3. First developed several decades ago by the U.S. government and research institutions, the Internet became widely popular after the development of **browsers**. A browser is a visual interface that interprets Web documents and allows for the display of graphics. Browsers, such as Netscape Navigator and Internet Explorer, enable graphics, sound, movies, and animation to be delivered to the user. The development of browsers helped spawn the **World Wide Web**, which supports delivery of multimedia, and provides for hyperlinking of content over the Internet. Together, browsers and the Web give the Internet multimedia capabilities. This lesson looks at multimedia on the Web.

DETAILS

▶ The fastest-growing area for multimedia delivery is online, including delivery via telecommunications and the Internet. Telecommunications involving phone line, satellite, wireless, and cable transmission is being used by educational institutions to deliver multimedia courseware to rural areas and by companies for teleconferencing and training. The use of the Internet is growing exponentially. Many companies are developing home pages for the Web that allow customers to access product data including video demonstrations, to purchase products, and even to subscribe to news services.

▶ One of the most compelling features of the Web is its immediacy. Events such as rock concerts, baseball games, and conference keynote speeches can be **Webcast**—that is, broadcast, in real time over the Web, as shown in Figure A-4. All Webcasts are audio and some include video.

▶ Animations, as simple as rotating text or as sophisticated as 3-D settings, are an exciting part of multimedia on the Web. They have proved especially useful for attracting attention and creating virtual learning environments. Animations can be created using simple HTML tags, animation software such as Macromedia Flash, or programming languages such as Virtual Reality Modeling Language (VRML).

▶ The "coding language" for Web documents is called **HyperText Markup Language** (HTML). Multimedia developers know that as long as their programs are written using HTML, the user should be able to run the application on the Web. Unfortunately, no standard hardware configuration exists for computers linked to the Internet. For example, the user's computer may or may not include a sound card. If it lacks a sound card, then the user cannot hear sound used in the multimedia application.

▶ HTML allows Web page developers to include **hyperlinks**, which consist of text or graphics that are coded to "jump" to another location. Hyperlinks give users the ability to "navigate" from place to place in a document or across documents.

▶ HTML uses **HTML tags** to mark text. For example, *Welcome!* would be coded as <i>Welcome!</i> in HTML. The HTML tags <i> and </i> display all text contained within the tags in italic.

▶ While HTML is used to create basic Web pages, other programming languages and development software are more appropriate for creating multimedia events. **Programming languages**, like Java, are used to produce sophisticated features such as animations and database searches. **Applets** are Java programs that are developed for a specific purpose and can be used in more than one application. For example, an applet might track stock prices and periodically display them on a Web page. Java applets are run within the browser on the user's computer and are downloaded from the Web when the browser opens a Web page that supports them. A person with programming knowledge can create applets. Applets are also available from commercial developers such as Sun Microsystems as well as third-party developers. Some are available free of charge and can be downloaded from the Web.

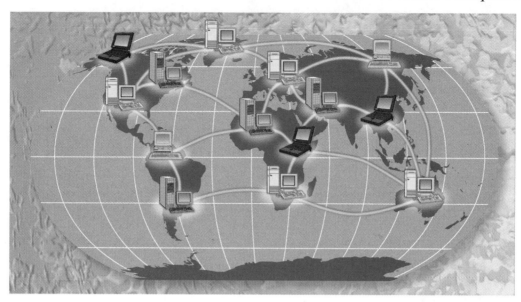

As the score changes in the real game, it is updated on this scoreboard

The program needed to receive the Webcast can be downloaded to your computer

This option allows you to hear a live broadcast of the baseball game using your computer

Web development considerations

Significant considerations when developing multimedia applications for the Web include file sizes and the playback system configuration (hardware and software). Today, most home computers connect to the Internet through modems and phone lines. A standard modem transfers data at a maximum rate of only 56 KB per second; by comparison, a CD may have a transfer rate as high as 7200 KB per second. Thus large files—especially video clips, sounds, and animations—can take an inordinately long time to move from the Web to a home or office computer. Certain techniques, such as **file compression**, can be used to speed up the transfer process and/or give the developer some control over the process.

Studying the growth of multimedia

Multimedia seems to be everywhere. There are entertainment sites on the Web, children's computer games, training materials with video clips, and educational material such as this textbook, which has both a CD-ROM and Web site with multimedia applications. The growth in multimedia has followed expansion of the use of computers, technological advances in hardware such as audio cards capable of playing CD-quality sound, and development of software that allows video to be delivered to the desktop computer. This lesson examines factors contributing to the growth of multimedia.

DETAILS

► One indication of the growth of multimedia is the number of households that own multimedia computer playback systems. As shown in Figure A-5, in 1997 only about one-third of the households in the United States had a computer. In just three years, the percentage of households with computers almost doubled. This growth corresponds to a decrease in the price of these computers from $2000 to as little as $500 during the same period.

► Another indication of multimedia's newfound popularity is the growth in the use of the Web and multimedia technologies used on the Web. As Figure A-6 shows, the percentage of households using the Internet doubled in the three years after 1997.

► Among the most significant technological developments that contributed to the growth of multimedia were programs that allow audio and video to be delivered over the Web. RealPlayer is one of the most popular of these programs.

► A dramatic decrease in price also contributed to the widespread distribution of multimedia CD-ROM titles. In 1992, the average price of a CD-ROM title was $100; today, it is less than $20.

► Marketing by computer companies was another reason for the growth in multimedia applications. The industry saw multimedia as the next "killer application." Why? Because companies knew consumers would spend billions of dollars on hardware components such as CD/DVD drives, audio cards, video cards, speakers, and software programs such as those for authoring, animation, and video and sound editing. To meet consumer demand, companies geared up to manufacture the components and software. Trade associations were formed to develop standards to help advance the industry, and book and magazines were published to educate and entertain consumers. Graphic artists, instructional designers, video producers, programmers, and musicians began to learn the new technology that would dramatically affect their professions.

► Adding value to an existing product is another reason for the growth of multimedia. Computer systems already existed and consumers were using them. Adding multimedia capability to basic computer systems then made multimedia accessible to all computer users. Consumers embraced multimedia and ensured its rapid growth; they quickly discovered that multimedia allows the user to control the content, to individualize the content, and to participate actively in the content.

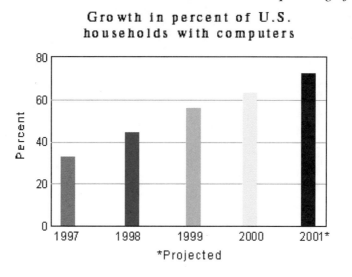

Source: U.S. Department of Commerce

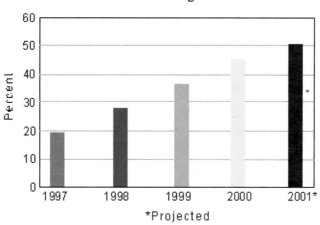

Source: U.S. Department of Commerce

Barriers to creating multimedia

When multimedia was first emerging in the 1980s, millions of desktop computers were already found in businesses, homes, and schools. As the technology improved to allow animation, sound, and video to be played on a desktop computer, dozens of companies became interested in developing multimedia titles. They faced a dilemma, however: so many different types of computer systems varying in speed, capacity, and display capabilities existed that they ran the risk of creating a title that would work on only a limited number of computers. The lack of standardization represented a barrier to entry into the industry for many developers. A second barrier was the lack of a way to deliver the large amount of data required for a multimedia title through the desktop computer. These barriers were overcome through the development of industry standards and the widespread use of CDs.

Examining educational applications

Various ways exist to classify multimedia titles. They can be classified by market (such as home, business, government, and school), or by user (such as child, adult, teacher, and student), or by other categories (such as education, entertainment, and reference). Many titles can be placed into more than one group. This lesson focuses on the use of multimedia in educational applications.

DETAILS

► A goal of the educator is to facilitate learning so as to help the student gain a body of knowledge, acquire specific skills, and function successfully in society. A major challenge to any educator is the diversity of ways in which students learn. Some people learn better through association, others by experimentation; some respond to visual stimulation, others to sound. Multimedia can accommodate a variety of learning styles.

► Often, students process new information in a nonlinear fashion. As they are reading in a textbook, they may come across a term that causes them to jump to another part of the book (for example, a glossary) before continuing. Multimedia, with its hyperlinking capabilities, can present the content in a way that allows the learner to jump from idea to idea in just such a nonlinear way.

► Because multimedia applications are user-controlled, students can proceed at their own pace and focus on those areas that are most interesting or helpful to them. For example, a student could watch an animation of the splitting of an atom over and over if necessary.

► Multimedia can be extremely motivating by allowing the user to take charge of his or her learning experience. In addition, it can provide immediate feedback, adjust the level of difficulty, and evaluate skills. For example, Pat, a student at Cascadia College, works in the computer lab on DNA replication for Biology 101. When she starts, the program asks whether she would like to take a pretest, review the process, or begin the tutorial. She selects the tutorial, then watches as a 3-D image of a double helix rotates on the screen. At any time, Pat can stop the process, review previous steps, ask for help, take a test, or quit the tutorial.

► Online courses and online enhancements to traditional courses, as shown in Figure A-7, are a rapidly growing part of higher education. Multimedia facilitates the user's desire for knowledge by providing pertinent information on demand, which creates a perpetual virtual-reality learning environment. Benefits of online courses include allowing students to access course material at any time and from virtually any location. In addition, audio lectures with accompanying PowerPoint slide presentations can be played; animations of complex processes such as DNA replication can be viewed, slowed down or speeded up, and replayed; and virtual labs allowing students to conduct experiments can be accessed.

► With the use of multimedia, students can easily access pertinent information in shorter timeframes. They can use multimedia to validate their results and obtain immediate feedback. As a consequence, students can spend more time focusing on pertinent information and less time wading through slower, manual-oriented processes. Figure A-8 depicts an award-winning educational title called A.D.A.M. that uses multimedia to teach human anatomy.

► **Edutainment**, as the name suggests, is the combination of education and entertainment. Many multimedia titles, especially children's games such as Sim City, fall into this category. Children like these titles because they are fun; parents like them because they have some educational value.

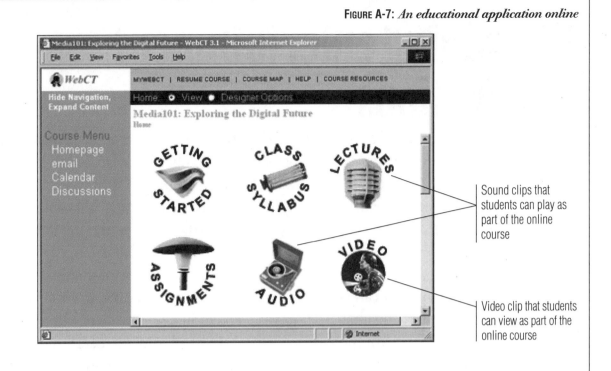

Sound clips that students can play as part of the online course

Video clip that students can view as part of the online course

Quiz feature

Hyperlinks to other images

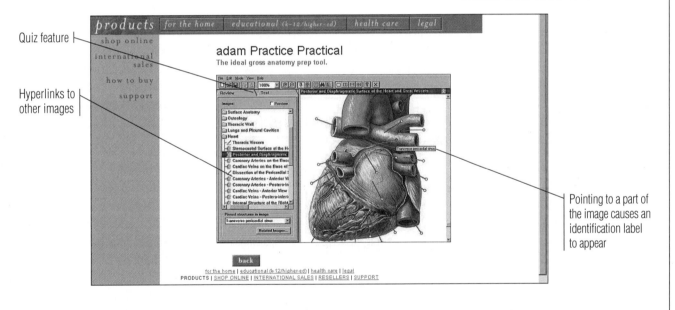

Pointing to a part of the image causes an identification label to appear

Multimedia enhances reference titles

Encyclopedias, census data, Yellow Pages directories, and dictionaries are examples of online and CD multimedia reference titles. In many cases, they represent "electronic" versions of existing reference books. The challenge to the developer is to make it easy for the user to find the desired information as well as to effectively use other multimedia elements such as sound, video, and animation. For instance, Microsoft Encarta includes more than 42,000 articles, 3000 audio clips, and 23,000 photos and illustrations. It also includes a timeline that helps you see how civilizations and events are related. When a subject interests you, you can simply click on it to access more information. Encarta also offers a browse function that you can use to skim through thousands of topics.

Examining entertainment applications

Game developers were pioneers in the use of multimedia. From large-style arcade video games to hand-held Nintendo Game Boys, the focus in this area has been on action and graphics. The developer of multimedia games needs to attract, engage, captivate, and challenge the user. Such developers have shifted the emphasis from pure action to action plus story-telling; from games to entertainment; and from the physical (hand-eye coordination) to the mental (solving the mystery, overcoming evil, outwitting the opponent). Multimedia incorporates all of the elements—fast action, vivid colors, 3-D animations, and elaborate sound effects—that are essential to entertainment. It can also be used to provide rewards, recognition, and a sense of accomplishment—components that are popular features in entertainment titles. For example, when a player wins a game, triumphant sounds might be played, the user's name might be flashed on the screen, and the score might be scrolled across the screen.

DETAILS

▶ Although CD-ROM-based games have been available for several years, online games (including multiplayer environments) are relatively new. Today, Web sites can be found that cater to almost any type of gaming interest. Myst, shown in Figure A-9, is an interactive adventure in which you search for clues to unravel the secrets of an island world. It includes high-resolution graphics, animations, and sound effects.

▶ One of the most interesting new fields in entertainment involves virtual worlds. Active Worlds, shown in Figure A-10, is a Web site that provides a variety of 3-D environments. Individuals can log on to the site and interact with other users in a virtual environment that includes chat sessions with others who have similar interests.

▶ Online entertainment titles can be classified into different categories. Sports sites include Beckett Interactive Football League. Mystery sites include Avalon, a mythological world in which you can develop your own characters and interact with other real-life and imaginary beings in real-time. Adventure sites include Webstrike, a real-time tactical war game. Fun sites include Playsites' backgammon, checkers, and chess.

▶ Recreation applications, another subset of entertainment applications, are similar to games but have a slightly different focus. They often give the user a vicarious experience such as being able to "play" the most famous golf courses in the world or "fly" over 3-D cityscapes. Hobbies and sports are examples of the types of titles that could be classified as recreation applications.

▶ One of the most popular and oldest multimedia games is the award winning Microsoft Flight Simulator. This virtual environment is so realistic that the U.S. Navy has used it to train pilots. Flight Simulator has become so widely used that an entire community surrounds the product, including Web sites, user groups, newsletters, and add-on products from third-party vendors, such as one that lets the user retrace Amelia Earhart's final voyage. Because of its realistic simulations, the most recent release of this product requires a more powerful computer setup than most games, including a Pentium 166 processor, 3-D graphics accelerator card, 500 MB of hard disk space, 64 MB of RAM, and a joystick or flight yoke game controller.

▶ Multimedia applications and titles do not fall neatly into categories. The dividing lines among categories are vague, which means that a multimedia title could be classified in more than one category. Table A-1 lists several titles and shows how they might be classified.

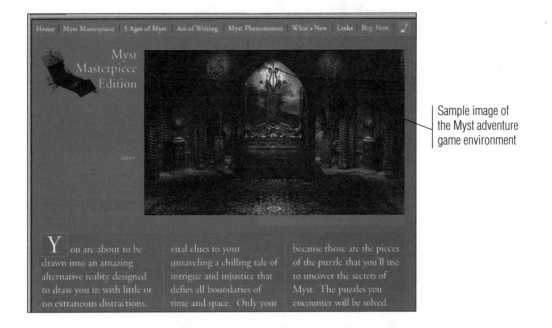

Sample image of the Myst adventure game environment

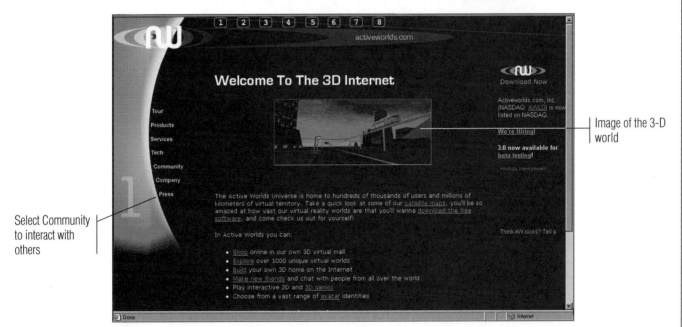

Image of the 3-D world

Select Community to interact with others

TABLE A-1: EXAMPLES OF HOW CD TITLES CAN FIT INTO MORE THAN ONE CATEGORY

MULTIMEDIA TITLE	ENTERTAINMENT	EDUCATION	REFERENCE	RECREATION
Myst (animated adventure)	√			
Encarta (encyclopedia)		√	√	
Bookshelf (reference title)		√	√	
Just Grandma and Me (children's story)	√	√		
Microsoft Golf (game)	√			√
A.D.A.M. (anatomy instruction)	√	√	√	
From Alice to Ocean (trek across Australia)	√	√		√

Examining business applications

Businesses and organizations have embraced the use of multimedia in marketing, training, and presentations. All of these areas share one thing—the need to communicate. For the marketer, the goal is to inform and to persuade the potential buyer as a way to sell a product, service, or idea. For the corporate trainer, the goal is to maintain a well-informed and productive work force. For the presenter, the goal is to inform and perhaps to motivate the audience. Using multimedia can help businesses and organizations achieve these goals.

DETAILS

► The Internet is the business world's dream come true. It provides an opportunity for every company to "go international" and to distribute its products and services directly to the end user at a reasonable price. Home pages on the Web provide interactive, online shopping through the Internet, as shown in Figure A-11. Often .com (pronounced dot-com) companies allow you to browse through a catalog and select merchandise to view. They might even provide video clips or 3-D animations to demonstrate their product line. Buyers can customize the product (change the color, add accessories, and so on) and then place orders.

► Certain magazines are now published and distributed online rather than in print. These online magazines can come alive with multimedia elements such as sound and video as well as links to related articles, products, and services.

► Corporate training is a multibillion-dollar industry. Training titles focus on developing specific skills usually related to a particular job. For example, the Boeing Company has an entire Training Division dedicated to developing multimedia applications, including computer simulations. Some of its multimedia applications are used to teach mechanics how to troubleshoot and repair equipment; others are used to instruct pilots on new aircraft systems. Employees of Holiday Inn are trained using a computer-based, interactive role-playing game, which is designed to help the employees improve customer service. Several online companies, including Click2Learn, have created Web sites to address corporate training needs by providing multimedia-based courses that prepare employees to take certification tests, such as the Microsoft Certified System Engineer exams.

► Thousands of business presentations are made each day. Company CEOs give annual reports at stockholder meetings. Sales representatives "pitch" their product line to potential customers. A conference keynote speaker tells an audience about industry trends. Multimedia can enhance presentations—sometimes, through the use of an "electronic" slide show (see Figure A-12) or an interactive video display. Multimedia gives the presenter a powerful tool with which to attract and focus the audience's attention, reinforce key concepts, and enliven the presentation.

► Another form of corporate communication involves training employees using multimedia-enhanced materials. Corporations now routinely provide new employee orientation via their intranets. An **intranet** is an internal computer network set up to facilitate communications among employees, customers, vendors, and selected others. Here new employees can access company history, goals, product information, and corporate policies. These interactive Web sites often include video segments, such as a welcome message from the company CEO.

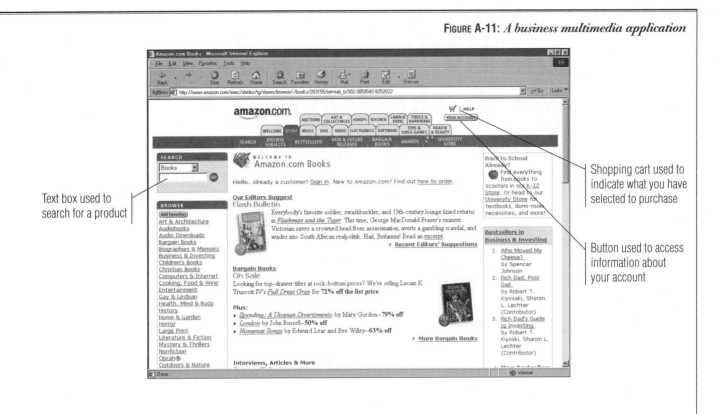

Text box used to search for a product

Shopping cart used to indicate what you have selected to purchase

Button used to access information about your account

Multimedia presentation developed on laptop computer, which is connected to a projector; presentation display matches display on monitor

Understanding multimedia computer playback systems

When studying computer systems with multimedia capabilities, it is useful to draw a distinction between those systems used for development and those used for playback. Development systems need to be the fastest and most powerful, and they should have the largest storage capacity that a company or individual can afford. The development process is people-intensive—and people's time costs money. The better tools developers have, the more quickly they can work. On the other hand, the type of computer system used for playback is related to the **installed market**—that is, the computers in use. This lesson looks at the components of a multimedia computer playback system.

DETAILS

▶ Every computer has a **processor**, which is the component that controls the operations of the computer system and performs calculations. The type of processor determines, among other things, how quickly data is processed and transferred. This issue becomes critical as the multimedia title becomes more graphic-, sound-, animation-, and/or video-intensive.

▶ The package containing a multimedia title will specify a minimum configuration. The lower the configuration, the larger the potential market. Often, the package will also specify a recommended configuration that will provide better-quality video, sound, and graphics as well as smoother animations.

▶ A computer has two basic types of memory: temporary (called **random-access memory**, or RAM) and permanent. Temporary memory stores instructions and data that are used while an application is running. For example, if you are playing a game on the computer, some of the game instructions are loaded into the temporary memory as the game is played. This approach helps to speed up the actions within the game and, in turn, makes the game more enjoyable for the player(s). When you quit the game, the instructions are erased from the temporary memory.

▶ The computer's hard drive is used to permanently store program instructions that are needed each time the program is run. When you install a program, a set of instructions is copied from the CD to the computer's hard drive. These instructions allow you to run the program without having to repeat the installation process. Then, the next time you want to play the game, you simply insert the CD and select the program's icon from the screen. While the program is running, instructions and data are loaded from the hard drive and CD as needed. Although the term "permanent" is used to describe the memory on the hard drive, you can, of course, erase programs from a hard drive.

▶ The monitor is critical to the playback system because it provides the primary communication with the user. Standards have been established regarding screen resolution and number of colors. Screen resolution is measured in terms of the number of dots, called **pixels** (picture elements), displayed on the monitor. Pixels are the smallest units that a monitor can display. Figure A-13 shows how the letter P is made up of several pixels in a grid pattern. The more pixels, the sharper the screen image.

▶ An earlier standard resolution was 640 pixels across and 480 down the screen. Figure A-14 shows the same image using two different screen resolutions, 640 × 480 and 1024 × 768; the latter resolution is now considered the standard. Notice the better quality of the image displayed in 1024 × 768 resolution.

▶ To display graphics, a computer must have a video graphics card. The video graphics adapter card and its memory capacity determine the number of pixels presented on screen. For Windows-based computers, VGA (Video Graphics Array) cards support a resolution of 640 × 480; SVGA (Super VGA) cards can support much higher screen resolutions. The video card also determines the number of colors that can be displayed on the screen, and hence the color quality. The more colors, the higher the image quality. Each pixel can display from one color to millions of colors.

▶ Whether used in games to provide "sound effects" or in education titles to teach foreign languages, sound is an important element in a multimedia title. To incorporate sound, the computer needs an audio card, such as Sound Blaster, and speakers. Just as a video card is used to display digital images, an audio card is used to play digital sounds. The quality of the digital sounds is determined by the binary digits (bits) used to represent the sound. A **binary digit** is the smallest unit used to represent the coding of data in a computer. The standard is now 16-bit sound.

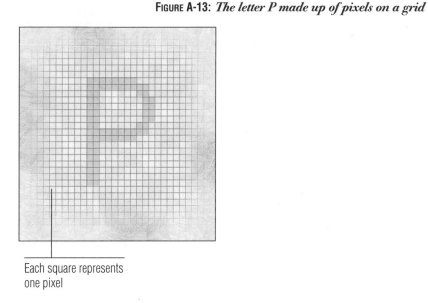

Each square represents
one pixel

FIGURE A-14: *Same image displayed on monitors with different screen resolutions*

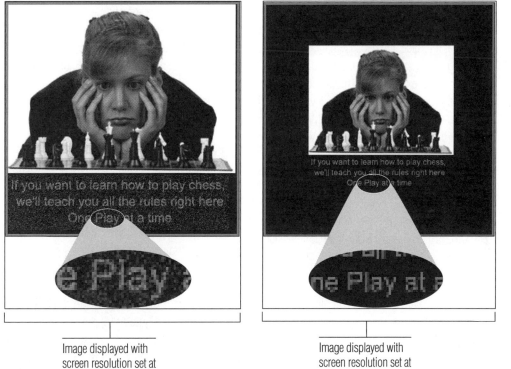

Image displayed with
screen resolution set at
640 × 480

Image displayed with
screen resolution set at
1024 × 768

CD-ROM and DVDs

CD-ROM (Compact Disc Read-Only Memory) and DVD (Digital Versatile or Video Disk) drives read data (graphics, sound, text, and so on) on a CD/DVD and transfer it to the computer. The drive determines the type of CD/DVD that can be played, the speed at which data can be located on the CD/DVD, and the speed at which data can be transferred from the disk to the computer. The data transfer rate is measured in kilobytes per second. A kilobyte (KB) is roughly equivalent to 1000 characters of data. The **seek time**—the time required to find a specific piece of data on the CD/DVD—is measured in milliseconds (ms); thousands of a second.

Understanding multimedia computer development systems

Developers realize that to produce commercial-quality titles that will keep up with the competition in terms of high-end graphics, sound, and video, they must invest in the best-quality equipment they can afford. Not only does high-end equipment provide the necessary development quality, but it also holds down production costs by reducing the time programmers, graphic artists, animators, and others spend in creating their part of the title. Figure A-15 shows a typical multimedia computer development system.

DETAILS

▶ Both Windows-based and Macintosh computers are used to create multimedia titles. Because the Macintosh was the first popular personal computer to provide a graphical interface and because it has superior handling of graphics and cross-platform capabilities, it has been used extensively in multimedia development. Software is available that allows a developer to choose either platform (Windows-based or Macintosh) for creating a multimedia title and for having the title play back on both platforms.

▶ Today, a Pentium III 500 processor is considered the minimum needed for development work. A Pentium III 750 or better is desirable. A Power Mac processor running at 500 MHz is the minimum Macintosh configuration.

▶ Multimedia titles are extremely memory-intensive. Consequently, 128 MB of RAM is considered the minimum needed, with 256 MB being more desirable. Hard drive disk space is a function of the number of programs that need to be stored on the drive. It is common to use several programs in multimedia development, including drawing, authoring and image, sound, and video editing software. All of these programs take up disk space. Add to this the space required for the various elements of the title, and you can quickly run out of room. Minimum hard disk space is 20 GB (20 billion bytes).

▶ When video will be used, it must be digitized using a video capture card. The card fits internally within the computer, and a video source (camera, VCR, TV) is then plugged into the card. As the video signal is sent from the source, it is captured, digitized, and stored. Later, it can be edited by deleting frames, adding text, adding sound, and so forth.

▶ While playback units typically have 15" or smaller monitors, developers need larger (19") models. This size monitor allows them to enlarge an image for detailed editing and to use the monitor as you would a desktop, with several items displayed and available.

▶ In addition to the basic computer system, several other hardware devices may be needed when developing a multimedia title.
  • Scanners are used to create digitized images so that the images can be incorporated into multimedia titles.
  • **External storage devices**, like the one shown in Figure A-16, provide additional storage space to relieve the pressure on a computer's hard drive.
  • A **digital camera**, as shown in Figure A-17, is used to capture still images just like a regular camera.
  • A microphone can be used to add narration, voice-over, or sound effects to the title.
  • Depending on the elements to be incorporated into the multimedia title, other hardware components might include a digital video camera or VCR.

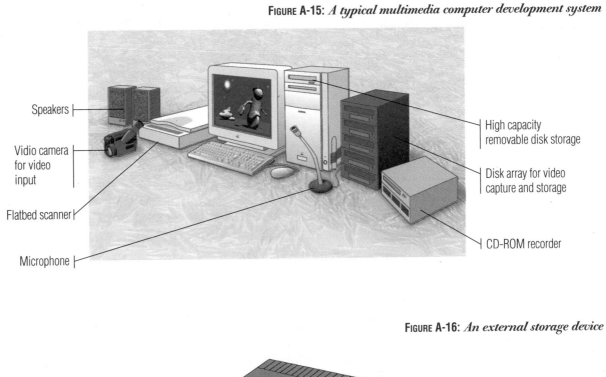

Speakers

Vidio camera
for video
input

Flatbed scanner

Microphone

High capacity
removable disk storage

Disk array for video
capture and storage

CD-ROM recorder

FIGURE A-16: *An external storage device*

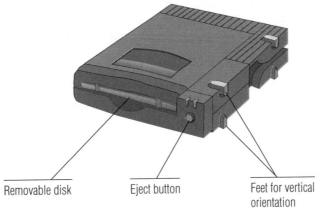

Removable disk

Eject button

Feet for vertical
orientation

FIGURE A-17: *A digital camera*

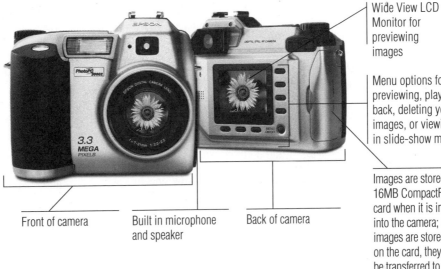

Wide View LCD
Monitor for
previewing
images

Menu options for
previewing, playing
back, deleting your
images, or viewing them
in slide-show mode

Images are stored on a
16MB CompactFlash™
card when it is inserted
into the camera; after
images are stored
on the card, they can
be transferred to a
computer using a cable

Front of camera

Built in microphone
and speaker

Back of camera

Issue: What is the appropriate use of multimedia?

Despite multimedia's many advantages, is it always appropriate to use multimedia? While the allure of multimedia is substantial, developers must weigh the development time and the costs of alternatives. All of the advantages associated with multimedia cannot compensate for a lack of content, poor design, targeting of the wrong audience, or delivery by a mediocre presenter.

Reading large amounts of text on a computer screen is tedious and tiring, both physically and mentally. Placing a book on a CD with some multimedia elements such as sound and expecting the user to read it "from cover to cover" is not a good use of multimedia. Developing interactive books in which the user becomes an active participant and can make choices that influence the storyline and outcome, however, can be effective. Similarly, multimedia reference titles can contain a great deal of text. But, by allowing the user control over the content and by adding other elements (such as animation, sound, and video), multimedia developers can overcome the drawbacks of text-intensive pages.

Is video an appropriate use of multimedia? First, simply watching a movie or any digitized video from beginning to end is not multimedia. In fact, using video inappropriately can be damaging rather than advantageous. Consider one company that wanted to showcase its high-tech image by sending out invitations to an upcoming conference on CDs. The content of the CD consisted of a well-developed video about the company, which included interviews, product demos, future plans, financial data, and so forth. Using a video for promotional purposes may have seemed like a good idea, but the result was a ten-minute video that played in a small window on a computer screen with poor resolution and no user control.

Before developing and distributing this title, the company should have asked the following questions: How many potential conference attendees will have multimedia computer playback systems? Will the user want to watch ten minutes of video on a computer screen? Will the user be impressed with the company's attempt at creating a "high-tech" image? A better approach would have been to design the CD content to play well on low-end user playback systems and to allow the user to choose from a menu what content to view. The menu might have included links to company background information, interviews, product demonstrations, and other options. After selecting a menu option, the user would see a short video clip associated with the menu choice. This approach would have permitted the user some control over the content of the video.

As a multimedia developer, you must always be up on the most recent "bells and whistles." But before incorporating them into a title, you must also ask: Should I use these multimedia elements? Are these elements appropriate in this title? Do these elements help us meet the title objectives?

EXPAND THE IDEAS

1. Write a one-page paper that presents your answer to the Issue question. Discuss the advantages and disadvantages of using multimedia. Provide a concrete example of multimedia used appropriately and another example of multimedia used inappropriately.

2. Work in small groups to develop guidelines for creating a multimedia presentation for class. Consider questions such as the following: Who is your audience? What is the topic of the presentation, and is it appropriate to use multimedia with it? What hardware and software considerations must be made? Discuss why these guidelines are important in helping to determine whether it is appropriate to use multimedia in a given situation.

As the personal computer (PC) industry was growing during the 1980s it became apparent that hardware standards were needed. The installed market, however, often thwarted the efforts of companies developing applications, including multimedia titles, for personal computers. These companies could not produce a different version of their application for every possible PC configuration (processor speed, memory capacity, monitor resolution). It is interesting to note that this development issue (for example, what computer configuration to develop for) was not as critical a concern for companies developing titles for the Apple computers. This is because the Apple Corporation controlled the specifications of each of its models and those developing applications that ran on Apple computers knew exactly what hardware components were included and could develop specifically to those components. Many companies, however, were manufacturing Windows-based computers with several different configurations. This created a definite development problem for companies creating titles for PCs.

In 1990 a group of companies agreed on the Multimedia Personal Computer (MPC) specifications for Windows-based machines. These specifications became known as the MPC Level 1 specifications. The MPC Level 1 specifications focused on the speed and capacity of the system unit, the resolution and colors for the display unit (monitor), and the quality of the CD-ROM drive and sound card. An MPC logo was developed and those companies that manufactured hardware that met the specifications or those companies that developed applications that ran on the MPC machines were allowed to use the logo. The logo was a great advantage to consumers, who could use the logo to tell at a glance if an application was compatible with their hardware.

In 1991 the Multimedia PC Marketing Council was formed to promote and revise the standards. This council was affiliated with the Software Publishers Association, the predominant industry trade group. The council included Microsoft, IBM, Philips Consumer Electronics, Comptons New Media, and NEC Technologies. Those developing the standards were faced with a trade-off: size of the market versus power of the computer system. If the standards were set high, developers could create more exciting and compelling titles — increasing the market appeal. On the other hand, the installed market consisted of computers at the low end of computing power. Understandably, consumers were hesitant to purchase entirely new systems to run applications. The challenge was to create standards that would allow companies to develop to the widest possible audience and still take advantage of newer computing technologies.

In 1993, the MPC Level 2 specifications were published. The MPC Level 2 specifications had a dramatic effect on the industry. The MPC Level 2 specifications reduced the risks involved in developers creating titles. As a developer, you knew that if you created a CD title that met the MPC specifications, the title would run on MPC machines. In addition, when you put the MPC logo on your product, consumers knew that your title would run on their MPC machines.

In 1995, the Software Publishers Group took responsibility for upgrading the MPC standards and released the MPC Level 3 specifications. MPC Level 3 specifications included a requirement for video compression that allows full screen and full motion video. What has happened since 1995? What role do the MPC standards play in the development of multimedia titles today?

1. This Issue makes a case for the benefits of standardization in the PC industry. However, some would argue that standards could stifle creativity and innovation especially by smaller companies. Develop a paper in which you explore the pros and cons of creating development standards.

2. The Macintosh computer was standardized long before the MPC guidelines were established and yet it has less than 10% of the market for PCs, while Windows-based PCs account for more than 80% of the market. In addition, the Macintosh is felt by many to be a higher quality computer. Work in a small group to create a report that explains the differences between developing titles for a Macintosh computer and developing titles for PCs. Do additional research as needed. Consider also the issue of cross-platform development.

3. The MPC standards are no longer promoted nor have they been revised since 1995. Research and write a report to answer the following questions: What role did these standards play in the growth of multimedia? Why have they not been revised since 1995? Have other standards been written to replace the MPC standards? If not the MPC standards, then what guidelines do developers use to address developing for the installed market?

End of Unit Exercises

STUDY TIPS

1. Based on the information presented in this unit, write your own definition of multimedia. Cite examples of multimedia and explain why they meet your definition.

2. Review the key terms in this unit. Over the next week, look for them in daily conversation and print. Are these words becoming more commonly used? In which situations do you encounter them?

3. Think about a concept you have studied in another class. How might a multimedia activity be used to help someone learn the concept? Be sure to include multimedia elements covered in this unit in your answer to this question.

4. Discuss this class with three friends who are not class members. Ask them to define multimedia and to give you examples of it. Compare what you have learned to their concept of multimedia. Do you feel that you can adequately explain what multimedia is to someone else? Why or why not?

5. List and explain the three most important concepts you have learned from this unit. Compare your list with that of another student in the class. Do you have any concepts in common? Would you include any of the other student's concepts in your list? Why or why not?

6. Do you think multimedia has more of an effect on education, business, or entertainment? Use examples to support your choice.

SELECT THE BEST ANSWER

1. Which of the following is NOT an element used in multimedia?

   a. Video

   b. Text

   c. Animation

   d. All are elements used in multimedia

2. Which of the following is associated with interactivity in multimedia?

   a. User control

   b. Nonlinearity

   c. CD-ROM

   d. Both a and b

3. The _____ is a vast communications system linking computers around the world.

   a. W3C

   b. Internet

   c. Netscape

   d. Cablescape

4. Internet Explorer is an example of a(n) _____.

   a. Intranet

   b. HTML program

   c. Webcast

   d. Browser

5. Screen resolution is measured in dots called
_____.

   a. Pixels

   b. Bits

   c. Bytes

   d. None of the above

FILL IN THE BEST ANSWER

1. Multimedia can be described as
_____
_____

2. The elements that can be combined to create a multimedia title are _____, _____, _____, _____, _____, and _____.

3. More than 50% of all U.S. households were using the Internet in the year _____.

4. Three reasons for the growth of multimedia from a marketing standpoint are _____, _____, and _____.

5. Three reasons for the growth of multimedia from a user standpoint _____, _____, and _____.

6. Four categories of multimedia titles are _____, _____, _____, and _____.

7. Two considerations for the appropriate use of multimedia are _____ and _____.

8. Screen resolution is measured in the number of dots, called _____, displayed on the screen.

9. VGA cards support a screen resolution of _____ by _____.

10. To display up to 256 different colors, you need a video card that can support a minimum of _____ bits.

INDEPENDENT CHALLENGE 1

Multimedia is an important part of a business environment—both in an office and on the Internet. The office environment applications are often used for training purposes. But why and how is multimedia used in business on the Web?

To complete this independent challenge:

Evaluate three Web sites that use multimedia for business. Develop a report that compares the sites. Include the following information in your report:

1. The name of the company, the type of business, and the URL for each site.

2. An example of how each site uses multimedia to enhance its site.

3. An example of how multimedia could be used to further enhance at least one of the sites.

4. An example of how multimedia is used poorly on one of the sites; explain why it is a poor use.

5. The best site in terms of use of multimedia; explain why it is so good.

INDEPENDENT CHALLENGE 2

The use of multimedia in education is valuable because students have different learning styles that can be addressed by delivering content in different ways. For example, sound and animation can enhance text material. Also, when the content is available on the Web, students may have the opportunity to access it at any time and from anywhere.

To complete this independent challenge:

1. Connect to the Internet.

2. Go to http://www.course.com, navigate to the Student Online Companion for this book, then click the link for Unit A.

3. The Unit A link contains links to Web sites providing information about learning styles. Click each link to visit the site and read about learning styles and how multimedia can be used to address various learner needs. Write a brief summary of each site — highlighting key points about learning styles and the use of multimedia.

4. After completing your research on learning styles and multimedia, evaluate three Web sites that use multimedia for education. Develop a report that compares the sites. Include the following information in your report:

  a. The URL for each site and its target audience.

  b. An example of how each site uses multimedia to enhance its site and address specific learning styles.

  c. An example of how multimedia could be used to address other learning styles.

  d. An example of how multimedia is used poorly on one of the sites; explain why it is a poor use.

  e. The best site in terms of use of multimedia to address learning styles; explain why it is so good.

INDEPENDENT CHALLENGE 3

Multimedia is constantly in the news as more and more applications, especially those intended for the Web, are developed.

To complete this independent challenge:

1. Submit a two-page (typed, double-spaced) review of a magazine or newspaper article related to multimedia. If you have access to the Internet, you might find an article using your favorite search engine. Include the following information in your review:

  a. Name and date of publication.

  b. Name of article.

  c. Review of article (in your own words).

  d. Conclusion: Do you agree with the author's point of view? Why or why not?

2. Be prepared to share your report orally.

INDEPENDENT CHALLENGE 4

CD-ROMs are a major source of multimedia titles. A search of the Internet or a trip to a computer store will show you just how popular CD titles have become.

To complete this independent challenge:

Choose a CD multimedia title to review (if possible, in a lab or one you have at home or work). Develop a report that includes the following information:

1. Product title and publisher information

2. Purpose of the product

3. Intended audience

4. Equipment required

5. Elements of multimedia used (sound, animation, and so on)

6. Design of the title screen

7. Information contained on the title screen

8. Method of navigation through the program

9. Approximate time needed to navigate the entire product

10. Way in which the product is divided if there is not time for the user to complete all of it

11. Strengths of the product

12. Weaknesses of the product

13. Ways you change the product to make it better

14. Cost of the product

INDEPENDENT CHALLENGE 5

The number of CD-ROM titles available has increased significantly in the past few years. This expansion is great news for the consumer. Unfortunately, having such a wide array of titles from which to choose can prove confusing for the consumer. Luckily, information is available to help you sort through the hype and find the titles that best suit your needs and your computer playback system.

To complete this independent challenge:

1. If you have access to the Internet, connect to the Internet and use a search engine to identify three CD-ROM titles on a specific topic (for example, personal finance or tax preparation). If you do not have access to the Internet, use other resources such as your local library.

2. Find at least two reviews of each title.

3. Analyze the reviews. Based on the reviews, include the following:

   a. Provide a brief summary of each title.

   b. Discuss how the titles are similar and how they are different.

   c. Discuss whether the reviewer provided an in-depth analysis of the title, including system requirements.

4. Summarize which title you would use, or list additional questions you would need answered before you would purchase one of these CD-ROM titles.

INDEPENDENT CHALLENGE 6

Multimedia can be classified into a variety of categories. This unit provided a discussion as well as examples of some of these categories. How would you define the various multimedia categories? Which multimedia titles would you assign to which categories?

To complete this independent challenge:

1. Create a table similar to the one shown previously in Table A-1.

2. Define each category.

3. Review six to ten multimedia titles.

4. Based on your review, state how you would classify the title. Write a brief comment explaining why you would use that classification. (*Note:* Some titles might be assigned to more than one category. Provide support for each classification that you assign to the title.)

INDEPENDENT CHALLENGE 7

An understanding of basic computer system configurations is useful in determining the appropriateness of a system for working with multimedia applications.

To complete this independent challenge:

1. Complete Table A-2 for each computer system that you use.

2. Leave blank those areas that do not apply.

3. Write a summary report based on the information in your computer table.

TABLE A-2

	HOME COMPUTER	WORK COMPUTER	SCHOOL COMPUTER	OTHER (SPECIFY)
Make and model				
Operating system, including version number				
RAM (in MB)				
Processor (type and speed)				
Hard drive (in MB)				
CD-ROM drive (access speed in ms and transfer speed in KB)				
Sound card (8-bit or 16-bit)				
Video display (resolution and number of colors)				

Use Figure A-18 to answer the following questions:

1. Which multimedia elements can you identify in the figure?

2. What opportunities exist for user interactivity? Describe them.

3. Write a step-by-step account of how you would progress from the search page to the audio clip associated with the didgeridoo.

FIGURE A-18

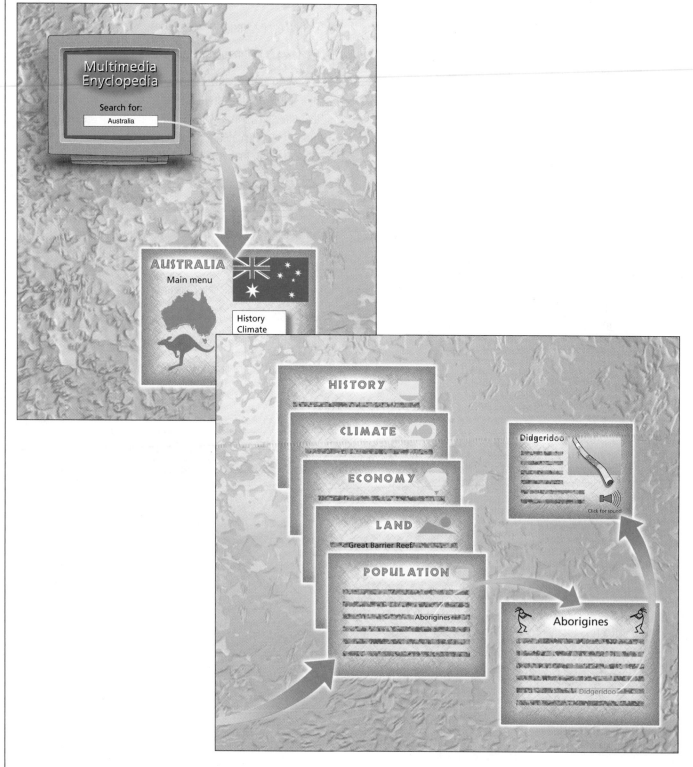

Multimedia Elements— Text and Graphics

Unit B

OBJECTIVES

Use text in multimedia applications

Use text on the Web

Understand software for working with text

Use graphics in multimedia applications

Understand graphic image file sizes

Understand software for working with graphics

Examine the sources of graphic images

Use graphics on the Web

In Unit A, you learned that multimedia titles incorporate text, graphics, sound, animation, and video. In this unit and Unit C, you will learn more about these elements, including how they are best used when developing a multimedia title. The way in which the elements are used depends on the intended audience and the objectives of the title. As you study these elements, keep in mind that the decision of what elements to use is often a trade-off between cost, time, or effect. This unit focuses on the appropriate use of text and graphics as well as a discussion of software for working with text and graphics to create special multimedia effects. In addition, you will learn about ways to decrease the size of graphic images so that they can be used efficiently on the Web. Finally, you will look at copyright issues and your responsibility as a multimedia user and developer.

Using text in multimedia applications

Text is perhaps the easiest of all multimedia elements to manipulate. Most computer users have had experience with word processing and are therefore familiar with the processes of entering and editing text and working with fonts and font sizes. This lesson takes a closer look at some considerations and guidelines to keep in mind when working with text.

DETAILS

▶ Be concise. Reading volumes of text on a computer screen is difficult and tiring. Moreover, it may not be the best way to communicate an idea, concept, or even a fact. The saying "A picture is worth a thousand words" (and perhaps more when sounds, simulations, and animations are added) is as true in multimedia as it is for the printed page. In some titles, where text dominates, such as reference works like encyclopedias, combining other elements with text can often reduce the amount of text needed to convey a concept. From a design standpoint, text should fill less than half of the screen.

▶ Use appropriate fonts. Text can be boring unless you enliven it by selecting **fonts** (which are analogous to **typefaces** in a print environment) and type sizes that are appropriate for the audience. Fonts help focus attention on certain text on the screen, enhance readability, set a tone (serious, lighthearted), and project an image (progressive, conservative). Fonts can be characterized as **serif**, **sans serif**, and **decorative**. Figure B-1 shows an example of each type of font.

  Figure B-2 shows Critter and ComicsCarToon, two fonts that may appeal to a younger audience because of their whimsical looks. It also shows Regency Script, a font that is appropriate for a formal look.

▶ Make the text readable. Perhaps the overriding concern with text is readability. For body text, a serif font is preferred because the serifs create a line at the top and bottom of a text line and guide the eye across the page. Sans serif text, however, does not have that line, so the eye has difficulty reading along the text line; it wants instead to leave the text line and wander through the body of the text. Research has shown that comprehension of text blocks with serifs is 75%–80%, whereas comprehension of text blocks set in sans serif fonts is 20%–30%.

Figure B-3 shows the same paragraphs from the Gettysburg Address set in serif and sans serif fonts.

▶ Fonts are measured in point sizes. There are 72 points per inch. Ten and 12 points are common point sizes for type displayed on the screen. The point size often depends on how the font is used—that is, as a title, as body text, and so on. Text that appears as a title at the top of a screen may be relatively large, whereas text that is used on a button might be quite small. Some guidelines follow:

Use	Point Size
Headings	14–48
Subheadings	Half the heading size, with a minimum that is not smaller than the text block
Text block	10–12

Headings and subheadings are used to attract attention and provide the user with quick identification of the screen content, while text blocks provide the substance. Subheadings must never be smaller than the text block.

▶ Consider using **font formats** and font colors. Three common font formats are **bold**, *italic*, and underline. These formats are often used for emphasis in print materials. In multimedia applications, however, they are more often used to indicate that clicking on the word will hyperlink (jump to another part of the program), to display additional text (such as a definition), or to cause some action (such as playing a sound or animation).

▶ Use restraint and be consistent. While it may be tempting and certainly easy to use a variety of fonts, sizes, and styles, it is important to exercise restraint. Avoid too many font sizes and styles on one screen. In addition, try to maintain consistency. For example, if several screens have a similar heading, use the same font, size, and style for all of the headings.

Sans Serif: The French word sans means "without," so a sans serif font is one without extensions. Sans serif fonts are best used for titles.

Bodoni
ABCDEFGHIJKLMNOPQRSTUVWXYZ

Avant Garde
ABCDEFGHIJKLMNOPQRSTUVWXYZ

Arnold Boecklin
ABCDEFGHIJKLMNOPQRSTUVWXYZ

Serif: A serif is a line or curve extension from the end of a letter. Serif fonts are best used for body text.

Decorative: Decorative fonts, such as script type, are more stylish and formal. They are best used for emphasis.

FIGURE B-2: *Examples of fonts*

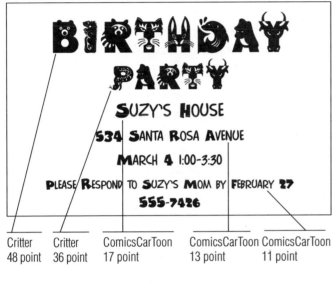

Critter 48 point

Critter 36 point

ComicsCarToon 17 point

ComicsCarToon 13 point

ComicsCarToon 11 point

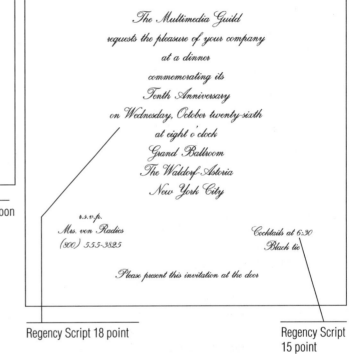

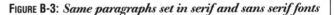

Regency Script 18 point

Regency Script 15 point

FIGURE B-3: *Same paragraphs set in serif and sans serif fonts*

▶ Serif Type

Fourscore and seven years ago our fathers brought forth on this continent a new nation, conceived in Liberty, and dedicated to the proposition that all men are created equal.

Now we are engaged in a great civil war, testing whether that nation, or any nation so conceived and so dedicated, can long endure. We are met on a great battlefield of that war. We have come to dedicate a portion of that field, as a final resting-place for those who here gave their lives that that nation might live. It is altogether fitting and proper that we should do this.

Fourscore and seven years ago our fathers brought forth on this continent a new nation, conceived in Liberty, and dedicated to the proposition that all men are created equal.

Now we are engaged in a great civil war, testing whether that nation, or any nation so conceived and so dedicated, can long endure. We are met on a great battlefield of that war. We have come to dedicate a portion of that field, as a final resting-place for those who here gave their lives that that nation might live. It is altogether fitting and proper that we should do this.

◀ Sans Serif

Using text on the Web

Research has shown that first-time visitors to a Web site spend less than 53 seconds on a Web page. If the Web page does not capture the visitor's attention in that time, then chances are good that he or she will leave the site. One challenge of using text on a Web page is getting the message across in an exciting, creative, and visual way. Meeting this challenge means recognizing how text is used on the Web differently than how it is used in print. Two considerations when using text in Web pages are how fonts will be displayed using different browsers and how to accommodate multimedia applications that are text-intensive.

DETAILS

- The two major Web browsers, Microsoft Internet Explorer and Netscape Navigator, essentially determine which fonts designers use. Why? Because most users will access a Web page using one of these two browsers. A designer must ensure that the Web page displays as expected by specifying fonts that are compatible with these two browsers. If the Web page designer specifies a font that is not available on the user's computer, then the browser substitutes a different font. A substitute font can have a negative effect on the page design. For example, it may take up more line space and thus wrap differently on the page—creating bad line breaks.

- To ensure that text is displayed in the desired way, Web page designers can use a **fontset**, which lists acceptable fonts in a specified order. If the first font is not available on the user's computer, then the second font in the list is used. If the second font in the list is not available, then the third font in the list is used, and so on. The use of fontsets is fairly common, but it does not give a great deal of control to Web page designers.

- One way to gain more control over the use of text on the Web is by using a **Cascading Style Sheet** (CSS). A CSS is a template that defines the appearance of a Web page, including text fonts. When a CSS is applied to a Web page, the Web page displays text and other style formats based on the information in the CSS. Web page designers can apply a CSS to all pages on a Web site so that all pages are formatted in the same way or to selected pages or even selected sections of pages within a Web site. Using a CSS provides consistency of style throughout a Web site. It also allows the designer to make a change in the CSS template, which updates all pages assigned to the CSS simultaneously.

- The most effective way to ensure that a specific font will work with various computer systems and browsers is to embed it into your Web pages. Two competing standards are **OpenType** (supported by Microsoft and Adobe) and **TrueDoc** (supported by Netscape and Bitstream).

Programs such as Microsoft's Web Embedding Fonts Tool and Bitstream's WebFont Wizard allow designers to embed fonts in a Web page.

- Another way to ensure that text will be displayed in a specific format is to change the text into an image—that is, to create the text and save it as a graphic format. The graphic will be displayed as created, irrespective of the fonts installed on the computer or the browser used. There are problems with this approach, however. For example, more development time is needed, which increases development costs; a graphic image is large, which increases the time it takes to display on the user's screen because of its size; and the developer cannot easily edit the text, which increases maintenance costs.

- There are times when the multimedia title must include a great deal of text—for example, in reference titles such as encyclopedias. However, there are ways to accommodate large amounts of text without overwhelming and perhaps turning off the user.
  - First, consider if there are other ways to communicate the message. For instance, can you show an animation or use narration rather than text to present the idea?
  - Second, consider including a small amount of text and then allowing the user to obtain more information as desired via a hyperlink. See Figure B-4. A hyperlink, allows the user to select a button (or word, graphic, or other element) that "jumps" or connects to another part of the title where more text and other information about the concept appear.
  - Third, consider dividing a Web page into sections, called frames, or using drop-down boxes. Figure B-5 shows frames with scroll bars that display more text as the user drags the scroll button. It also shows a text box with a list arrow, which displays more text when clicked.

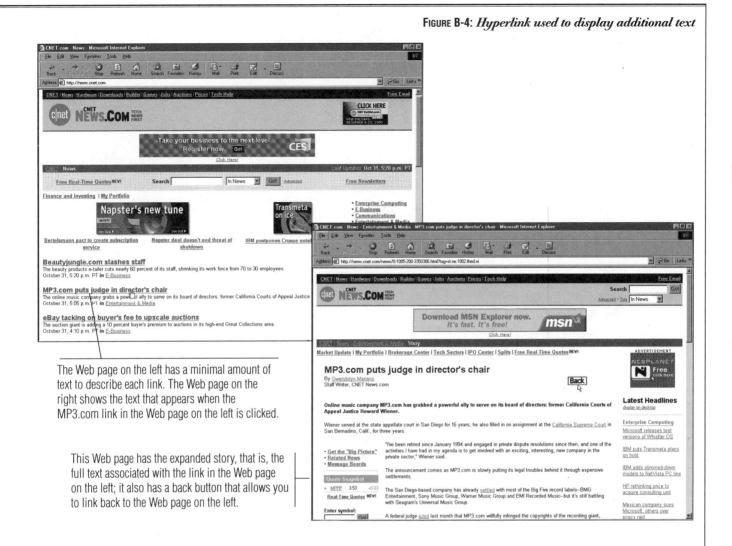

The Web page on the left has a minimal amount of text to describe each link. The Web page on the right shows the text that appears when the MP3.com link in the Web page on the left is clicked.

This Web page has the expanded story, that is, the full text associated with the link in the Web page on the left; it also has a back button that allows you to link back to the Web page on the left.

FIGURE B-5: *Accommodate large amounts of text using text boxes*

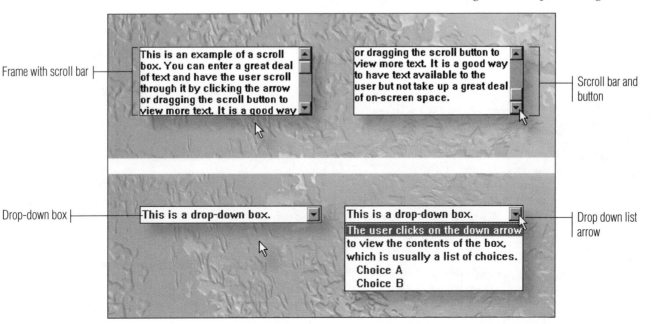

Understanding software for working with text

Word processing programs, such as Microsoft Word and Corel WordPerfect, are useful in generating text for text-intensive multimedia titles. Once text is created in a word processing program, it can easily be copied to a multimedia title. In addition, word processing programs now allow you to save a document in HTML format so that it can be used on the Web. When you want text in your multimedia title to have a special effect such as animation, however, you can use other programs designed specifically for working with text.

DETAILS

▶ You might use two types of programs for multimedia titles that are not text-intensive: graphics programs (software used to draw and paint images, such as CorelDRAW and Adobe Illustrator) and authoring programs (software used to create multimedia titles, such as Macromedia Director and Authorware). These programs have text tools that allow you to enter and edit text—for example, by selecting fonts, font sizes, and type styles and colors. Figure B-6 shows the type effects of Adobe Illustrator. These programs also allow you to create special effects with text, such as distorting or animating it.

▶ You can expand the font library associated with these graphics programs by purchasing font packages, which provide a variety of specialized fonts. The Web is an excellent source of font packages because you can search various Web sites, select the fonts you want, and download them to your computer. Figure B-7 shows a Web site that sells fonts.

▶ Programs such as Macromedia Fontographer, which is shown in Figure B-8, allow you to create your own fonts or to modify existing ones. You can create fonts by using a calligraphic pen tool or a pressure-sensitive **drawing tablet** that will generate fonts using your handwriting.

▶ Multimedia titles that are text-intensive often use electronic copies of documents. For example, if you were creating an online Yellow Pages directory for a particular geographical area, you would not type in all of the text from the current directory. Instead, you would obtain the electronic files used to publish the current paper-based directory and then simply import or copy the data into your title. In some cases, electronic copies of printed documents may not be available. In such cases, or when only small parts of a document are needed, you can use a scanner and an **optical character recognition** (OCR) program to capture the desired text. As the document is scanned, the OCR program translates the text into a format that can be used by a word processing program.

Fonts and playback systems

An important consideration in selecting fonts for use on a Web page is whether the user has the same fonts available in his or her software program. Multimedia designers must consider whether their titles will be played back on a Macintosh or Windows-based computer and whether their titles will be accessed via the Web using Internet Explorer or Netscape Navigator. All of these playback systems have built-in (default) fonts. **PostScript** fonts for the Macintosh and **True Type** fonts, such as Helvetica and Times on the Macintosh and Arial and Times New Roman on Windows-based computers, are usually installed with the operating system and thus are available on most of these computers. If you use a font that is not on the playback system, the system will substitute a default font. It will try to match the developer's font with a substitute font that resembles it. Unfortunately, even a close match can have disastrous effects on the appearance of the text—for example, it might change word spacing, wrap the text inappropriately, or even alter the size of the text. To avoid these problems, you can bundle the font with your title so that it is always available.

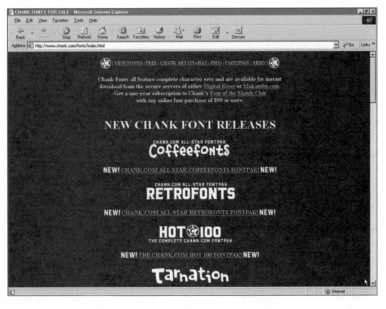

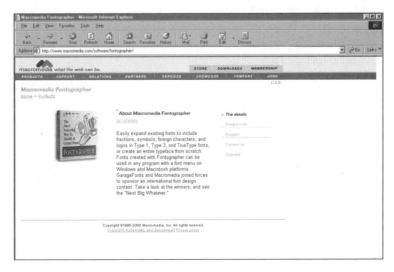

Using graphics in multimedia applications

The introduction of the Apple Macintosh computer and the Microsoft Windows program simplified the way we interact with computers. Using a mouse and a desktop metaphor on our computers, we use graphical images such as icons, drop-down menus, folders, and windows. We are accustomed to interacting with graphical images on the screen and, in fact, we now expect to see them. Visualization can be an important part of the communications process, and graphical images can be used to add emphasis, direct attention, illustrate concepts, and provide a background for the content. Just as graphical images are important in our day-to-day encounters with computers, graphics—such as illustrations and photographs—are integral to multimedia titles. Two types of graphics are used in multimedia titles: draw-type and bitmap.

DETAILS

▶ **Draw-type graphics** (also called **vector graphics**) represent an image as a geometric shape made up of straight lines, ovals, and arcs. When you draw a line, a set of instructions is written to describe its size, position, and shape. If more than one line is drawn, it has a precise relationship to the other parts. Figure B-9 shows a graphic, a pie chart, composed of arcs and lines. The instructions that create the arcs and lines establish the relationship between them. If a change is made, such as a modification of the size of the arcs, then the relationship between the arcs and the lines stays the same. Figure B-9 also shows the graphic reduced in size and rotated. The reduced graphic keeps the same relationship (relative position and relative size) as the original graphic.

▶ There are advantages and disadvantages to using draw-type graphics. The ability to resize and rotate a graphic without distortion is a major advantage of a draw-type graphic. Another advantage of a simple draw-type graphic is its smaller file size. Because each draw-type graphic is stored as a set of instructions, its file size may be significantly smaller than bitmap graphics. One disadvantage of draw-type graphics is that the more complex the graphic is, the larger the file size and the longer it takes to appear on the screen. Another disadvantage is that draw-type graphics cannot be displayed in photo quality.

▶ Draw-type graphics are often used for graphics that need to retain distinctive lines when their sizes change, such as in a company logo.

▶ A **bitmap graphic**, as shown in Figure B-10, represents the graphic image as an array of dots, called pixels.

As you learned in Unit A, the screen is made up of a grid, and each part of the grid is a pixel. Color information, called **color depth**, is recorded for each pixel. Unlike a draw-type graphic, which keeps the same relationship (relative position and relative size) among its parts when its size or placement is changed, a bitmap graphic becomes distorted under those same circumstances. To avoid distortion, bitmap graphics need to be redrawn using different resolution settings.

▶ Bitmap graphics are often used with photographic images because they can represent subtle gradients in color.

▶ A clear difference exists between draw-type graphics and bitmap graphics. Because draw-type graphics are displayed using a set of instructions that define each line in the graphic, they are not as discrete as bitmap graphics, which are displayed using a set of instructions that define each pixel in the graphic. Consequently, the quality of the draw-type image is lower than the quality of the bitmap image. For example, creating a circle with a draw-type program allows you to specify only one color for the entire circle, whereas creating a circle with a bitmap program allows you to change the color of every pixel in the circle. Thus the bitmap graphic can have a photo quality. The trade-off is that a bitmap graphic file is larger than a draw-type graphic file.

▶ Commercially available programs for creating draw-type graphics include CorelDRAW and Adobe Illustrator. Commercially available programs for creating bitmap graphics include Adobe Photoshop and Jasc Paint Shop Pro.

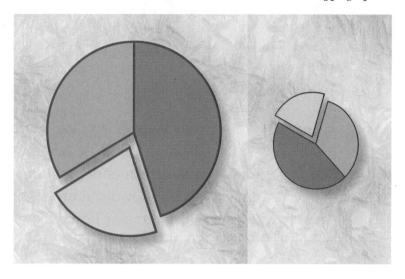

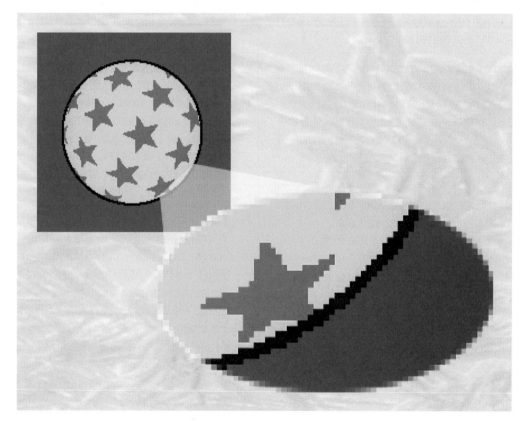

Understanding graphic image file sizes

Graphic image file sizes can become unproductively large depending on the complexity of the images and the way the images are developed. The multimedia designer must balance the need for quality images with the need to keep file sizes small. An understanding of graphic image file sizes can help the developer reduce the time it takes to download images and display them on the computer screen. This lesson takes a closer look at graphic image file sizes.

DETAILS

▶ Screen resolution. Screen resolutions are measured in horizontal and vertical pixels with 640 × 480 being the lowest standard. The larger the pixel count and the smaller the pixel diameter are the higher the image resolution. A screen resolution of 1024 × 768 will display a much better-quality image than a screen resolution of 640 × 480 on the same size monitor.

▶ Image size. The **image size** is determined by the number of pixels making up the image. The screen resolution and the image size determine how much of the screen is occupied by the image. For example, if the image size is 640 × 480 and the screen resolution is 640 × 480, then the image will occupy the entire screen.

▶ Color depth. Each pixel can display from one color to millions of colors. The number of colors is determined by information associated with the pixel. Various numbers of colors can be associated with each pixel, depending on the number of bits specified (8-bit for 256 colors, 16-bit for 65,000 colors, and 24-bit for 16.7 million colors). The range of colors available for pixels is called the color depth.

How is the range of colors available for each pixel determined? The information is coded in **bits**, which means binary digits. Computers operate on the basis of the flow of electricity and the sensing of electrical impulses. The symbols used to represent this are 1 for "on" and 0 for "off." Because there are two symbols (1 and 0), this is a **binary system**. Everything that is done by the computer can be represented by this binary system—including determining how many colors can be displayed by a pixel.

Let's say that you want to use 16 different colors in your graphic. Each pixel in the graphic would need to be able to display each of the 16 colors. Each color could be assigned a number ranging from 0 to 15 (16 total colors).

The question then becomes, "How many bits are needed to represent 16 colors?" Using a binary number system, 4 bits in different combinations of "on" and "off" can represent 16 different numbers (colors). The process requires assigning each bit a value based on its position relative to the other bits, as shown in Table B-1.

▶ File size. The file size of a bitmap graphic is related to the image size and color depth. It can be estimated using the formula:
   Image size in pixels × color depth in bits / 8
   You divide by 8 because the file size is measured in bytes and there are 8 bits per byte. Table B-2 shows examples of file sizes for particular image sizes and color depths. Figure B-11 shows the image quality of various bitmap graphics. The more colors, the higher the image quality.

▶ File formats. Graphic images can be saved in a variety of **file formats**. The more popular **file formats** include **TIFF** (Tagged Image File Format), **BMP** (Bitmap), **PCX** (Windows Paint), and **PICT** (Macintosh picture format), which are the standard file formats for multimedia development; **JPEG** (Joint Photographer Experts Group), **GIF** (Graphics Interchange file format), and **PNG** (Portable Network Graphics), are the standard file formats for the World Wide Web. The file format determines how the file will be displayed. Some file formats are more space-efficient than others. For example, a file saved in the TIFF format generally has a smaller file size than a file saved in the BMP format. You select the file format based on the intended use. For example, TIFF is used to exchange files between applications and computer formats, and JPEG is used when preparing photographs for display on the Web.

► The 8, 4, 2, and 1 represent the values associated with each bit. The 0s and 1s indicate whether the bit is turned "on" or "off." The sum of the bit values that are turned "on" represents the number associated with the pixel color. This example is intended merely to illustrate the relationship between the binary system and the display of different colors. In practice, 16 colors would be too few to provide quality images. In most cases, 256 colors would be a minimum.

BIT VALUES				PIXEL COLOR
8	4	2	1	
0	0	0	0	0
0	0	0	1	1
0	0	1	0	2
0	0	1	1	3
0	1	0	0	4
0	1	0	1	5
0	1	1	0	6
0	1	1	1	7
1	0	0	0	8
1	0	0	1	9
1	0	0	1	10
1	0	1	1	11
1	1	0	0	12
1	1	0	1	13
1	1	1	0	14
1	1	1	1	15

TABLE B-2: *File sizes of bitmap graphics given the image size and color depth*

IMAGE SIZE IN PIXELS	SCREEN SIZE	COLOR DEPTH IN BITS	NUMBER OF AVAILABLE COLORS	FILE SIZE IN BYTES (APPROXIMATE)
640 × 480	Full screen	8	256	300,000
320 × 240	Quarter screen	8	256	77,000
1024 × 768	Full screen	24	16.7 million	2,400,000

FIGURE B-11: *The image quality of various bitmap graphics*

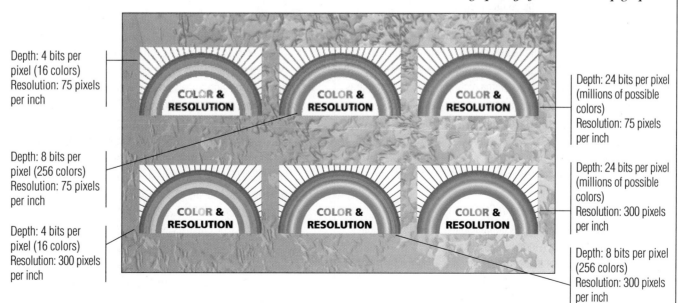

Depth: 4 bits per pixel (16 colors)
Resolution: 75 pixels per inch

Depth: 8 bits per pixel (256 colors)
Resolution: 75 pixels per inch

Depth: 4 bits per pixel (16 colors)
Resolution: 300 pixels per inch

Depth: 24 bits per pixel (millions of possible colors)
Resolution: 75 pixels per inch

Depth: 24 bits per pixel (millions of possible colors)
Resolution: 300 pixels per inch

Depth: 8 bits per pixel (256 colors)
Resolution: 300 pixels per inch

Understanding software for working with graphics

Graphics programs are the tools that allow an artist to create and edit all graphic elements used in multimedia titles. There are dozens of graphics programs. The most basic programs are those that come with operating systems (such as Microsoft Paint, which comes with Windows 95 and Windows 98) and those that are included in authoring programs used to create multimedia applications. These programs are relatively unsophisticated and, as a result, lack many features found in high-end programs. Generally, graphics programs can be categorized as drawing, paint, or image editing programs. You will probably need to use a combination of these programs when designing a multimedia title. Several of the high-end programs include features from all three of these categories (drawing, painting, and image editing).

DETAILS

▶ **Drawing programs** are used to create draw-type graphics. They provide for freehand as well as geometric shapes. Consequently, they are useful in creating designs where precise dimensions and relationships are important. Figure B-12 shows an example of a drawing program, Illustrator.

▶ **Paint programs** are used to create bitmap images. They are useful in creating original art because they provide the tools (such as brushes and pens) used by artists. Figure B-13 shows an example of a paint program, PaintShop Pro.

▶ **Image editing programs** are useful in making changes, such as changing the brightness or contrast, or applying textures or patterns to existing images. Figure B-14 shows an example of an image editing program, Photoshop.

▶ Features of graphics programs. Since features available in graphics vary, you should ask yourself questions such as those listed here and on Table B-3 when analyzing which graphics programs to use. Some high-end graphics programs address all of the issues raised in these questions.
  • *Types of images.* Which type of images (draw-type or bitmap) will the program support? Is the program primarily a drawing, paint (bitmap), or image editing program? Many graphics programs allow you to create both draw- and paint-type graphics.
  • *Cross-platform compatibility.* Does the graphics program support cross-platform compatibility? Does the program comes in both Windows and Macintosh versions? Can it create graphics that can be used on both Macintosh and Windows-based computers?

  • *File format support.* Which graphics file formats does the graphics program support? Does the program allow saving and/or converting graphic images using the more popular file formats, including TIFF, BMP, PCX, PICT, JPEG, GIF, and PNG?
  • *Object layering.* Does the graphics program support object layering? **Object layering** allows you to include more than one bitmap in an image and edit each bitmap independently of the others.
  • *Image enhancements.* Does the graphics program allow you to make image enhancements with painting tools? Does the program have a pencil, a brush, an airbrush, and text and line tools? Does it allow you to define brushes and to preview the brush size? Does the program have an option to paint with textures and patterns and to retouch using smudge, sharpen, and blur features?
  • *Selection tools.* Which selection tools does the graphics program include? Does the program allow selection of any part of an image using a freehand tool? Programs that allow for the most precise development of graphic images permit you to select all pixels of a certain color, which allows for fine detail work. Does the program support the use of **masks**, which are used to isolate parts of an image so that you can work on them separately? Finally, does the program have selection tools that will allow you to apply a special effect such as a drop shadow.
  • *Color adjustments.* To what extent can color adjustments be made? Does the graphics program allow adjusting of image color and choosing from a range of colors simultaneously? Can you selectively change hue (the shade or color itself), saturation (the relative brilliance or vibrancy of a color), and brightness?

FIGURE B-12: *A drawing program—Illustrator*   FIGURE B-13: *A paint program—PaintShop Pro*

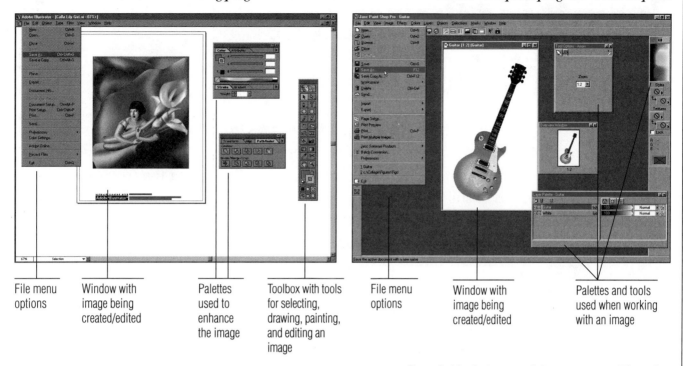

File menu options   Window with image being created/edited   Palettes used to enhance the image   Toolbox with tools for selecting, drawing, painting, and editing an image   File menu options   Window with image being created/edited   Palettes and tools used when working with an image

FIGURE B-14: *An image editing program—Photoshop*

File menu options

Palettes and tools used when working with an image

Window with image being created/edited

TABLE B-3: *More Graphics Programs Features*

FEATURE	QUESTIONS
Image manipulation	Does the graphics program allows you to stretch, skew, and rotate an image?
Filters	Does the graphics program have filters for sharpening, softening, and stylizing the image?
Anti-aliasing	Does the graphics program support anti-aliasing? Anti-aliasing smoothes edges by blending the colors on the edge of the image with the adjacent colors. Because bitmaps are made up of rectangular pixels, the outside edge of the image can appear jagged. Anti-aliasing adjusts for this problem.
Text support	How extensive is the text support? Does the graphics program support manipulation of PostScript and TrueType fonts?
Graphics tablets	Does the graphics program support pressure-sensitive graphics tablets, which are peripheral devices that can be used for freehand drawing?
Open architecture	Does the graphics program support open architecture? Is it compatible with third-party software such as programs that provide special effects?

Examining the sources of graphic images

Draw and paint programs are used to develop graphic images from scratch. But what are other ways to obtain graphic images for multimedia titles? For example, can you use as a graphic image a photograph that you took or a picture that you created not using the computer? Can you use photographs or still images that others have created? Can you use images that are found on other multimedia titles or the Web? This lesson takes a closer look at alternative ways to generate graphics that can be incorporated into multimedia titles.

DETAILS

▶ Copyright. The first question to ask when using a graphic image is, Who owns the copyright to the image? A **copyright** provides legal protection and grants certain rights to its owner. The author of the image is usually the owner of the copyright, unless the author has transferred copyright ownership. You have full copyright protection for any image that you create. You must always honor the copyright of any graphic image, regardless of its source.

▶ Clip art, stock photographs, and fine art. Some graphics programs come with **clip art** (ready-to-use illustrations) and **stock photographs** (ready-to-use photos), although these are often of limited variety or poor quality. Several companies specialize in providing images for multimedia titles.

- The largest image provider is Getty Images, which has acquired 25 stock-photo companies that together have over 70 million images. Many of these images can be purchased on CDs or accessed from the Getty Images Web site, as shown in Figure B-15.
- CD and Web site catalogs allow you to search for an image using descriptive words. If you want photos of sunsets, you might search using "sun" or "sunsets." A list of photos appears based on the keyword search.
- The companies that sell clip art and stock photographs often allow you, as part of the purchase agreement, to use the images in a multimedia title and to distribute the title without paying a royalty. Sometimes the purchase agreement requires you to give notice that you obtained the image from the company that sold you the image.
- Always make sure that you understand the terms of the use agreement before you incorporate any clip art or stock photos into your Web pages.

▶ Video images. Pictures from video sources such as videotapes, video cameras, and digital video cameras can be transferred to a computer. Then individual frames can be saved as graphic images. Some companies specialize in selling video footage.

▶ Still images. Digital cameras capture images in a digital form and are useful in generating graphics. You use a digital camera to take a picture just as you would take a picture with any still camera. The image can be saved to a computer disk or the camera can be connected to a computer using a special cable, so the images (pictures) can be downloaded from the camera to the computer.

▶ Scanned images. One of the most useful pieces of equipment for generating graphics is a scanner. Figure B-16 shows a scanning program. To scan an image, you place the material in the scanner and run the scanning program. Depending on the type of scanner and the sophistication of the program, you can zoom in and select (crop) specific parts of the image before capturing it. You can edit the image by adjusting colors, contrast, and brightness. Scanned images provide a way to generate graphics that can be used for backgrounds in a multimedia title, as shown in Figure B-17.

▶ Photo CDs. A photograph that is taken with a regular still camera can be made into a graphic image by scanning it directly into a computer or by writing the scanned image to a photo CD. Photo CDs can hold approximately 100 images.

▶ Screen-capture programs. Both Macintosh and Windows-based computers allow you to capture whatever is on the computer screen as a graphic. In addition, programs such as Hijack Pro and Collage Plus can capture a screen or part of a screen and save it as a graphics file of a type you specify.

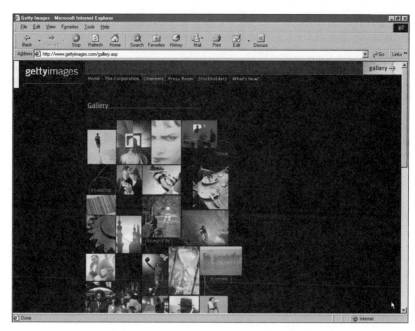

FIGURE **B-16:** *A scanning program used to digitize images such as photos and illustrations*

FIGURE **B-17:** *Examples of scanned objects that can be used as backgrounds*

Using graphics on the Web

Many home computers are connected to the Internet using modems that transfer data at relatively slow speeds. Today, most computers are sold with modems capable of transferring data at a rate of 56 kilobits per second (Kbps)—that is 56,000 bps. Thus a photo-quality image with a file size of 600 kilobytes (KB) could take more than a minute to appear on the screen. For those users with older 28.8 modems, the transfer time is doubled. This delay could be extremely frustrating to a user who is accustomed to faster transfer rates when accessing images from sources other than the Web, such as from a CD. As you can see, an important consideration when using graphics (illustrations and photographs) on the Web is file size. Certain techniques can be used to speed up the transfer time and give the developer and user some control over the transfer process.

DETAILS

► File compression is a process that reduces the file size of a graphic and therefore reduces the transfer time to the user's computer. Files are compressed before they are sent to the user's computer and decompressed before they are displayed. In fact, the standard graphics file formats for the Web (GIF, JPEG, and PNG) are automatically compressed when they are created. GIF is a prevalent graphics file format for images, both illustrations and photographs, on the Web. JPEG is used when still photographic images are digitized. PNG is a relatively new bitmap graphics file format that is similar to GIF. One advantage of PNG is that, unlike GIF, it is licensed for free to developers.

► File compression is achieved by analyzing the image and noting repeating patterns (see Figure B-18). For example, a block of the image may be solidly colored with red pixels. When this file is compressed, the pattern of repeated red pixels is reduced to a single unit. When the file is later decompressed the single unit is repeated to replicate the original pattern. The compression ratio varies from file format to file format, with JPEG file compression ratios ranging from 10:1 to 100:1. By comparison, the GIF file compression ratio averages 4:1, so an image with a file size of 200 KB would be reduced to 50 KB.

► Another technique that can be useful when dealing with large image files is to have them load in stages. That is, a faint representation of the complete image appears first, and the image gets sharper until it is completely loaded, as shown in Figure B-19. This approach gives the user an idea of the image's contents and allows him or her to decide whether to wait for the entire image to appear. Files that can load in stages are saved as **interlaced GIFs** and **progressive JPEGs** using a program such as Adobe Photoshop. If this process is not used, the image will load from top to bottom.

► A technique used by Web page designers to avoid having the user wait for a large image to be displayed is to use a small image, called a **thumbnail**, that is linked to a large image. The user can then decide whether to click on the thumbnail and display the large image. Figure B-20 shows an example of a thumbnail image and its linked full-size image.

► The file size of a graphic is a function of the image size, quality, and colors. These factors can be adjusted by using an image editing program such as Photoshop. It is important to always start with the best image possible. Then you can make adjustments, such as decreasing the contrast or reducing the image dimensions, until the trade-off between the image quality and the file size is acceptable.

The information (color, size, location) for the block of pixels is stored together

During decompression the block of pixels is reassembled from the stored information

FIGURE B-19: *Loading a graphics image in stages*

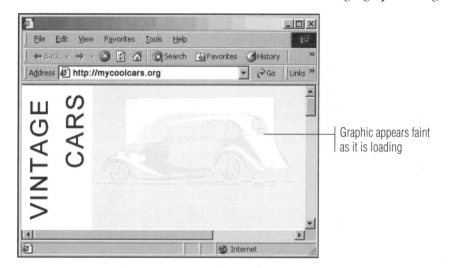

Graphic appears faint as it is loading

FIGURE B-20: *A thumbnail image linked to a larger image*

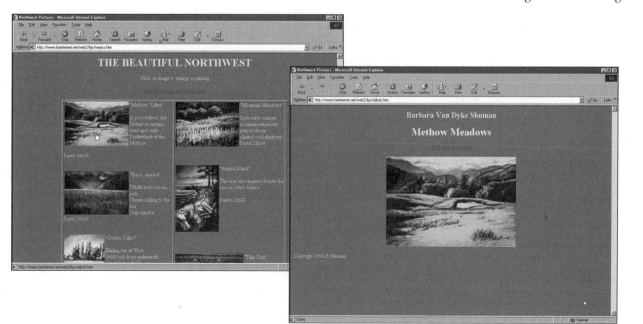

"Everybody's doing it! Everybody's copying images off the Web."
"If it's posted on the Web, it must be OK to use."

The ease with which material can be copied, digitized, manipulated, incorporated into a multimedia title, and delivered to a mass market has raised concerns about the adequacy of existing copyright laws as they apply to the multimedia industry. This issue has become especially evident with the popularization of technology, such as scanners, that allows for easy digitization of images and graphics programs. Once in digital form, any image can be easily manipulated and changed. For example, the Mona Lisa can be given blue eyes, Mickey Mouse can be shown with a Nike logo on his hat, and Darth Vadar can be shown embracing the pope.

Another concern relates to the ease with which images can be captured and downloaded from the Web. Merely pointing to a picture and clicking the right mouse button allows you to save the image to your hard drive. The images can then be posted on a Web site or distributed through e-mail. All of this activity is possible from a desktop computer. But is it legal?

Copyright laws are designed to protect intellectual property rights and provide potential monetary rewards for inventiveness and hard work. In this way, they foster creativity. Original material that is essentially permanent can be copyrighted, including images found in print material, on CDs, and on the Web. Business models providing licensing agreements and royalty fees have been in place for many years to provide protection and payment to those in the publishing industry. Indeed, entire industries revolve around the acquisition and sales of copyrighted material. However, concerns have been expressed that copyright laws that apply to printed material cannot be applied to digitized material. Because of those concerns and because of the potential for abuse to digital material, the issue of providing worldwide digital and transmission rights to an image has been approached cautiously. Organizations such as the Electronic Frontier Foundation (EFF) have been and continue to be instrumental in helping to define copyright laws for the digital age.

A copyright is essentially a monopoly. The copyright holder can choose to freely distribute the material, license or sell it, or withhold it from a particular use. In some situations, termed "**Fair Use**," materials can be used without infringing on the copyright. These situations are called "fair use" and include use in news reporting, parody, research, and education. Special restrictions apply even in "Fair Use" situations, however.

Materials that have no copyright are said to be in the **public domain** and can be used without the author's permission. Either no copyright was issued (such as with certain government-generated materials), the copyright has expired (for some works, expiration occurs 75 years after publication), or it was not renewed. Legal considerations may arise when using public domain materials, especially those related to derivative works, trademarks, and individuals. **Derivative works** are based on an original work, such as adaptations and dramatizations. A **trademark** is a name, symbol, or other device identifying a product; it is officially registered with the U.S. government, and its use is legally restricted to its owner or manufacturer. The rights of individuals include what's known as the **Right to Publicity**; this is a legal basis for requiring permission and/or payment for using a person's name, image, or persona.

In order to keep the focus on the issue of copyright in the digital age, questions such as the following need to be raised:

- What are appropriate and inappropriate uses of copyrighted material in multimedia applications?

- Do copyright laws need to be revised to reflect the new technologies related to digitization and Internet distribution? If so, in what ways?

- Should instructors be able to use copyrighted material under "Fair Use" guidelines that are intended to allow access to copyrighted material for educational purposes? If so, what rights should the guidelines include? How much of a copyrighted work should be used? How often can the material be used? How can copyrighted materials used in online courses be protected from widespread use?

- Should a presenter be able to use copyrighted material in a multimedia-based presentation during a keynote speech at a conference? If so, under what guidelines?

- Should members of the entertainment industry be able to parody material by changing a copyrighted image or song? If so, under what guidelines?

- Under what situations might copyright holders benefit from the use of their materials without compensation?

EXPAND THE IDEAS

1. Should software developers eliminate the function that allows users to copy and paste graphics in their work to help protect copyright images? Write a brief paper explaining your position.

2. Should images on the Web be governed by the same protection as print images? Why or why not? Research how companies are protecting images on their Web sites. Write a summary of your research.

3. As the saying goes, "Necessity is the mother of invention." New businesses are emerging that alert customers when copyright infringement is suspected. Use your favorite search engine to explore these companies. What services do they offer? How do they help their customers protect their copyrighted materials?

4. What is being done to evaluate current copyright laws and how those laws apply to the digital age? Investigate organizations that provide forums for exploring copyright laws. Select one organization and create a poster explaining its positions on copyright issues.

5. Research and discuss another example of copyright infringement. Did the dispute go to court? How did the court rule? Will the ruling stand, or is it being challenged?

End of Unit Exercises

STUDY TIPS

1. Make a list of the key terms used in this chapter. Classify them as related to text, graphics, or both. Review the key terms and do additional research on any that are not clear to you.

2. Describe various ways to present text, including font type, font format, and font size. What decisions must you make related to the subject matter of the text and the intended audience?

3. Summarize the issues related to software used for working with text and software used for working with graphics. Answer the following questions: What features should you look for in each program? Why would you want to use programs designed especially for working with text and graphics rather than using word processing software or the software that comes installed with your operating system?

4. Review the discussion about graphics file sizes. Answer the following questions: What must you consider when determining the graphics file size? Which file types are more space-efficient? Why might you want to reduce a graphic image file size? How might you do so?

5. Review image sources. List possible sources of images you might want to use in the development of a multimedia title. Then for each source, list the following: potential cost, ways to obtain it, advantages, disadvantages, ways that copyright issues affect use, and additional comments. You may need to do more research to complete your chart.

SELECT THE BEST ANSWER

1. Font formats include all of the following EXCEPT:

   a. Bold

   b. Color

   c. Italic

   d. Underline

2. The French word "sans" means _____.

   a. With

   b. Without

   c. Type

   d. Font

3. Which of the following is not a category of fonts?

   a. Serif

   b. Sans serif

   c. Decorative

   d. Times New Italian

4. Which of the following is not a font format?

   a. Bold

   b. Serif

   c. Italic

   d. Underline

5. A _____ is used to specify an order of fonts to be used in a Web page.

   a. Hyperlink

   b. Cascading Style Sheet

   c. Fontset

   d. Typeset

6. One way to control the use of text on the Web is by using a _____.

   a. Cascading Style Sheet

   b. Web template

   c. Fontmap

   d. All of the above

7. Which of the following file formats does not work for graphic images displayed on the Web?

a. PNG

b. JPEG

c. GIF

d. PCX

8. Which of the following file formats is best used for photographs?

a. PCX

b. TIFF

c. GIF

d. JPEG

9. The process of smoothing the edges of a graphic by blending colors on the edge of the image with adjacent colors is called _____.

a. Anti-aliasing

b. Color depth

c. Object layering

d. File compression

10. Which of the following is not a source of graphic images for multimedia applications?

a. Scanned images

b. Photo CDs

c. Screen-capture programs

d. All of the above are sources

FILL IN THE BEST ANSWER

1. Two guidelines to keep in mind when using text in a multimedia title are _____ and _____.

2. A(n) _____ font provides better readability for body text.

3. Some graphics programs allow you to save text as a(n) _____.

4. _____ is a way to accommodate text-intensive titles.

5. The two categories of graphics are _____ and _____.

6. A(n) _____ graphic represents the image as an array of dots, called pixels.

7. A bitmap graphic can be closer to _____ quality than can a draw-type graphic.

8. Bitmap graphics are _____ in size than draw-type graphics.

9. The file size of an image is a function of _____ and _____.

10. The approximate file size in kilobytes of a 16-bit color image that is 640×480 is _____.

INDEPENDENT CHALLENGE 1

There are a number of graphics programs available. It is important to research and compare the different products before purchasing one. To select the product that best suits your needs, you will need to know exactly how you plan to use the program.

To complete this independent challenge:

1. Research two popular graphics programs (such as Illustrator, Freehand, or CorelDRAW).

2. Prepare a report that compares the programs based on the features of graphics programs listed in this chapter. Explain how the programs are similar and how they are different. Provide an example of when you might use each product. Include reviews by users, if possible. State the prices for each program.

3. Prepare an oral presentation of your report and be prepared to present it to your class.

INDEPENDENT CHALLENGE 2

Some graphics programs, such as the Paint program that comes with Windows, are fairly easy to use but do not have the features of the more powerful (and costly) programs. The best way to grasp the advantages and disadvantages of a program is to use it.

To complete this independent challenge:

1. Experiment with a graphics program, like Window's Paint program. If you do not have a graphics program installed on your computer, you may want to use your school computer lab.

2. Write a report based on your analysis of the graphics program. Answer the following questions in your report. Include any other observations specific to your analysis.

   a. What are the name of the program, the version number, and the platform used (Windows-based, Macintosh)?

   b. Is it a paint program, a draw-type program, or combination? How did you make this determination?

   c. What features are available?

   d. In which file formats can you save graphics?

   e. Create a simple graphic with the program. How did you do it? What tools did you use?

   f. What did you like about the program? What did you dislike about it?

   g. Would you use this program to create graphic images? Explain.

INDEPENDENT CHALLENGE 3

As you have learned, effective multimedia titles are developed with the audience in mind. A wide variety of titles are available—so wide, in fact, that the choices might seem overwhelming. A little research can help you decide which titles are best suited to meet your needs.

To complete this independent challenge:

1. Study two multimedia titles: for example, a children's title and a reference title (such as an encyclopedia).

2. Prepare a report comparing the titles in their use of the following:

   a. Fonts (font sizes, font colors, serif, and so on).

   b. Text (too much, too little, techniques used to accommodate large amounts of text, and so on).

   c. Graphics (difference in the number of colors used, the quality of the graphics, and so on).

   d. Provide specific examples of fonts, text, and graphics to support your comments.

3. Prepare an oral presentation of your report and be prepared to present it to your class.

INDEPENDENT CHALLENGE 4

The purpose of this independent challenge is to compare your computer with a computer at your school lab or classroom. You want to determine how the configurations (especially modem connections and transfer speeds) affect the time it takes to display graphics.

To complete this independent challenge:

1. Connect to the Internet and visit a Web site that is rich in graphics. Use the same site for the comparison between the computers.

2. Complete the following table using your computer and a computer in your school's computer lab:

3. Use the information you gathered to make some observations about the use of graphics in multimedia titles.

Feature	Your Computer	School Computer	Notes
Type of modem or Internet connection			
Speed of Internet connection			
Processor			
Operating system			
Web browsers			
Site visited (URL)			
Time to load			

Bitmap graphics will become distorted when they are resized. Some graphics programs have features that allow you to resize the image by cropping it. In some programs, you may be able to zoom in on a portion of the image and save this magnified area.

To complete this independent challenge:

1. Display an image on your monitor, such as a Web site.

2. Perform a screen capture of the image. (*Hint*: When you hold down the Command and Shift keys and press 3 on the Macintosh, whatever appears on the screen will be captured as a graphic file, which you can save and import into a software program. When you press the Print Screen button on a Windows-based computer, whatever appears on the screen is placed on the Clipboard; it can then be pasted into a graphics program and saved as a graphics file).

3. Paste the image into a paint program, such as Windows Paint.

4. Save the image as Test 1[insert your name here].

5. Use the pointer or menu options to resize the image. (*Hint*: Use Help to read about resizing images.) Notice how the image changes.

6. Save the image as Test2[insert your name here].

7. Use the program's options to zoom in on the image. Notice how the image changes.

8. Save the image as Test3[insert your name here].

9. Compare the images. Write a brief statement about the effect of resizing and magnifying the original image.

The Web is an excellent source of graphic images, including photographs, that can be used in multimedia applications. Several companies sell images from the Web that can be downloaded directly to a user's computer. Before using any such images, it is important to understand the conditions of the site's terms of use policy.

To complete this independent challenge:

1. Connect to the Internet.

2. Go to http://www.course.com, navigate to the Student Online Companion for this book, and then click the link for Unit B.

3. Notice that the Unit B link contains links to Web sites offering images. Click each link to visit the site. Write a summary of each site. Include the following information in your summary:

a. What are the names of the company and the URL?

b. What is the approximate number of photos available?

c. How are the photos organized?

d. Search for a particular type of photo, and evaluate the search process: How easy is it to perform the search? How satisfied are you with the results?

e. How much does an image cost?

f. Are the images available on CD-ROM? On the Web?

g. What are the terms of use? Do they differ depending on how the images will be used?

h. Who would be likely to secure images from this site?

1. Describe what you see in Figure B-21. What type of program would you be using if you see a screen similiar to the one shown in Figure B-21?

2. Why would you be using the program shown in Figure B-21?

3. Label three features shown in Figure B-21. Tell how/why these features would be used.

FIGURE B-21

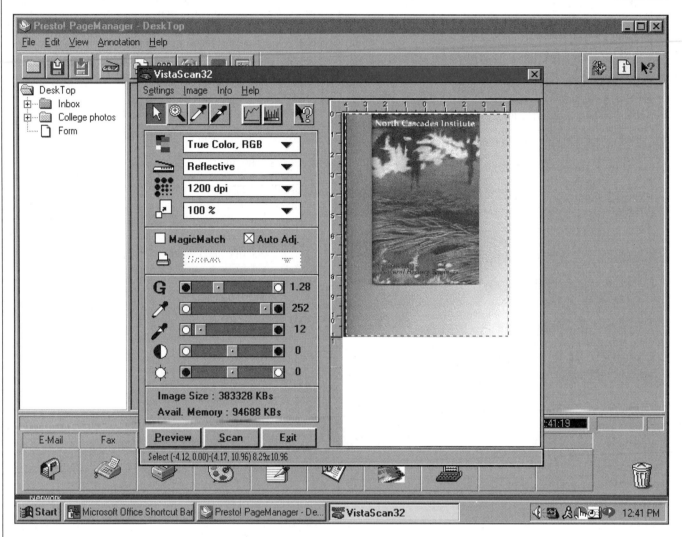

Understanding Multimedia Elements – Sound, Animation, Video

OBJECTIVES

Understand sound

Explore sound on the Web

Understand 2-D animation

Understand 3-D animation

Explore animation on the Web

Understand video

Understand video compression and video editing

Explore video on the Web

In Unit B you learned how text and graphics are used in multimedia titles. In this unit you will learn about the other multimedia elements: sound, animation, video and virtual reality. These elements are relatively new to desktop computers and can greatly enhance the effectiveness of multimedia titles. The way in which the elements are used depends on the intended audience and the objectives of the title; for example, sound is critical for teaching a foreign language. As you study these elements, keep in mind that the decision of which elements to use is often a trade-off between cost, time, or effect; for example, it might be more cost- and time-efficient to create a series of photographs with narration than to film a video of a tour of the pyramids in Egypt. This unit also discusses ways to decrease file size. Finally, it looks at the issue of intellectual property rights and emerging Web technologies.

Understanding sound

In the early days of desktop computers, usually the only sound that you heard from a computer was a beep—often accompanied by an error message. Now an entire range of sounds can be played through a computer, including music, narration, sound effects, and original recordings of events such as a presidential speech or a rock concert. The element of sound is fundamental to multimedia. This lesson examines how sound is used in multimedia applications.

DETAILS

▶ To study the use of sound in multimedia applications, you need a basic understanding of sound. When we speak, vibrations, called **sound waves**, are created. These sound waves have a recurring pattern, as shown in Figure C-1, that is called an **analog wave pattern**. The wave pattern has two attributes that affect how you work with sound on a computer: volume and frequency. The height of each peak in the sound wave relates to its **volume**—the higher the peak, the louder the sound. The distance between the peaks is the **frequency** (sometimes referred to as pitch)—the greater the distance, the lower the sound. Frequency is measured in hertz (Hz). A pattern that recurs every second is equal to one hertz. If the pattern recurs 1000 times in a second, it would be equal to 1000 Hz or 1 kHz (kilohertz).

▶ For sound to be included in a multimedia application, the sound waves must be converted from analog (sound waves) to digital (bits) form. This conversion is done through a process called sampling, in which every fraction of a second a sample of the sound is recorded in digital bits. Two factors that affect the quality of the digitized sound are (1) the number of times the sample is taken, which is called the **sample rate**, and (2) the amount of information stored about the sample, which is called the **sample size**. Figure C-2 shows an example of an analog wave pattern that has been sampled.

▶ The three most common sample rates are 11.025 kHz, 22.05 kHz, and 44.1 kHz. The higher the sample rate, the more samples that are taken and thus the better the quality of the digitized sound. The two most common sample sizes are 8 bit and 16 bit. An 8-bit sample allows for 256 values that are used to describe the sound, whereas a 16-bit sample allows for 65,536 values. The higher the sample size, the better the quality of the digitized sound and the larger the file size.

▶ A sound card and software program are used to digitize sound. A sound from an external source is sent to the card.

The external source could be a cassette tape, videotape player, CD, or a person speaking into a microphone. The card samples the sound based on the sample rate (11.025, 22.5, or 44.1 kHz) and bit value (8 or 16), and then produces the digital approximation of the analog signal. The user determines, through settings provided in the software program, the sample rate and bit value used by the sound card.

▶ Once a sound has been digitized, it can easily be manipulated using a sound-editing program. Figure C-3 shows a sound-editing program and some of its features. Sound files can be saved in several file formats. Popular audio file formats include the following: **WAV** – a format developed by Microsoft and IBM that has become widely used for audio on the Web. WAV files can be played on Windows-based and Macintosh computers. **AIFF (Audio Interchange File Format)** and **AIFFC (AIFF Compressed)** – a format developed by Apple and used as a standard for Macintosh computers. AIFF files can be played on a Windows-based computer. **RealAudio (.ra)** – a compression format developed by Real Networks that allows streaming of the sound file over the Web. **MP3 (MPEG Layer 3)** – a format that compresses large audio files (entire songs) for playback on the Web at near stereo quality.

▶ **MIDI (Musical Instrument Digital Interface)** is a standard format that enables computers and electronic musical instruments to communicate sound information. A MIDI file begins with an event, like pressing a key on a MIDI keyboard, and codes the event (including which key was pressed as well as how hard and long it was pressed) as a series of commands. This information is stored in a file, which can be sent from the computer to an instrument, such as a synthesizer, for playback. Because MIDI files contain code instead of the actual digitized sounds, they can be hundreds of times smaller than audio files. Working with MIDI requires specialized software and may require specialized equipment for recording and playback or a MIDI-compatible audio card.

FIGURE C-1: *An analog wave pattern*

This analog wave pattern represents the volume and frequency of a sound

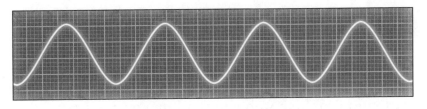

FIGURE C-2: *A digital sampling of an analog wave pattern*

Each bar represents one sample of the sound

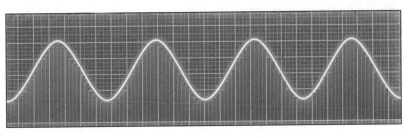

FIGURE C-3: *A sound-editing program*

With a sound editing program, you can perform tasks such as selecting and cutting. You can also choose to add sound effects such as an echo, fade-in, or fade-out.

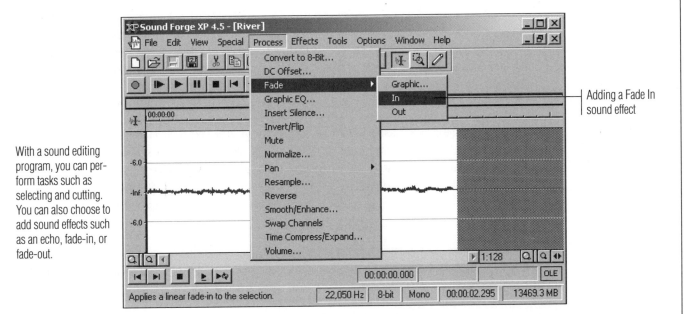

Adding a Fade In sound effect

Exploring sound on the Web

The use of sound on the Web is becoming increasingly more prevalent. Companies use sound to draw attention to their Web sites and market their products; developers search the Internet for sound files to use in their multimedia applications; educators deliver audio lectures in their online courses; musicians provide sample versions of their latest songs; and Web-based game developers use sound to enhance their entertainment sites. This lesson examines how sound is used on the Web.

DETAILS

► A primary consideration when using sound on the Web is file size. Uncompressed audio files can be extremely large, requiring unacceptable playback time when delivered through the Internet. For example a 10-second recording of CD-quality audio in stereo would be nearly 2 MB in size and take as long as 30 seconds to download from the Internet using a 56K modem. Through a process called **file compression**, the size of a file can be reduced significantly. File compression is automatically performed when audio files are saved using certain file formats, such as RealAudio, or when they are converted from one format to another, such as when converting a WAV file to an MP3 file.

► Sound files delivered via the Web are stored on a server. A **server** is a computer with software that responds to other computers and makes data and programs available to them.

► **Streaming media** is a technology that allows audio and video to be played in real time, as shown in Figure C-4. Ordinarily, sound files are delivered from a server to a user's computer in the same way that a Web page is delivered. That is, the user clicks on a link within a browser, which sends a request to the server to transfer the audio file. Once the document has been sent, the link between the server and the user's computer is disconnected. The audio file has essentially been transferred (downloaded) to the user's computer. Downloaded audio files do not begin playing until the transfer is complete, which can take several minutes. With streaming media, however, the file is sent from the server to the user's computer after the user requests the audio file (perhaps by clicking the name of the sound clip or an icon representing an audio file), and it starts playing after only a few moments—before the entire file is downloaded to the computer. The connection from the server to the user's computer is continuous. An advantage of streaming media is its greater speed in starting the media file.

► While some of the standard audio file formats, such as WAV, can be played on the Web, other audio formats have been developed specifically for use on the Web and for streaming audio files. MP3 (MPEG Layer 3) is a popular file format standard for delivery of music on the Internet because it can compress very large files, including complete songs, into small file sizes while maintaining CD-quality audio. RealAudio (.ra) is a file format developed by Real Networks specifically for streaming. When sounds are saved in this format, they are automatically compressed to reduce the file size.

► A media player must be installed on a computer to stream sound files through the Web. These players are usually available for free from various download sites on the Internet. Among the most popular are RealPlayer (see Figure C-5), Windows Media Player, MP3, and QuickTime.

FIGURE C-4: *Example of streaming media*

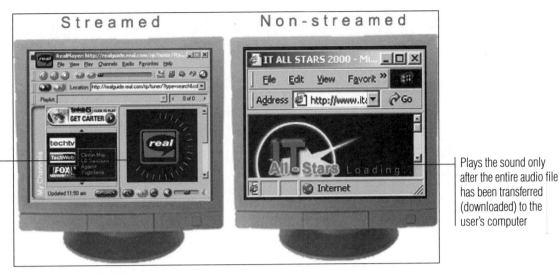

Plays the sound as the audio file is being transferred to the user's computer; if video is available, plays the video while the video is being transferred

Plays the sound only after the entire audio file has been transferred (downloaded) to the user's computer

Figure C-5: RealPlayer Media Player

Play

Pause

Stop

Rewind

Controls

TABLE C-1: *Tips for using sound on the Web*

REGARDING	DESCRIPTION
Appropriate use	Consider the appropriateness of using sound. Some sounds are content-related, such as hearing a foreign phrase pronounced. Other sounds are for effect, such as creating a mood or setting a scene. Avoid using sound when there is no compelling benefit.
Quality	Start with the highest-quality sound available and reduce the file size by converting the audio file to a compressed format. When possible, avoid using free sound clips available from the Internet. These are often of poor quality and overused.
Cost considerations	When recording audio files, it may be cost-prohibitive to contract with a recording studio and hire professional talent. Investing in reasonably high-end equipment (such as a sound card, microphone, and recording and editing software), however, will prove worthwhile.
Alternative methods	Consider using sound and still images as an alternative to video to reduce file sizes. It may be just as effective to show a photograph of a speaker and play the sound file of the speech as it is to show a video of a "talking head."
Streaming	Consider streaming the audio, especially for large files.
User control	If appropriate, provide a way to give the user some control over the audio. Consider allowing the user to skip a sound clip or adjust the volume. This issue is especially important if a musical introduction is played when the user first enters a Web site. The second time visiting the site, the user may not want to hear the musical introduction.

Understanding 2-D animation

Television programs, movies, and videotapes with animation are part of our daily lives. Animation plays a huge role in entertainment (providing action and realism) and in education (providing visualization and demonstration). Entertainment titles in general and children's titles in particular rely heavily on animation. But animation can also be extremely effective in other titles, such as training applications. For example, if a mechanic needs to be trained on the hydraulic system for the landing gear of a jet plane, a training video might be used to provide information on the flow of hydraulic fluid through the system. While it might be impossible to videotape the actual flow of the fluid inside the landing gear, an animation could provide a simulation of the process and dramatize how pressure is created during the process. This lesson examines how 2-D animation is used in multimedia applications.

DETAILS

▶ The perception of motion in an animation is an illusion. The movement that we see is made up of many still images, each in its own frame, which is like a movie. Movies on film run at 24 frames per second, whereas television uses 30 frames per second. Computer animations can be effective at 12 to 15 frames per second; anything less than 12 frames per second, however, creates a jerky motion as the eye detects the changes from one frame to the next.

▶ Two types of 2-D animation exist: cel animation and path animation. **Cel animation** is based on changes that occur from one frame to another, which give the illusion of movement. Figure C-6 shows an example of cel animation. "Cel" comes from the word *celluloid,* which is a clear sheet material on which images were drawn by movie animators. The celluloid images are then placed on a stationary background. The background remains fixed as the object changes from frame to frame. You can have more than one object move against a fixed background. Computer-based cel animation usually employs animation programs such as TOONZ, although some multimedia authoring programs can create cel animations.

▶ **Path animation** moves an object along a predetermined path on the screen. The path could be a straight line or it could include any number of curves. Often the object does not change, although it might be resized or rotated. Figure C-7 shows path animation used to create the movement of a bouncing ball. Path animation can be relatively easy to create as compared with cel animation, because you need only one object (the ball), instead of several objects (the chipmunk in various positions). In addition, you can use a multimedia authoring program to create the path simply by dragging the mouse pointer around the screen

or by pointing to different locations on the screen and clicking the mouse button. Some authoring programs even allow you to set the object's beginning position on one frame and its ending position on another frame. Then the program uses a technique called "**tweening**" to automatically fill in the intervening frames.

▶ Generally, you will use cel animation when you want to create a 2-D animation. Path animation is useful when an object should move along some predetermined course.

▶ Software used to create 2-D animations ranges from shareware products, to low-cost, easy-to-use programs that can create basic cel animations quickly, to sophisticated multimedia authoring programs that cost hundreds of dollars. These programs allow you to determine the **frame rate**, which sets the speed of the animation, and allow you to include **transitions**, which determine special effects such as fade-in and fade-out. In addition, these programs allow you to define user control for playback and to specify how many times to run the animation; in **looping**, for example, the animation continues to play over and over until the user stops the animation, or the loop is complete.

▶ The more powerful 2-D animation programs allow the developer to draw an object, animate the object, provide a sound clip such as a narration, and provide controls for the user such as play, pause, and quit. There are even GIF animation programs, which allow you to assemble a series of GIF images that are then displayed in rapid succession to give the appearance of motion.

▶ 2-D animation can be an acceptable alternative to the expense of creating video, especially in those applications in which the realism provided by video is not critical.

FIGURE C-6: *Example of cel animation*

Stationary background

The placement and action of the chipmunk varies from frame to frame, creating the illusion of movement as the frames are displayed in rapid succession

FIGURE C-7: *Example of path animation*

A path animation created by placing the ball at the first and last position of each path segment and using the "in between special" function of the authoring program.

Clip animation

The Web is an excellent source for animations of every conceivable category. Many of the sites have hundreds of free clip animations available for downloading and use in a multimedia application. Often, these free animations are "cute," but generally they are fairly low-quality and easy to spot as "clip animation." Professional developers will want to create their own animations rather than using clip animation.

Understanding 3-D animation

While 2-D animation can be effective in enhancing a multimedia title, 3-D animation takes the entire multimedia experience to another level. 3-D animation is the foundation of many multimedia CD games and adventure titles. Top-selling products such as Myst and 7th Guest use 3-D animation to bring users into the setting as participants, not spectators. Creating 3-D animation is considerably more complex than creating 2-D animation. This lesson examines how 3-D animation is developed and used in multimedia applications.

DETAILS

► 3-D animation involves three steps: modeling, animation, and rendering.

► **Modeling** is the process of creating the broad contours and structure of 3-D objects and scenes. One technique, shown in Figure C-8, is drawing various views of an object (top, side, cross section) by setting points on a grid. This is done by creating a polygon mesh. These views are used to define the object's 3-D shape.

► **Animation** is the process of defining the object's motion. This step defines how the lighting and perspective views also create change during the animation.

► **Rendering** is the final step in creating 3-D animation. It involves giving objects attributes such as colors, surface textures, and amounts of transparency. Figure C-9 shows an image that has been rendered. Initially, animators may render the animation using a quick, lower-resolution process as a test. They will then analyze the test and make adjustments accordingly. Once they are satisfied, they will use a slower, higher-quality process to render the finished animation. This is changing with videographics equalizers such as Sony's GSCube that allow animators to create complex scenes in real time. Strata 3D, LightWave 3D, 3D Studio Max, Maya, and Houdini are examples of programs that can produce quite sophisticated 3-D animations.

► A commonly used special effect for animations is morphing. **Morphing** is the process of blending together two images into a series of images, as shown in Figure C-10. Morphing is useful in showing not only how two images blend together, but also how an image might change over time. Morphing can be done in 2-D animation, but is more commonly carried out in 3-D animation because of the subjects used—people.

► **Warping** is a related special effect that allows you to distort a single image. For example, you could warp a facial feature to change a frown into a smile.

► **Virtual reality** (VR) creates an environment that surrounds the user so that he or she becomes part of the experience. The term *virtual reality* has been used to describe various types of applications, some of which are more experiential than others. Examples of virtual reality include the following:

- The Boeing Corporation uses flight simulators that are cockpits of actual airplanes. These cockpits are mounted on hydraulically controlled legs that can simulate every motion of an aircraft. Flight crews training in these simulators can be presented with any number of virtual reality environments (airports, weather conditions, landing approaches) on displays viewed through the cockpit windows. These simulators are so realistic that the FAA will approve current pilots for certification on a specific model using the simulator alone.

- CD-based adventure games, such as Myst and 7th Guest, create scenes by having the user point the mouse cursor and walk through doors, go up stairs, turn left or right, or otherwise move through the changing surroundings. The goal for the multimedia developer is to make it seem as though the user is standing in the middle of a room, in an arcade, in a haunted house, and so on.

- Some VR applications, such as the Zion National Park CD-ROM, allow a "virtual tour" of a site. Arcade-type games, such as BattleTech and the Red Planet, require special equipment—some games even require headgear with goggles that allow the user to "step into" a virtual world. As the user turns his or her head, a different view of the world appears. Gloves and hand-held equipment can be used to allow the person to interact with the environment. Haptic interface devices and virtual reality caves are being used in medical, engineering, and other fields.

FIGURE C-8: *Various views: 3-D modeling process*

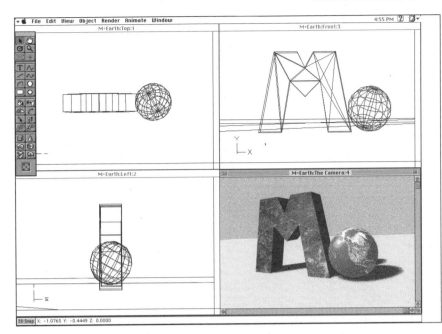

FIGURE C-9: *Results of the rendering process in a 3-D animation*

Rendering can take considerable time (days) depending on the complexity of the animation and the tools being used. The various rendering processes differ in terms of time needed and quality of the completed animation.

FIGURE C-10: *Example of morphing*

Animating the Morph

First image

You can create a series of bitmap images that can be used in an animation. In this case 18 images were created.

The morphing process involves selecting sets of corresponding points on each of the two starting images. For example, in morphing two faces, the sets of points might include eyes, lips, ears, and head. Based on these sets of points, the morphing program rearranges the pixels to blend the original two images into a series of images.

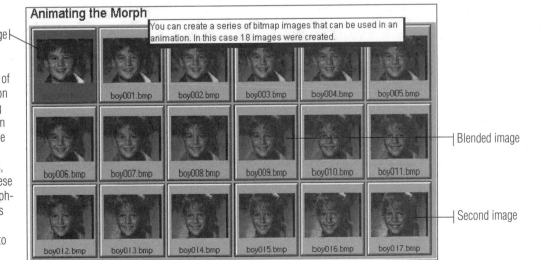

Blended image

Second image

Exploring animation on the Web

Animation is an excellent way to increase the appeal of a Web site and to help ensure return visits. Animations can be as simple as blinking text, marquee-like scrolling headlines, rotating logos, and 2-D action figures, or they can be as complex as 3-D virtual reality environments with user control. This lesson presents an overview of animation on the Web.

DETAILS

▶ Animated text. Text can be animated in several ways. These actions include rotating, zooming in and out, scrolling across the screen in a marquee-like action, distorting, and blinking. Software, including multimedia authoring programs, is available to help you animate text. The process can be as simple as typing in the word or phrase and selecting the desired action or as complex as writing HTML code for the desired action. For example, the HTML tags <blink>...</blink> will cause text entered between the HTML tags to blink. The HTML code <blink>YEAR-END SALE </blink> will cause the words YEAR-END SALE to blink.

▶ Animated GIF. As you read earlier, GIF is a standard graphics file format for the Web. GIFs are still images that can be combined to create an animation. The Animagic GIF Animator Program (see Figure C-11) allows you to create an animation by displaying a series of still GIF image files. In addition to ones you create, hundreds of free GIF animations are available for downloading from the Web. These free GIF animations are often low-quality animations, and, because they are free, they seem to pop up everywhere. For this reason, a multimedia developer should be careful in using them. Even though these free animations may not be exactly what the multimedia developer had in mind, they can be a valuable resource. For example, they can stimulate ideas for creating new animations or be modified to be more appropriate.

▶ Macromedia Director applications. Macromedia Director is an authoring program that has been used for years to create multimedia applications that run on CD-ROMs. Now developers use Director to create applications that can be played on the Web by saving Director files in a Web-ready format. To run a Director application from the Web, a user must have the Shockwave plug-in installed on his or her computer. A **plug-In** is a program that permits a Web browser to access and execute files that the browser would not normally recognize. If the user's computer does not have the Shockwave plug-in, it can be downloaded from the Internet. Flash, another Macromedia program, (see Figure C-12) was created specifically for the development of animations that can run on the Web. Flash also uses the Shockwave plug-in.

▶ 3-D environments. **Virtual Reality Modeling Language** (VRML) is a computer language used to create interactive 3-D multimedia environments on the Web that allow the user to move through a space or explore an object. Instead of the object moving, the user is moving through the environment, much as we do in our everyday 3-D world. It allows the environment to be dynamic and always changing. Using a VRML browser, the user can move around the world zooming in and out, rotating direction, and interacting with the virtual environment.

   Now that you have explored 2-D animation, 3-D animation, and animation on the Web, you can see that the possibilities for making multimedia titles come to life are limited only by the designer's imagination and creativity. Before using any animation in a multimedia title or on the Web, however, the multimedia designer should ask these questions: Is the animation appropriate for the multimedia application? Does it add value, or is it simply for show? What is the best way to animate the concept? How unique can the animations be?

FIGURE C-11: *The Animagic GIF Animator program*

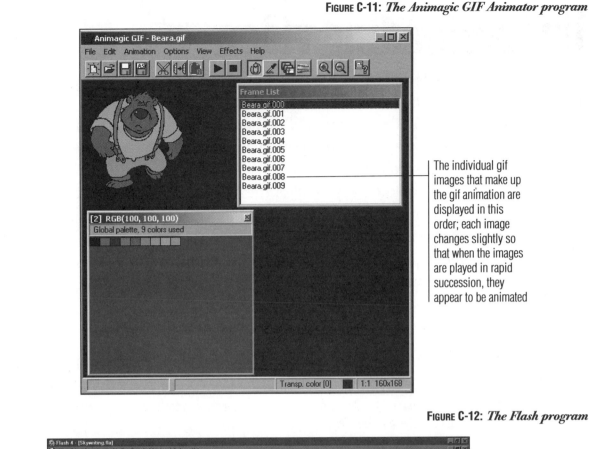

The individual gif images that make up the gif animation are displayed in this order; each image changes slightly so that when the images are played in rapid succession, they appear to be animated

FIGURE C-12: *The Flash program*

Tool panel with text, drawing, selection, and other tools

Control panel for playing the animation

Object panel for setting properties (such as size) of an object

Timeline and the objects that will appear during the animation

Work area

Color Panel for selecting colors

Accessing animation on the Web

To view certain animations on the Web, your computer playback system must have the appropriate plug-in. For example, to play an animation created using the Macromedia Flash software, you need the Shockwave plug-in. Often Web pages that use animation will alert you when you start to play the animation and the plug-in is not available on your computer. These alerts usually provide a link to a site where you can download the plug-in needed to run the animation.

Understanding video

The ability to incorporate digitized video into a multimedia title marked a significant achievement in the evolution of the multimedia industry. Consider the following scenario: You are developing a report on the civil rights movement in the United States. You want to include excerpts from Martin Luther King, Jr.'s "I have a dream..." speech. As part of your presentation, you could do any or all of the following: type part of the speech and hand it out (text); show a photo of Martin Luther King, Jr. (graphics); play an audio excerpt of the speech (sound); or play a video excerpt of the speech (video). Those viewing the video would recognize the impact of seeing the actual event rather than reading about it or listening to it. This lesson examines how video is used in multimedia applications.

DETAILS

► Video can be extremely costly and time-consuming to create, and video files can become extremely large; so careful planning is critical when using video in multimedia elements.

► Many sources provide ready-made video clips such as Web sites and stock film companies. The developer may find that these stock videos are not appropriate for the intended effect, however.

► Video, like sound, is usually recorded and played as an analog signal. Analog video must be digitized in order for it to become incorporated into a multimedia title. Figure C-13 shows the process for digitizing an analog video signal. A video source such as a video camera, VCR, or TV is connected to a video capture card in a computer. As the video source is played, the analog signal is sent to the video card and changed into a digital file that is stored on the hard drive. The sound from the video source is digitized at the same time using the video capture card.

► Analog video, such as a videotape, is linear. That is, it has a beginning, middle, and end. If you want to edit it, you need to rewind, pause, and then fast forward the tape to display the desired frames. Conversely, digitized video allows random access to any part of the video. Editing digitized video can be as easy as the process used to cut and paste text in a word processing program. In addition, the process to add special effects such as transitions to digitized video is relatively simple.

► Although digitized video has many advantages, there is an important consideration: file size. Digitized video files can be extremely large. One second of high-quality color video that takes up only one-quarter of a computer's screen can be as large as 1 MB. Several elements determine the file size, including the frame rate, image size, color depth, and length of the video.
  • Frame rate. Earlier you learned that animation is an illusion caused by the rapid display of still images (frames). Television plays at 30 frames per second, but acceptable playback can be achieved with 15 frames per second.
  • Image size. When a full-screen resolution is set at 640 × 480 pixels, video is more appropriately displayed in a window that is one-fourth (320 × 240) the size of the full screen.
  • Color depth. Digitized video is really made up of a series of still graphic bitmaps. Thus the quality of video depends on the color quality (related to the number of colors) for each graphic bitmap. As you learned earlier, 8-bit color provides 256 colors, 16-bit color provides more than 64,000 colors, and 24-bit color provides more than 16 million colors.

► Using the following formula, you can estimate the file size of one second of digitized video:
Frames/second x image size x color depth / 8 = file size

► While it might be desirable to run several minutes of photo-quality, full-screen video at 30 frames per second, it may not feasible. The file size would be prohibitive and the current playback multimedia systems would not support the processing power required. Table C-2 provides tips for reducing video file size. In the final analysis, the use of video becomes a trade-off between quality and file size.

FIGURE C-13: *Digitizing an analog video signal*

Video camera   Analog signal   Video card   Digital signal   Hard drive storage

FIGURE C-14: *Minimizing the use of video*

The flame is the only moving part of the scene. Instead of creating a video of the entire scene, you could use the scene for a background still image and videotape only the flame; you could then play the flame in a window, giving the impression that the entire image is a video.

TABLE C-2: *TIPS FOR REDUCING VIDEO FILE SIZE*

REDUCE	RAMIFICATIONS
Color depth	Reducing the color depth to less than 256 colors gives a markedly poorer-quality image.
Frame rate	Reducing the frame rate to less than 15 frames per second causes a noticeable and distracting jerkiness that is usually unacceptable.
File size	A technique for reducing file size is to minimize the use of video in the image that appears on the screen—that is, to create video only for the parts of an object that are changing, such as a flickering candle. The video could be played over and over to create the motion of a flickering candle. Figure C-14 shows how to minimize the use of video to reduce file size.
Display size	In most multimedia titles, you do not need to show full-screen video. The video can be played in a window that can be as small as one-fourth or even one-sixteenth the size of the screen.

Conclusion: Changing the image size and compressing the file become the primary ways of reducing file size. In most cases, a one-quarter screen image (320 x 240), an 8-bit (256 colors) color depth, and a 15 frames per second frame rate are acceptable in a multimedia title.

Understanding video compression and video editing

Because of the large sizes associated with video files, video compression/decompression programs, known as **codecs**, have been developed. These programs can substantially reduce the size of video files, which means that more video can fit on a single CD and that the speed of transferring video from a CD to the computer can be increased. Video editing is used to incorporate compressed video into a multimedia application. This lesson presents an overview of video compression and video editing.

DETAILS

▶ There are two types of compression, lossless and lossy. **Lossless** preserves the exact image throughout the compression and decompression process, but the resulting file can be very large. **Lossy** compression actually eliminates some of the data in the image and, therefore, provides greater compression ratios than lossless compression. The greater the compression ratio is, however, the poorer the decompressed image is. The trade-off is file size versus image quality. Lossy compression is applied to video because some drop in the quality is not noticeable in moving images.

▶ Certain standards have been established for compression programs, including files created with the JPEG (Joint Photographic Expert Groups) and **MPEG** (Motion Pictures Experts Group) formats. Programs used to create JPEG and MPEG files reduce the file size of graphic images by eliminating redundant information. Often areas of an image (especially backgrounds) contain similar information. JPEG compression identifies these areas and stores them as blocks of pixels instead of pixel by pixel, thereby reducing the amount of information needed to store the image. Compression rations of 20:1 can be achieved without substantially affecting the image quality. A 20:1 compression ratio would reduce a 1 MB file to only 50 KB.

▶ MPEG adds another step in the still image compression process when working with video. It looks for changes in the image from frame to frame. Figure C-15 shows, in a simplified way, how this process works. Key frames are identified every few frames, and the changes that occur from key frame to key frame are recorded.

▶ Two widely used video compression software programs are Apple's QuickTime (and QuickTime for Windows), and Microsoft's Windows Media Player. QuickTime is popular because it runs on both Apple and Windows-based computers. It uses lossy compression coding and can achieve ratios ranging from 5:1 to 25:1. Windows Media Player uses a format called Audio Video Interleave (AVI) that, like QuickTime, synchronizes the sound and motion of a video file.

▶ Several steps are needed to prepare video to be incorporated into a multimedia title, including capturing and digitizing the video from some video source such as a video camera, VCR, or TV; editing the digitized video; and compressing the video. Some software programs specialize in one or more of these steps. Other programs, such as Adobe Premiere, as shown in Figure C-16, can perform all of them.

▶ While capturing and compressing video are necessary, editing video receives the most attention. Features that may be included in video-editing programs include the following:
- Incorporating transitions such as dissolves, wipes, and spins
- Superimposing titles and animating them such as a fly-in logo
- Applying special effects such as twisting, zooming, rotating, and distorting to various images
- Synchronizing sound with the video
- Applying filters that control color balance, brightness and contrast, blurring, distortions, and morphing

FIGURE C-15: *Video compression process*

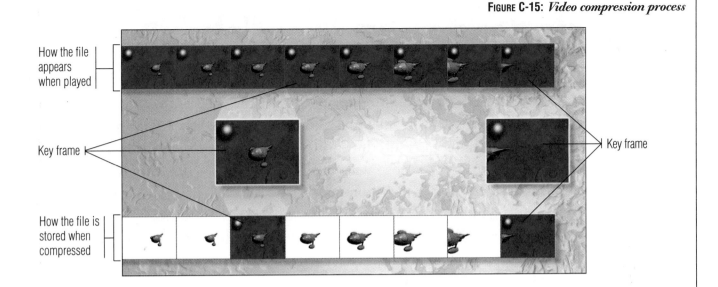

How the file appears when played

Key frame

Key frame

How the file is stored when compressed

FIGURE C-16: *Adobe Premiere video-editing program*

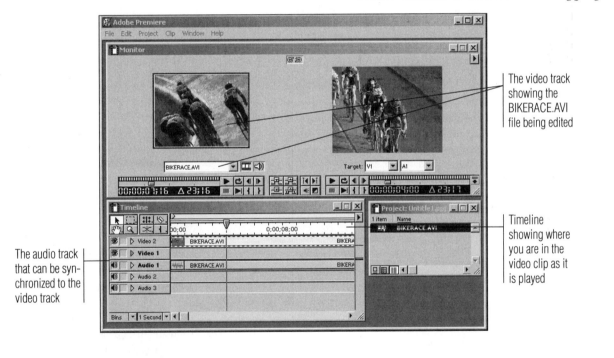

The video track showing the BIKERACE.AVI file being edited

Timeline showing where you are in the video clip as it is played

The audio track that can be synchronized to the video track

Synchronizing multimedia elements

Using a video-editing program such as Adobe Premiere allows you to easily synchronize video elements such as audio and video. When using several multimedia elements such as audio, video, and graphics within the same streaming presentation on the Web, these elements must be coordinated so that, for example, the sound is synchronized with the video.

SMIL (Synchronized Multimedia Integration Language) is a markup language (like HTML) and is used to solve the problems of coordinating the timeline of displaying multimedia on Web sites. The start and end times of different elements are specified relative to events in other media elements. For example, in a narrated presentation, a particular video clip is played when the narrator in the audio starts talking about it; a program such as SMIL ensures that the two events happen synchronously.

Exploring video on the Web

Using video on the Web provides a level of realism not possible with animation or still images. For example, there are Web sites that allow you to view streaming real-time or archive video of news, entertainment, and education programming. Realistically, however, video on the Web is practical only for those with fast Internet connections (56K minimum) and high-end computers (for example, Pentium processors for PCs, PowerPC for the Macintosh). The primary challenge for using video on the Web is the **transfer rate**—the amount of time it takes to transfer video from a server on the Internet to the user's computer. This challenge can be addressed in the planning, creation, and delivery stages for video content. This lesson examines how video is developed for and used on the Web.

DETAILS

▶ Without careful planning, the use of video on the Web can be a drawback rather than an asset. Lack of planning often results in poor-quality video.

▶ When planning the use of video on the Web, alternatives such as animation or still images with sound should be explored. These alternatives will provide smaller file sizes and quicker download times; they may also reduce costs and development time.

▶ Video files in various formats, including AVI, MPEG, and QuickTime, can be downloaded from the Web and played on a user's computer. Many Web sites and companies offer stock video clips for sale that can be transferred over the Web. Two concerns that must be addressed when considering stock videos are the quality-versus-cost issue and the relevance of the video to the multimedia application.

▶ There are essentially two types of video transfer through the Internet: HTTP and RTSP.

▶ **HTTP (HyperText Transfer Protocol)** downloads the entire video to the hard drive on the user's computer. The user must wait for the download process and does not have the ability to jump from one location to another on the video being played. Because the video is downloaded, it can be played repeatedly and copied if necessary.

▶ **RTSP (Real-Time Streaming Protocol)** is a continuous-playing, streaming technology in which the user's computer is in constant contact with the server playing the video. The video is broadcast to the user and, after being displayed, discarded. Even with real-time streaming, some delay (depending on the connection speed) occurs between the time that the user starts the process and the time that the video begins playing, even though a few seconds of data are stored on the user's computer to compensate for any transfer interference. RTSP allows the user to randomly access any part of the video by moving a slider left or right, which indicates to the server which part of the video to start streaming. Overall, HTTP is best suited for playing small video clips, and RTSP is best for large video files and live broadcasts.

▶ Streaming video via the Web is popular because it can reduce significantly the amount of time required for the video to begin playing. RealPlayer from Real Networks, Windows Media Player from Microsoft, and QuickTime Player from Apple are the leading programs used to display streaming video. All three players work with popular video file formats such as AVI and MPEG. Figure C-17 shows two Windows Media Players running the same video clip.

▶ Users have different Internet connection speeds (28.8K, 56K, 256K, and so on). One way to help optimize the streaming process is for the server to transfer the video at the same rate as the user's connection speed. Some programs, such as SureStream from Real Networks, are able to adjust dynamically to the user's connection speeds.

▶ Webcasting of video events in real time, such as concerts, keynote speakers at conferences, and interactive, computer-based chat sessions, is a form of streaming media. HorizonLive, shown in Figure C-18, is a product that supports live video presentations.

FIGURE C-17: *Two Windows Media Players with different skins*

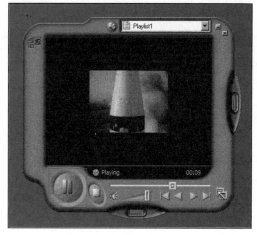

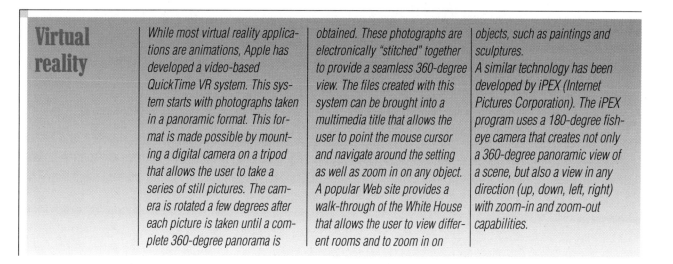

The Media Players have the same controls (start, pause, volume, and so on) but different designs. These designs are called **skins**. There are many skins from which a user can choose.

FIGURE C-18: *A program that provides for streaming video and interaction*

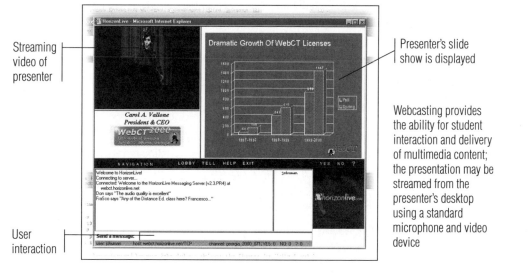

Streaming video of presenter

Presenter's slide show is displayed

Webcasting provides the ability for student interaction and delivery of multimedia content; the presentation may be streamed from the presenter's desktop using a standard microphone and video device

User interaction

Virtual reality

While most virtual reality applications are animations, Apple has developed a video-based QuickTime VR system. This system starts with photographs taken in a panoramic format. This format is made possible by mounting a digital camera on a tripod that allows the user to take a series of still pictures. The camera is rotated a few degrees after each picture is taken until a complete 360-degree panorama is obtained. These photographs are electronically "stitched" together to provide a seamless 360-degree view. The files created with this system can be brought into a multimedia title that allows the user to point the mouse cursor and navigate around the setting as well as zoom in on any object. A popular Web site provides a walk-through of the White House that allows the user to view different rooms and to zoom in on objects, such as paintings and sculptures.

A similar technology has been developed by iPEX (Internet Pictures Corporation). The iPEX program uses a 180-degree fish-eye camera that creates not only a 360-degree panoramic view of a scene, but also a view in any direction (up, down, left, right) with zoom-in and zoom-out capabilities.

In 1999, a nineteen-year-old "techie" developed a software program that enabled the "sharing" of MP3 files through the Web. In a few short months, 20 million individuals were downloading CD-quality songs at the rate of 1400 per minute—for free. How was this situation possible? Who was responsible for this incredible feat? Both questions can be answered with one word—Napster.

The Napster Web site allowed anyone connected to the Web to download its software and then link up to a virtual community of individuals willing to make their MP3 libraries available to others. The Napster Web site provided a search function that allowed visitors to the site to find songs by artist and/or title. In addition, it offered a free MP3 player that allowed users to listen to the MP3 files they downloaded. It also provided an instant messaging system and chat feature so users could communicate in real time about current music titles and trends.

In July 2000, Napster had more than 5.4 million visitors to its Web site, ranking it as the 47th most popular site in the United States. This was an astounding achievement, but the clouds of controversy overshadowed this success. The Recording Industry Association of America (RIAA) had filed suit against Napster, claiming that it violated copyright laws by facilitating the exchange of copyrighted material. The suit raised important questions about intellectual property rights and emerging technologies.

Those against Napster make these points:

1. The music that is being downloaded via the Napster Web site is copyrighted, and the copyright holders are not receiving compensation. (RIAA estimated $300 million in lost sales.)

2. Artists are losing money on "pirated" songs. (The band Metallica found more than 300,000 users trading its songs online.)

3. CD sales are down 13% at stores within a mile of the "Top 40 Wired Colleges" as identified by *Wired* magazine as well as at those stores near colleges that had formally recognized they were having problems with Napster-induced network overloading.

Those for Napster make these points:

1. Those downloading files are only sampling them, which does not affect sales. One study showed that users of Napster were 45% more likely to increase their music purchasing than those not sharing files. Another study found that two-thirds of students polled said they download songs to preview them before purchasing.

2. Some artists (for example, Courtney Love) view the process as sampling rather than stealing and see it as a way for unknown artists to gain a following.

3. Some artists see Napster as a way of forcing the major recording labels to deal more fairly with recording artists.

4. Downloads are up, and CD sales are up. In fact, according to industry estimates as reported by Wired News, year-to-date U.S. sales of albums in compact disc and cassette form were up more than 7% at the time the suit was filed.

5. Napster is not copying and distributing the music; it merely provides a way for individuals to share. A message appears when Napster is launched stating: "Neither the MP3 file format nor the Napster software indicates whether a particular MP3 file has been authorized for copying or distribution…Compliance with copyright laws remains your responsibility." This message places the responsibility in the lap of the user; in other words, it is not Napster's responsibility, and Napster should not be held responsible.

During July 2000, Napster attorneys participated in a U.S. Senate hearing on Internet services and technologies. At the end of July, a judge ordered Napster "to remove all copyrighted material from its service pending the trial for the copyright-infringement lawsuit." Less than 24 hours after the court order was issued, Napster filed a stay—stating that if the company was forced to shut down its Web site, that action would effectively put Napster out of business. At the eleventh hour, the U.S. District Court of Appeals in San Francisco granted Napster a temporary stay. The court ruled that Napster could continue to maintain its Web site while the case proceeded through the appeals process.

Some see this case as the first big legal battle over intellectual property rights and emerging technologies. Its outcome will have a far-reaching impact—not only on the parties involved in the case, but also on copyright laws and their relationship with emerging technologies.

EXPAND THE IDEAS

Work individually or in small groups. Research the following questions. Be prepared to provide support for your position on each in class discussion.

1. Design a poster that addresses the issues for and against Napster. Highlight points argued by both sides presented in the Issue. Research the case. Add more points for Napster (Napster's and its supporters' views) and against Napster (RIAA's and recording artists' views) to your poster.

2. Do you think that the Napster message that appears when its product is launched should protect the company from copyright suits? Why or why not? Are there other situations where disclaimers are used to protect the provider (for example, the disclaimers posted near roller-coaster rides, coat checks in restaurants, or whirlpools)? Have those disclaimers been challenged in court? If so, what was the outcome? Will those court cases have any effect on Napster's claim that its posted message protects it? Prepare an oral report of your findings.

3. Do you agree or disagree that Napster should be shut down? Why or why not? If you disagree with shutting down Napster, what would you say to the artist whose songs are being shared? Summarize your ideas in a written report.

4. If Napster were shut down, do you think it would end the controversy? Why or why not? Provide a written report, and be prepared to share and support your ideas in a class discussion.

5. Napster believes that its site helps the music industry. What is the Napster business model? What compromise could be made to the business model currently employed by Napster that would allow it to continue to service its users and satisfy the music industry? Make a poster presenting your ideas.

6. Many feel that this debate is not really about Napster, but rather the larger issue of how our society deals with the impact of Internet technologies on the distribution of copyrighted materials. What do you see as the impact, and how can it be a win-win situation? Summarize your ideas in a written report.

7. There have been many news articles regarding the Napster case. Connect to the Internet and read five articles. Provide the article source information and a brief review of each article. Summarize your reading by answering the following questions: Did the articles present the information fairly and objectively? Was the voice consistent from source to source? Were there discrepancies in the information reported?

End of Unit Exercises

STUDY TIPS

1. Review key terms from this unit. You might use online resources to gather additional information or to clarify any terms that you would like to explore in more depth.

2. Make a poster presentation about sound waves. Describe an analog sound pattern and explain how an analog sound wave is converted to a digitized sound.

3. Make a table listing sound and video file formats. Include these column heads: Acronym; Meaning of Acronym (if appropriate); Description/Notes.

4. Review Table C-1, Tips for using sound on the Web. Create a third column for the table called Examples. Work with a partner to brainstorm examples for each tip. Share your examples with the class. Were the examples similar? Did any surprise you?

5. Define 2-D animation. Create simple sketches to illustrate both types of 2-D animation described in this unit.

6. Summarize the steps involved in creating 3-D animation.

7. Discuss why planning is a critical factor when incorporating video into a multimedia title. Identify at least three considerations you must take into account when using video.

8. Write a report defining file compression. Define and discuss lossless compression and lossy compression.

9. Describe transitions used in videos. Why are they important? When might you use them? What are some you have seen used?

10. Name the two types of video streaming. Explain differences between the two.

SELECT THE BEST ANSWER

1. The final step in creating a 3-D animation is
_____.

 a. Modeling

 b. Rendering

 c. Programming

 d. Testing

2. The process of blending together two images is called
_____.

 a. Cloning

 b. Merging

 c. Morphing

 d. Integrating

3. The process of playing audio and video in real time over the Internet is called _____.

 a. Downloading

 b. Transferring

 c. Streaming

 d. Serving

4. For most multimedia applications, acceptable playback can be achieved with _____ frames per second.

 a. 30

 b. 15

 c. 45

 d. 55

5. JPEG and _____ are file compression program standards.

a. AWA

b. MPEG

c. GIF

d. WWW

6. A process called _____ automatically fills in the intervening frames in a path animation that flows from one frame to another frame.

a. Morphing

b. Tweening

c. Warping

d. Rendering

7. A(n) _____ is a program that allows a Web browser to access and play files that the browser would not normally recognize.

a. Server

b. MPEG

c. Plug-in

d. Looping

8. _____ is a computer language that is used to create interactive 3-D multimedia environments.

a. VRML

b. SMIL

c. HTTP

d. RTSP

9. _____ compression eliminates some of the data in the image.

a. Lossless

b. Lossy

c. Skin

d. Server

10. Sound files can be saved as _____.

a. WAV

b. AIFF

c. .ra

d. all of the above

1. The three most common sample rates used to digitize sound are _____, _____, and _____.

2. The two types of 2-D animation are _____ and _____.

3. The three steps involved in creating 3-D animations are _____, _____, and _____.

4. The file size of digitized video is determined by _____, _____, _____, and _____.

5. A(n) _____ _____ and software program are used to digitize sound.

6. A(n) _____ is a computer whose software responds to other computers and makes data and programs available to them.

7. _____ is used to synchronize sound and video in a multimedia presentation on the Web.

8. Before a sound is digitized, it is represented as a(n) _____ wave pattern.

9. Digitizing sound is done through a process called _____.

10. _____ is a standard format that enables computers and electronic musical instruments to communicate sound information.

INDEPENDENT CHALLENGE 1

Sound is a fundamental element in a multimedia title. We may tend to overlook the importance of sound because it is so much a part of our daily life—participating in conversations, listening to lectures, playing music on the radio—that we take it for granted. Successful multimedia developers understand the significance of sound and use it in a variety of ways, such as attracting attention, communicating an idea, and creating a mood.

To complete this independent challenge:

1. Choose an application (CD-ROM, Web site) that includes sound, and study it.

2. Prepare a report with the following information:

a. Name of CD title or Web site URL.

b. Purpose of the application (for example, entertainment, commerce).

c. Intended audience.

d. What types of sound are used (content-related, such as narration, and/or background)?

e. How does the use of sound improve or degrade the quality of the application? Be specific.

f. What would be the effect on the application if sound were not used?

g. If you were asked for ideas about replacing the sound, what would you suggest?

INDEPENDENT CHALLENGE 2

Animation is a fundamental element in a multimedia title. Multimedia developers find animation especially useful in attracting attention, communicating complex concepts, and instilling fun into a title.

To complete this independent challenge:

1. Choose an application (CD-ROM, Web site) that includes animation, and study it.

2. Prepare a report with the following information:

a. Name of CD title or Web site URL.

b. Purpose of the application (for example, entertainment, commerce).

c. Intended audience.

d. What types of animation are used (2-D: cel or path; 3-D)?

e. How does the use of animation improve or degrade the quality of the application? Be specific.

f. What would be the effect on the application if animation were not used?

g. If you were asked for ideas about replacing the animation, what would you suggest?

INDEPENDENT CHALLENGE 3

Video is a fundamental element in a multimedia title. Multimedia developers use video to convey a sense of realism and to provide an effect that may not be achievable through animation or sound alone.

To complete this independent challenge:

1. Choose an application (CD-ROM, Web site) that includes video, and study it.

2. Prepare a report with the following information:

a. Name of CD title or Web site URL.

b. Purpose of the application (for example, entertainment, commerce).

c. Intended audience.

d. How is video used to improve the application? Be specific.

e. What would be the effect on the application if video were not used?

f. If you were asked for ideas about replacing the video, what would you suggest?

INDEPENDENT CHALLENGE 4

WEB WORKS

Stock clips for sound, animation, and video are available from both commercial vendors and individuals. Some clips cost money to use, whereas others are offered free of charge. Stock clips are available via CD distribution and via the Web. The quality of these clips varies widely. Because of their easy accessibility, some clips have become overused—that is, they no longer capture the audience's attention and imagination, which means that they lose their effectiveness and value. As a developer of multimedia titles, it is critical that you use sound, animation, and video wisely. It is important to familiarize yourself with stock clips—their sources and the terms of their use—before you need them.

To complete this independent challenge:

1. Connect to the Internet.

2. Go to http://www.course.com; navigate to the Student Online Companion for this book; and then click the link for Unit C.

3. Notice that the Unit C link contains links to Web sites offering stock sound, animation, and video clips. Click each link to visit the site. Write a summary of each site. Include the following information in the summary:

a. Name of the company and URL.

b. What types of clips are available (sound, animation, video)? Approximately how many clips are available?

c. How are the clips organized?

d. Preview a variety of the clips. Are there any that you have seen before? If yes, which ones? Where? Would you consider using these clips? Why or why not?

e. Search for a particular type of clip and then evaluate the search process, including how easy it was and how satisfied you were with the results.

f. What information is provided about the file (size, sample rate, file format)?

g. If possible, play one of the clips, and evaluate its quality.

h. What are the conditions of use? Royalty? Free? Licensing agreement required? Copyright considerations? How much does a clip cost?

i. Are the clips available on CD-ROM? On the Web?

INDEPENDENT CHALLENGE 5

Streaming is an important technology used on the Web. Both audio files and video files can be streamed.

To complete this independent challenge:

1. Connect to the Web.

2. Find three Web sites that provide streaming audio or video, and analyze the delivery of the audio or video.

3. Write a report that includes the following information for each Web site:

a. Web site URL.

b. Types of content available for streaming (radio show, sports broadcast, music, entertainment, and so on).

c. The steps you followed to stream content from the site.

d. Which media player (such as RealPlayer or Windows Media Player) did you use to complete the streaming? Was the player installed on your computer, or did you need to download it?

e. How long did it take to start playing the file?

f. What controls are available to you as you play the file (for example, start, pause)?

g. Summarize the quality of the file that is being streamed.

h. Draw a sketch of the skin.

1. What is pictured in Figure C-19?

2. When would you use this application?

3. What controls are available? Label them.

FIGURE C-19

Multimedia Authoring Programs

OBJECTIVES

Explore multimedia authoring programs

Examine slide show programs

Examine card or book metaphor programs

Examine icon-based programs

Examine time-based programs

Explore programming languages

Explore scripting languages

Use Web-based multimedia development programs

Now that you are familiar with multimedia applications and their multimedia elements—text, graphics, sound, video, and animation— you are ready to study **authoring programs** used to create multimedia applications. Multimedia authoring programs vary in the features they provide, in their cost, and in their ease of use. In this unit, you will learn about different types of authoring programs, their advantages and disadvantages, and their most appropriate uses. In addition, you will learn about programming and scripting languages used to develop multimedia. You will also learn how multimedia is developed for the Web. Finally, you will consider the issue of censorship as it relates to multimedia titles.

Exploring multimedia authoring programs

Multimedia authoring programs help the developer do the following tasks: produce content with paint, text, and animation tools; design screen layouts using templates; create interactivity; incorporate text, graphics, sound, video, and animation; and create hyperlinks. This lesson explores the way multimedia is used—either to create a presentation or to produce an interactive title—because the way multimedia is used affects its design, development time, cost, and often the authoring program used to create it.

DETAILS

► **Multimedia presentations** involve a presenter and an audience of one or more persons. Generally speaking, a sophisticated authoring program is not needed to create a multimedia presentation.

► In a multimedia presentation, the presenter has control over the multimedia title. It is primarily a one-way communications process, as shown in Figure D-1. Interactivity, such as allowing the presenter to quickly "jump" to various parts of the content, can be built into a multimedia presentation. For example, a sales representative might start with a relatively linear presentation including her company's history and product line, and then "jump" to information about pricing, product availability, or video clips of testimonials from current customers. Multimedia presentations are useful when the presenter wants to take advantage of the power of multimedia while keeping control of the presentation. They are similar to slide shows, but have more bells and whistles; they can be developed easily, quickly, and inexpensively.

► **Interactive titles** are intended for use by individuals in a one-on-one situation or, in cases such as Web-based games, by two or more individuals. For example, a computer-based simulation of a biology lab procedure might teach students how to dissect a frog, or an Internet-based sports game might allow two individuals to interact on the Web.

► A major advantage of interactive titles is that users have control over the applications and can determine what to view based on their needs. For example, if a student is studying for an anatomy test and wants to review the respiratory system, he or she might use hyperlinks to advance to the appropriate lesson on the anatomy CD. Giving control to the user makes him or her an active rather than a passive participant.

► In addition to hyperlinks, the developer might build into these titles conditions that the user must satisfy before proceeding along a certain path. Now the program is making decisions based on user performance. For example, in an educational title the user might be required to take a pretest (see Figure D-2) that determines which tutorial can be accessed. Similarly, in an adventure game the user might be required to solve a puzzle before being allowed to move through a certain door.

► Because control is turned over to the user or programmed to respond to user input in interactive titles, the developer of interactive titles must address several design, navigation, and "what-if" issues. For example, how do you design the application so that the user does not get confused or lost? Should a tutorial on how to use the application and/or a Help feature be included? Should the user be given the option to quit the application at any time? These types of considerations make interactive titles generally more difficult, expensive, and time-consuming to develop than presentation-type titles.

► Generally speaking, the difference between multimedia presentations and interactive titles relates to the issue of who has control. In multimedia presentations, the presenter has control, and generally the intended audience remains passive. In interactive titles, the user (intended audience) has control. As multimedia titles become increasingly more sophisticated, the lines separating them blur.

FIGURE D-2: *Example of a program making a decision based on user performance*

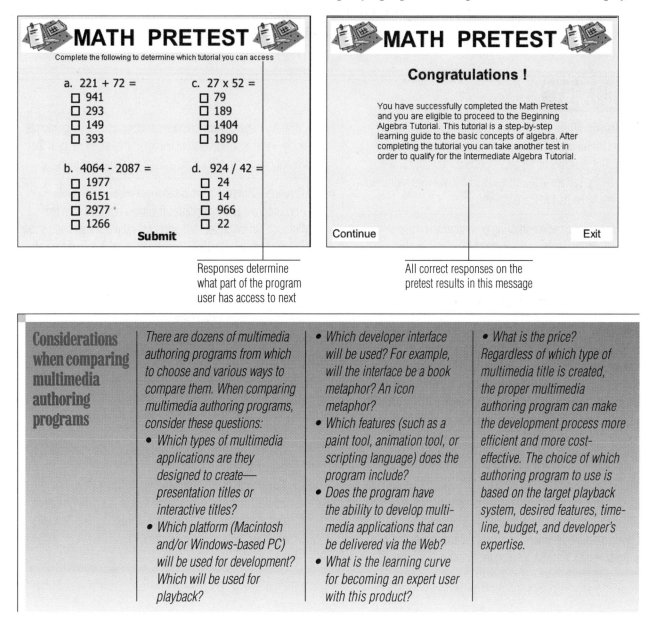

MATH PRETEST

Complete the following to determine which tutorial you can access

a. 221 + 72 =
- [ ] 941
- [ ] 293
- [ ] 149
- [ ] 393

c. 27 x 52 =
- [ ] 79
- [ ] 189
- [ ] 1404
- [ ] 1890

b. 4064 - 2087 =
- [ ] 1977
- [ ] 6151
- [ ] 2977
- [ ] 1266

d. 924 / 42 =
- [ ] 24
- [ ] 14
- [ ] 966
- [ ] 22

Submit

MATH PRETEST

Congratulations !

You have successfully completed the Math Pretest and you are eligible to proceed to the Beginning Algebra Tutorial. This tutorial is a step-by-step learning guide to the basic concepts of algebra. After completing the tutorial you can take another test in order to qualify for the Intermediate Algebra Tutorial.

Continue   Exit

Responses determine what part of the program user has access to next

All correct responses on the pretest results in this message

Considerations when comparing multimedia authoring programs

There are dozens of multimedia authoring programs from which to choose and various ways to compare them. When comparing multimedia authoring programs, consider these questions:

- Which types of multimedia applications are they designed to create—presentation titles or interactive titles?
- Which platform (Macintosh and/or Windows-based PC) will be used for development? Which will be used for playback?

- Which developer interface will be used? For example, will the interface be a book metaphor? An icon metaphor?
- Which features (such as a paint tool, animation tool, or scripting language) does the program include?
- Does the program have the ability to develop multi-media applications that can be delivered via the Web?
- What is the learning curve for becoming an expert user with this product?

- What is the price? Regardless of which type of multimedia title is created, the proper multimedia authoring program can make the development process more efficient and more cost-effective. The choice of which authoring program to use is based on the target playback system, desired features, time-line, budget, and developer's expertise.

Examining slide show programs

Multimedia authoring programs can be categorized loosely by the way in which they work—that is, by the metaphor used. These metaphors include electronic slide show programs, card stack or book programs, icon-based programs, and time-based programs. The electronic slide show programs are perhaps the easiest to understand because they are based on a process that is familiar to the developer—that is, the process of creating slides to show one at a time. Electronic slide shows can include all of the multimedia elements and provide for hyperlinking. In addition, the companies that develop the programs realize that, in most cases, the people who are creating the slide shows are not programmers or even computer power users, but rather content experts. As a result, they have tried to make these types of authoring programs as intuitive as possible. Most multimedia presentations are electronic slide shows. In this lesson you will learn how multimedia presentation titles can be developed using authoring programs based on the electronic slide show metaphor.

DETAILS

▶ **Electronic slide show presentations** are similar to presentations using traditional overhead transparencies or slides, but they can be far superior because of the power of the delivery system—the computer, which allows multimedia elements to be part of the presentation.

▶ While any multimedia authoring program can create an electronic slide show, some authoring programs are specifically designed for this purpose. Multimedia authoring programs such as Microsoft PowerPoint and Corel Presentations use a slide show metaphor.

▶ Authoring programs used to create electronic slide show programs offer several advantages. They are relatively inexpensive, easy to learn, and easy to use. These programs provide templates with different background colors and graphics. They even allow you to create your own backgrounds, allowing you to tailor the application to your audience. Most programs run on both Macintosh and Windows-based computers; many include run-time modules that allow presentations to be played on computers that do not have the program.

▶ Electronic slide shows can be designed to be self-running and delivered through a kiosk, distributed to users on CD, or played from the Internet. They are used extensively as a supplement to Web-based lectures in online courses.

▶ A disadvantage of slide show presentations is their predominantly linear, non-interactive nature. It makes them ideal for presentations, but not so attractive for interactive titles.

▶ Microsoft's **PowerPoint** is the most widely used slide show program (partly because it comes bundled with the Microsoft Office Suite). Although not all electronic slide show programs are exactly like PowerPoint, a brief discussion of PowerPoint will provide insight into the basic characteristics of electronic slide shows. Note: This overview is not intended to cover all characteristics of the program, and the characteristics listed here and in Table D-1 may also exist in other authoring programs.

Some PowerPoint terms:

Presentation – the completed file that contains all of the slides

Slide – a single page of content as displayed on the screen

Objects – elements such as headings, bullets, charts, and images

Development environment – in Normal view, PowerPoint displays a slide that is ready to be edited and also displays Standard, Formatting, and Drawing toolbars, as shown in Figure D-3

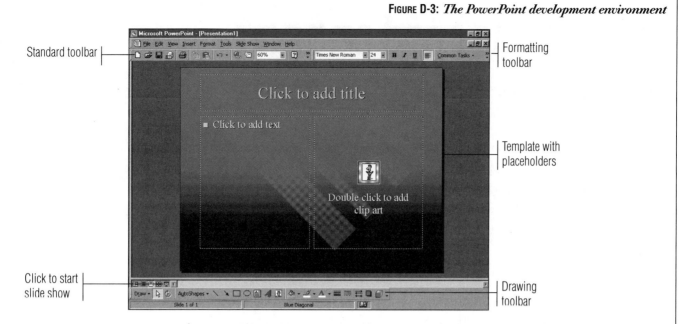

Standard toolbar

Formatting toolbar

Template with placeholders

Click to start slide show

Drawing toolbar

FIGURE **D-4**: *Adding multimedia elements to a PowerPoint application*

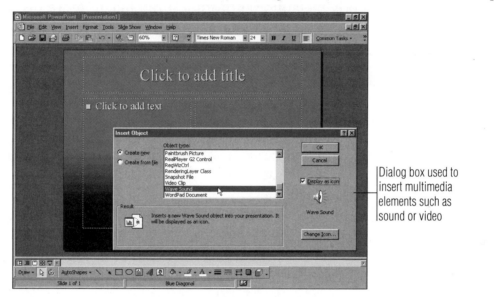

Dialog box used to insert multimedia elements such as sound or video

TABLE **D-1**: *Some PowerPoint Features*

FEATURE	DESCRIPTION
Design templates	dozens of prebuilt designs with backgrounds, color schemes, bullet styles, and font types and sizes
Auto Layouts	several prebuilt slide layouts used to organize the placement of various objects, such as headings, charts, and pictures
AutoShapes	used to create diagrams and drawings
Customization	content such as organization charts, company logos, Excel spreadsheets, clip art, WordArt drawings, and tables can be easily incorporated into a slide
Animation	used to animate objects such as slides and bullets
Multimedia	in addition to text and graphics, sound, animation, and video can be included in a slide, as shown in Figure D-4
View	the ability during the development of the presentation to use three different modes to view the slides: Normal—the view used when working on the slides
Sorter	the view that shows thumbnails of several slides at a time; Slide Show—the view that the user sees as the presentation is running

Examining card or book metaphor programs

Authoring programs based on card or book metaphors can be used to create interactive titles. Two advantages of these authoring programs are the ease in understanding the metaphor and the straightforward relationship between what is created on a card or page, as shown in Figure D-5, and what is displayed on any particular screen based on the card or page, as shown in Figure D-6. These programs are relatively easy to use and often provide templates that can streamline the development time. A major disadvantage is that some programs run on only one platform (Macintosh or Windows-based computers). In addition, some program features, such as animation and paint tools, are not as powerful as the corresponding features found in other types of multimedia authoring programs. This lesson looks at card and book metaphor authoring programs in more detail.

DETAILS

▶ **HyperCard**, which was developed in 1987 to run on Apple computers, was one of the first multimedia authoring programs to use a card metaphor. Using HyperCard, you develop cards that have different elements associated with them, and then you put the cards in stacks. You link the cards with buttons or other elements. Later, when a user clicks on a linked button or other element, the user jumps to a different card in the stack. HyperStudio, which is a more recent version of HyperCard, provides more opportunities for including multimedia elements.

▶ **Toolbook** is an example of an authoring program based on a book metaphor in which pages are used to represent different screens; the pages make up a book. Toolbook has two levels of interaction, the author level and the reader level. You use the author level to create the title; you use the reader level to interact with the program. Toolbook, which was developed by Asymetrix and was one of the first multimedia book metaphor programs, is an easy-to-use program that provides several useful tools for multimedia developers. Although not all authoring programs based on a book metaphor are exactly the same, a brief discussion of Toolbook will provide insight into basic characteristics of this type of authoring program. Note: This overview is not intended to cover all characteristics of the program, and the characteristics listed here and in Table D-2 may also exist in other authoring programs.

Some Toolbook terms:

Book – a collection of pages that make up an application; for example, a company that wanted to create a sales training CD would create a book and save it in a file format appropriate for the intended delivery process (for example, an HTML document for Web delivery); related books can be combined to create larger applications

Page – the basic unit of a book; pages are similar to a screen view of content; therefore, as the content changes, new pages are created to display the content

Object – visual elements in a book; pages, buttons, graphics, text, and backgrounds are all objects

Properties – features of an object that define its appearance and action; properties can be as simple as specifying the color of text or as involved as specifying an animation to play when a Start button is selected; the multimedia developer determines the properties for objects

Development environment – developers work at the author level, which displays a work area that is similar to the screen display that the user will see (see Figure D-5); a menu bar and toolbar border the work area

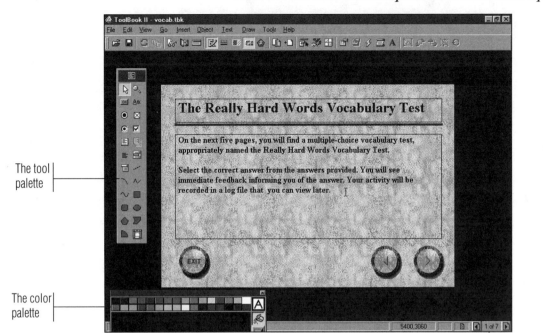

The tool palette

The color palette

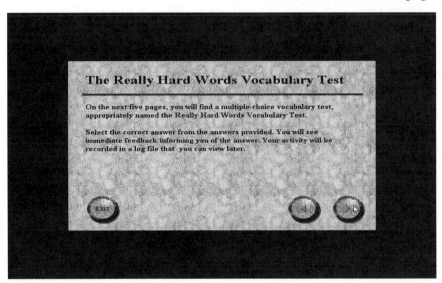

TABLE D-2: *Some Toolbook features*

FEATURES	DESCRIPTION
Template	a prebuilt book that includes objects such as backgrounds and navigation panels
Animation Editor	an animation program that is used to create path and cel animations
Media Player	an object that allows multimedia elements such as sound and video to be played from a page
Coach	a reference tool that provides context-sensitive information as you are working with Toolbook; Coach provides step-by-step procedures as well as tips and suggestions
Catalog	a file containing more than 1000 useful predefined objects such as buttons, navigation panels, and Media Players, which can be added by merely "dragging and dropping" them in the desired location on a page
OpenScript	the scripting language for Toolbook
Distribution	the way Toolbook applications can be delivered, such as through the Internet, on CD-ROM or DVD, and through company intranets

Examining icon-based programs

Icon-based programs are another category of multimedia authoring program used to create interactive applications. **Icon-based programs** use a flowchart scheme, as shown in Figure D-7. Each icon (symbol) represents content or a particular event. For example, in an icon-based program the Wait icon stops a process until an action occurs, such as the user clicking the mouse button, the user pressing a key, or the passing of a previously specified amount of time. In this lesson you will learn the advantages and disadvantages of authoring programs using an icon metaphor and some basic characteristics of a popular icon-based program.

DETAILS

► An advantage of authoring programs based on the icon metaphor is that you can see how a title is structured—you can see the flow of a program, especially the branching. This visualization of the program structure makes it easy to edit and update the program by simply adding or deleting icons.

► Disadvantages of authoring programs based on the icon metaphor are that they are less intuitive than other programs (slides, cards, books, movies); they can be fairly difficult to learn; and they are often more expensive.

► Macromedia Authorware is a popular icon-based authoring program for development of media-rich learning applications delivered on CD-ROM or through intranets and the Internet. Although not all authoring programs based on an icon metaphor are exactly the same, a brief discussion of Authorware will provide insight into basic characteristics of this type of authoring program. Note: This overview is not intended to cover all characteristics of the program, and the characteristics listed here may also exist in other authoring programs.

Some Authorware terms:

Application – the completed multimedia file
Design window – the area that is used to create an application; it contains the flowchart
Presentation window – displays what the user will see when running an application
Flowchart – the visual representation of the application's flow and logic
Flowline – the part of the flowchart that maps out the sequence of events and the relationship between elements; icons are placed on the flowline, and, when the application starts, Authorware begins traveling down the flowline and interpreting the icons in the order of their placement on the flowline
Icons – representations of the various elements that make up the application, such as text, graphics, animation, sound, and video, as well as representation of the flow of the application, such as branching and interactivity
Knowledge objects (KO) – prebuilt functions, interactions, and navigation structures that aid in the authoring process; for example, the Movie controller KO icon can be placed on the flowline, which causes a control panel to be displayed and allows the user to view a video
Development environment – an area that includes an icon palette, menu bar, tool bar, and two windows, Design and Presentation, as shown in Figure D-8

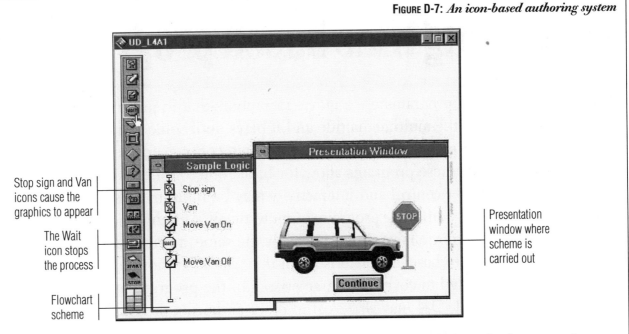

Stop sign and Van icons cause the graphics to appear

The Wait icon stops the process

Flowchart scheme

Presentation window where scheme is carried out

FIGURE D-8: *The Authorware development environment*

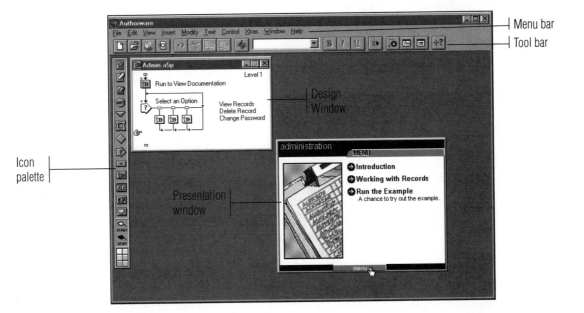

Menu bar

Tool bar

Design Window

Icon palette

Presentation window

TABLE D-3: *Some Authorware features*

FEATURES	DESCRIPTION
"Drag and drop" process	permits development of applications without programming
Text and graphics editing	allows for quickly modifying, adding, deleting, replacing, and repositioning of text and graphics within the Presentation window
Text search and spell check	allows searching for specific text and automatic checking for spelling errors
Knowledge Object Wizard	provides a step-by-step guide used to lead the developer through the process of working with knowledge objects
Path animation	allows for dragging objects around the Presentation window to create a path animation
Data tracking	supports automatic capture and access to user information, such as a test score
Packaging	allows royalty-free distribution of the application for CD-ROM/DVD, intranets, and the Internet without requiring the user to have a copy of Authorware
Web packager	automatically prepares the application for streaming over the Internet by dividing the file into smaller segments

Examining time-based programs

Time-based authoring programs use a movie metaphor—that is, just like a movie on a videotape, you start the multimedia title and it plays until some action causes it to pause or stop. At first glance, this approach may seem contrary to the nonlinear nature of multimedia; however; these programs allow for branching to different parts of the "movie," and any amount of user control and interactivity may be built in. This lesson discusses Director, a time-based authoring program, in more detail. Although not all authoring programs based on a movie metaphor are exactly the same, a brief discussion of Director will provide insight into basic characteristics of this type of authoring program. Note: This overview is not intended to cover all characteristics of the program, and the characteristics listed here and in Table D-4 may also exist in other authoring programs.

DETAILS

▶ **Macromedia Director**. Macromedia Director is a widely used time-based, authoring program, which uses a movie metaphor.

▶ Instead of cards or pages, Director movies consist of a series of individual frames. Each frame can contain several objects—such as graphics, buttons, and text—placed on a stage (the computer screen). As the movie is played, frames are displayed revealing their elements. A brief overview of Director follows.

Some Director terms:

Movie – the multimedia application created using Director

Stage window – the visible portion of the movie that allows you to determine where the objects appear in the movie, all action occurs on the stage

Score window – organizes and controls the movie's content over time using channels

Cast window – displays the cast members in either thumbnail or list form

Cast members – objects such as sound, animation, text, graphics, video, and scripts that become the content or that control the actions within a movie

Sprite – a cast member that has been placed on the stage; Sprites control when, where, and how a cast member appears in a movie.

Channel – rows in the Score window that control the tempo of the movie, sounds, background images, the color palette, and transitions within the movie

Frames – individual areas of the Score window that contain objects

Lingo – the scripting language for Director

Development environment – consistent with the movie or theater metaphor, Cast, Stage, and Score windows are used when developing a movie, see Figure D-9

TABLE D-4: *Some Director features*

Animation	used to change an object's position, size, and orientation (flip, skew, rotate, and so on)
Property inspector window	used to assign or change attributes (or behavior) of objects in a movie, such as assigning a sound to a button click
Paint window	see Figure D-10 – used to create and edit graphic images and text, assign properties to them, and add them to the Cast window
Cast manager	used to sort cast members by name, size, creation and modification date, type, and comments; facilitates the management of large projects that may include hundreds of objects
Projector	stand-alone applications that can be freely distributed and run on both Macintosh and Windows-based computers
File format support	Director can import more than 40 different file formats, including MP3 audio, AIFF, WAV, Flash, QuickTime, AVI, JPEG, and animated GIFs
Multiuser support	Director allows for the creation of movies that include chat sessions, whiteboards, and multiuser games
Web delivery	using the Shockwave player, a Director movie can be delivered through the Web

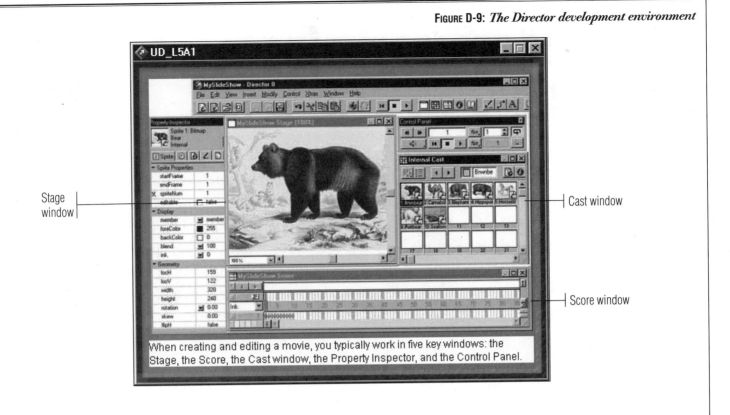

Stage window

Cast window

Score window

When creating and editing a movie, you typically work in five key windows: the Stage, the Score, the Cast window, the Property Inspector, and the Control Panel.

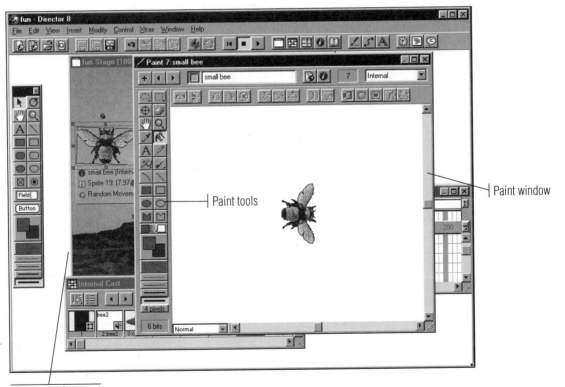

Paint tools

Paint window

Director environment behind Paint window

Exploring programming languages

In addition to authoring programs, traditional programming languages can be used to create multimedia titles. Programming languages are used to generate **programming code**, which consists of the instructions carried out by the computer. Among the most popular programming languages are C++, Visual Basic, Perl, and, more recently, Java and JavaScript. The latter two languages are used extensively for Web applications. **C++** is perhaps the most popular programming language. This lesson examines the advantages and disadvantages of using programming languages and provides a brief overview of several programming languages, including those designed for delivery through the Web.

DETAILS

▶ The advantage of using a programming language is its flexibility. Because you are writing programming code when you use a programming language to create a multimedia title, you can be very specific in how you tailor the application. This consideration is especially important when you are developing titles that may run on different operating systems.

▶ The disadvantage of using programming languages to create multimedia titles is that they are not specifically designed to create multimedia applications. This lack of specificity makes it more difficult and more time-consuming to develop multimedia applications using a programming language rather than a multimedia authoring program.

▶ Programming languages, like **Java**, offer the ability to use sophisticated features such as creating animations and searching a database. Java, developed by Sun Microsystems, is a powerful language similar to C++ that has become popular for programming Web-related applications because of its cross-platform compatibility. Java can extend the functionality of HTML through Java applets.

▶ Applets, which are small programs that can be shared with other applications, are developed for a specific purpose. Figure D-11 shows a Java applet that creates a clock. Applets can be used in applications that will be delivered via the Web and are run within the browser on the user's computer. They are downloaded from the Web when a browser opens a Web page that supports them.

Although a person with programming knowledge can create applets, this task requires a high level of programming expertise. You may want to determine whether an existing applet meets your needs before attempting to create your own. One source of custom codes, such as applets, is user groups.

User groups, which often operate through the Internet, are composed of individuals who share their custom codes. Custom codes—specifically applets—are also available from commercial developers such as Sun Microsystems as well as third-party developers. Some applets are available free of charge and can be downloaded from the Web.

▶ **JavaScript** is scripting language that is specifically designed to add interactivity to Web pages. JavaScript can be used to provide users with feedback as they move through a Web site. One type of feedback is a rollover. In a rollover function, the action of rolling the mouse over an object results in an action—for example, a button changing color when the user's mouse pointer rolls over it.

JavaScript can also add interactivity to a Web page by interacting with a Java applet on a Web page. For instance, you could use JavaScript to create a dialog box that allows the user to enter text. Then a Java applet could check the text and modify the font so that the text fits on the screen.

▶ Different programming languages can be used to produce the same end result.

▶ In addition to programming languages such as Java and JavaScript, another consideration when programming for the Web is the **Common Gateway Interface** (CGI). CGI is a specification that allows programs to be written using various programming languages. Programs written to CGI specifications run on a server and provide a way to obtain information from the user and to return information to the user. A typical program written to CGI specifications might allow users to search a database. Figure D-12 shows a Web page with a search function that lets the user enter text to search a database.

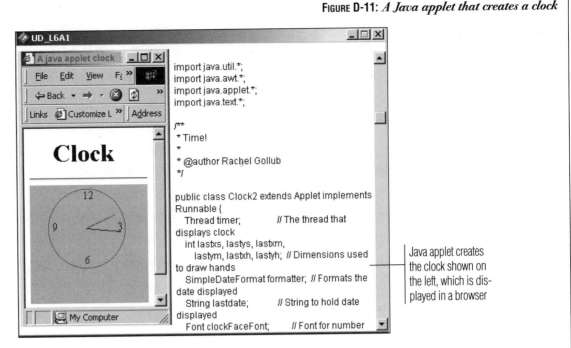

FIGURE D-11: *A Java applet that creates a clock*

```
import java.util.*;
import java.awt.*;
import java.applet.*;
import java.text.*;

/**
 * Time!
 *
 * @author Rachel Gollub
 */

public class Clock2 extends Applet implements
Runnable {
    Thread timer;            // The thread that
displays clock
    int lastxs, lastys, lastxm,
        lastym, lastxh, lastyh;  // Dimensions used
to draw hands
    SimpleDateFormat formatter;  // Formats the
date displayed
    String lastdate;         // String to hold date
displayed
    Font clockFaceFont;      // Font for number
```

Java applet creates the clock shown on the left, which is displayed in a browser

FIGURE D-12: *A Web page with a search function*

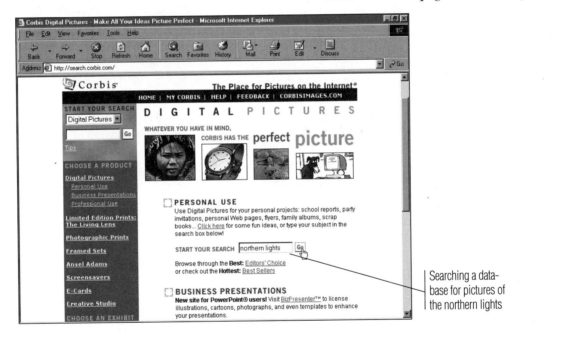

Searching a database for pictures of the northern lights

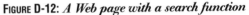

HTML: a markup language

In this discussion of programming languages, you may have wondered why HTML has not been mentioned. Although HTML (and its derivatives such as DHTML, XHTML) has become the standard for creating Web pages, it is a markup language and not a programming language. A markup language uses tags to mark elements, such as text and graphics, so that they can be displayed using a Web browser; in contrast, a programming language generates the programming code. HTML has limited capabilities and requires a programming language like Java to produce sophisticated features such as animations. HTML is not used to create multimedia applications, but it is used to incorporate multimedia elements into Web pages.

Exploring scripting languages

In Lesson 6 you learned how programming languages are used to develop the program code that serves as the foundation for multimedia titles. When you use an authoring program, how is the code generated? Does the authoring program generate the code automatically as the title is created, or does the developer need to write the code? Because authoring programs are designed specifically to develop multimedia titles, they try to make it easy for developers to produce and edit content, create hyperlinks and interactivity, and incorporate text, sound, graphics, animation, and video. **Scripting languages** are programming languages used to create **scripts**, which are the program code for specific tasks. In this lesson you will learn about features, such as scripting languages that are available to help the developer customize the multimedia application.

DETAILS

▶ Some authoring programs are promoted on the basis of their ease of use and the fact that you do not have to be a programmer to take advantage of the product. As a developer works with it, the authoring program automatically generates the programming code needed to perform the tasks identified by the developer. The programming code is transparent to the developer.

▶ Many authoring programs provide their own scripting languages to create scripts. Scripts allow the developer flexibility in designing the program. They are used to access external media such as CD-ROMs, to create interaction (for example, specifying what happens when a user types a certain response to a question), to control the speed of an animation, and so on. Scripts for common tasks are often included with the authoring program.

▶ Scripts can be as brief as a few lines of code or as complex as many pages of code. One advantage of using them is that script program code can be easily read, interpreted, and edited by developers. Although each scripting language has its own characteristics, a discussion of simple scripts from two different authoring programs provides a broad overview of scripts.

Example 1 — Toolbook's **OpenScript**

Figure D-13 shows two screens in a Toolbook application. In the first screen, the user selects an option by clicking a button. Each button is scripted to cause an action (in this case, branch to a different page). If the user clicks the button labeled True, the script directs the application to display the second screen, as shown in Figure D-13. The script that causes this action to happen and an explanation of the script follow:

```
to handle buttonClick
    go to page "Correct"
end buttonClick
```

This script consists of three lines of scripting language (code). The first line indicates that the script executes when the user clicks the mouse button (assuming the mouse pointer is on the button named True). The second line causes the program to go to a page named "Correct." The third line ends the script. Another script tells the program what to do if the user clicks the False button.

The first screen in Figure D-13 also shows the Script window that the developer uses to create the script. The developer would select the appropriate button (True) and then use the Script window to write the script for the button. The Script window is not viewable by the user.

Example 2 — Macromedia Director's **Lingo**

In this example, a function called rollOver is used. A **rollover** function is performed when the mouse pointer rolls over (points to) an object and some action occurs. In this case, when the mouse pointer rolls over the car at the top of the page, the word Roadster appears in a message box (see Figure D-14).

```
if rollOver(5) then
        put "Roadster" into field "Message"
    end if
```

In this script the object is the car at the top of the page. The object has been assigned a number (5), which appears after the word rollOver in the first line of the script. The first line of code indicates that if the mouse pointer is positioned over object number 5, then the program should continue to the next line of code. The second line of code instructs that the word "Roadster" be displayed in a field called "Message." The field "Message" has been designated previously to be an area on the screen that will display text. The last line of code is the end if statement, which ends the script.

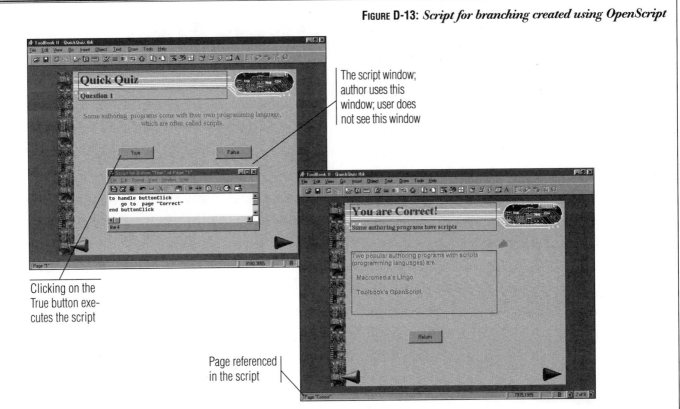

The script window; author uses this window; user does not see this window

Clicking on the True button executes the script

Page referenced in the script

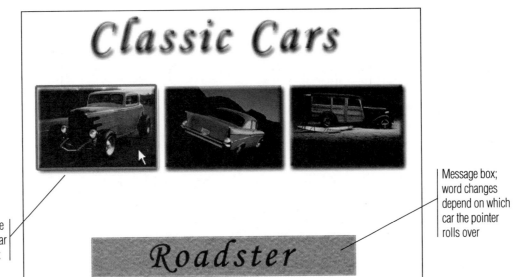

Pointing to a picture causes text to appear in the message box

Message box; word changes depend on which car the pointer rolls over

Multimedia development steps: an overview

Regardless of how you develop your multimedia title—using an authoring program, programming languages, or a combination of both—there are basic steps to follow for good title design. They include planning your title, selecting or creating a template, choosing a layout, adding special effects and assigning properties, testing the application, and saving the application in an appropriate format for delivery. Some of these steps are more complicated than others, depending on which authoring program you use, but the same basic principles of design always apply. Unit E provides an in-depth look at the process of developing a multimedia title.

Using Web-based multimedia development programs

A useful guideline for multimedia developers is to "author once for delivery in many forms." Long before the popularity of the Web, developers were producing multimedia applications to be delivered on CD-ROMs or installed on company network systems and desktop computers. Many of these applications were highly sophisticated titles involving sound, animation, and video elements. As the Internet evolved into a viable delivery system, the challenge for the developers was how to adapt authoring programs so they could accommodate existing titles for use on the Web. In this lesson, you will learn how companies developed ways for delivering multimedia applications—existing titles as well as new titles—on the Web.

DETAILS

▶ Companies found ways to adapt their existing titles by creating programs that translated them for delivery over the Web. For example, Macromedia provides a utility program called **Shockwave** that allows an Internet user to play applications created with Director; Microsoft provides **ActiveX controls** that allow movies, animations, and sounds to be delivered over the Internet.

▶ Many companies provide free, downloadable **players** that allow users to run multimedia applications on their computers. For example, you can download (see Figure D-15) and use Shockwave to play Director movies on the Web. Four steps are involved in preparing and playing Director movies on the Web:

Step 1 – The multimedia developer uses the Publish option in Director to save the movie in a compressed format. Figure D-16 shows compression settings available in the Publish Settings dialog box.

Step 2 – The developer inserts the compressed Director file into an HTML document so that a browser can read it. An example of the HTML coding for embedding a compressed Director movie into a Web document follows:

```
<EMBED SRC="mymovie" WIDTH="200" HEIGHT="45"> </EMBED>
```

In this case the Director movie called mymovie will be displayed in a window on the screen that is 200 pixels wide and 45 pixels high.

Step 3 – The developer uploads the file to a server.

Step 4 – The user views the movie using the Shockwave player. Shockwave must be installed on the user's computer to view the movie.

▶ Some companies sell authoring programs intended specifically for the development of multimedia applications that run on the Web. Macromedia's **Director Shockwave Studio** is a comprehensive authoring package that allows developers to create multimedia applications for CD-ROM, DVD, and Web delivery. In addition, **Macromedia Flash** has become popular as an animation tool for developing 2-D animations delivered on the Web.

▶ Authoring programs also allow you to save new applications in a format that can be used on the Web—for example, via the PowerPoint "Save as Web Page" option and the Director "Publish" option.

▶ In addition to using an authoring program's options to make an application Web-ready, you can add multimedia elements directly to Web pages. Although you would not use HTML code to create multimedia titles, you can use HTML code to add multimedia elements such as sounds, animation, and video to a Web page. When you are working with various media files, the file extension indicates the type of media being called by the HTML code. For example, a .mov file extension indicates a QuickTime movie, and a .wav extension indicates an audio file. See Table D-5 for examples of HTML code used to add multimedia elements to Web pages.

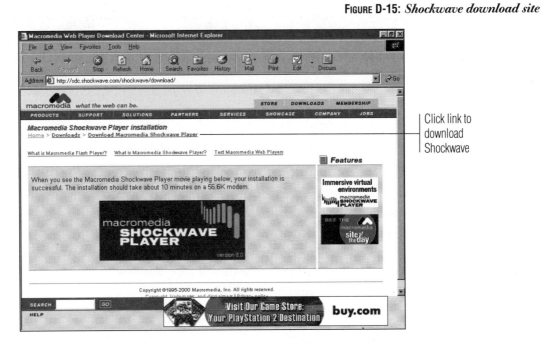

Click link to download Shockwave

FIGURE D-16: *The Director Publish Settings option*

When saving a Director movie using the Publish option, this dialog box appears allowing the user to set the compression options; for example, selecting the "Convert Stereo to Mono" will reduce the size of the size of the audio files

TABLE D-5: *Examples of HTML code used when working with audio files*

DESCRIPTION OF ACTION	CODE
The HTML code to the right causes the jazz.wav audio file to be played when the user clicks on a picture of a saxophone	`<A HREF="jazz.wav"><IMG SRC="sax.gif"></A>`
The HTML code to the right causes the jazz.wav audio file to be played when the Web page is displayed and repeats the sound five times.	`<BGSOUND SRC="jazz.wav" loop=5>`
The HTML code to the right causes a set of controls to appear, with the specified dimensions; these controls allow the user to start, pause, and stop the playing of the jazz.wav audio file	`<EMBED SRC="jazz.wav" width=144 height=74>`

The content of CD-ROM/DVD titles and multimedia applications on the Web is essentially no different from the content of other media. Consequently, pornography, violence, and racism are as much a concern in multimedia titles as they are in television, movies, and music. This statement is especially true of titles, such as games, that may be directed toward children.

The movie and music industries have long had rating systems and labeling to provide the consumer with an indication of the appropriateness of the content for various audiences. The Motion Picture Association of America's (MPAA) ratings range from G (General), indicating that all ages are admitted, to N-17, indicating that no one 17 years or younger is admitted to the theater. The Recording Industry Association of America (RIAA) has a voluntary Parental Advisory logo that record companies can place on recordings indicating that they contain strong language, depictions of violence, sex, or substance abuse.

Now the Entertainment Software Rating Board (ESRB) has begun to rate software titles as well as online games and Web sites. Its ratings are age-based and go from Early Childhood through Adult. They include content descriptors for language, violence, and sexual content. These systems were instituted partly in response to research that has linked violence in the media with violence in children and partly in response to the threat of government controls. In reality, potential consumers of CD-ROM/DVD titles may have little more than the company's own promotional material on the packages to inform them of the content and its appropriateness for a particular audience.

In 1996, Congress passed the Communications Decency Act in an attempt to ban the transmission of obscene or indecent material over the Internet. A year later, the U.S. Supreme Court unanimously over-turned the act on the grounds that it violated First Amendment free speech rights. However, more than 20 state legislatures have since passed legislation in an attempt to regulate Internet speech. Many organizations have been involved in opposing these acts, including the American Civil Liberties Union, the Citizens Internet Empowerment Coalition, and the Electronic Frontier Foundation.

The Internet provides the opportunity for developers to deliver their content to users without the need for a publisher, distributor, retailer, or other intermediary—those entities that have, in the past, provided some screening by determining what to market. As a result, the issue of censorship has intensified as multimedia applications have become more prevalent on the Internet.

The issue of censorship as it relates to multimedia titles is under scrutiny today. At the heart of the issue are these questions: Should censorship—the official and authoritative examination, and possible expurgation, of material for appropriateness of content—be applied to multimedia titles? If so, then who will control the content—the multimedia industry or the government? Along those same lines, should rating systems and labeling be required? If so, who will determine the ratings and the labels? How can consumers be assured that they are applied consistently?

1. Define censorship. Based on your definition, should censorship be applied to multimedia titles? If yes, under what conditions? If no, why?

2. Research ratings and labels currently used to identify multimedia content. Write a brief report that addresses the following: Who called for the ratings or labels? How did they come about? Are they effective—explain your answer. Were you aware of the ratings or labels before reading the Issue?

3. Australia has taken steps toward censoring information available on the Internet. Research Australia's position. What does the government act specify? Who is responsible? What effect could this legislation have on multimedia titles delivered via the Web? How has the worldwide community reacted to this legislative act? Be prepared to use your notes to participate in a class discussion on Australia's Broadcasting Services Amendment (Online Services) Act 1999, which became effective in January 2000. Summarize your findings in a report.

4. What does research say about the effect of violence on children's behavior? Have studies been done to relate multimedia applications to children's behavior? What does the research say? Do the research findings support censorship? Prepare a poster presentation to support your position.

End of Unit Exercises

STUDY TIPS

1. Review the vocabulary presented in this unit. Use additional resources as needed to add depth of understanding to terms.

2. Multimedia titles can be created using multimedia authoring programs, programming languages, or a combination of both. Explain the advantages and disadvantages of each method.

3. Four types of authoring programs exist: electronic slide show, card or book metaphor, icon-based, and time-based. Make a poster explaining each type. Be sure to include the following: situations where each type is used, the advantages of each type, the disadvantages of each type, and an example of a product that can be used to create that type.

4. Write a summary report regarding scripting languages. When are they used? Why are they used? What are some examples.

5. Delivery of multimedia on the Web requires some special considerations. Summarize delivery of multimedia on the Web. Use the following questions as points of discussion: What are the delivery methods? What was done to accommodate existing titles and make them available? How are new titles developed for delivery via the Web?

SELECT THE BEST ANSWER

1. Two ways in which multimedia applications are used are as interactive titles and as _____.
   a. Presentations
   b. Movies
   c. Videos
   d. Games

2. A major advantage of interactive titles is that they _____.
   a. Promote passive interaction
   b. Are linear
   c. Provide user control
   d. Are easy to develop

3. Multimedia titles can be classified according to the way they work—that is, based on the _____ used.
   a. Programming language
   b. Metaphor
   c. Interactivity
   d. Scripting language

4. Which of the following would not be a classification of multimedia titles?
   a. Slide show
   b. Icon-based
   c. Time-based
   d. Video-based

5. A disadvantage of an electronic slide show application is that it _____.
   a. Cannot include video clips
   b. Must have a presenter
   c. Is predominantly linear
   d. Cannot be delivered through the Web

6. Which of the following is not a view in PowerPoint?
   a. Normal
   b. Slide Show
   c. Presentation
   d. Sorter

7. With authoring programs, a book metaphor uses _____ to build the application.
   a. Slides
   b. Novels
   c. Pages
   d. Cards

8. An icon-based authoring program uses a _____.
   a. Flowline
   b. Stage
   c. Frame
   d. Sorter

9. Director is an example of a(n) _____.

  a. Time-based authoring program

  b. Scriptless program

  c. Icon-based program

  d. Slide show

10. The advantage of using an authoring program is that it is

  _____.

  a. Easy to use

  b. Flexible

  c. Easy to learn

  d. All of the above

FILL IN THE BEST ANSWER

1. Multimedia _____ are used to create both interactive titles and multimedia titles.

2. Microsoft's _____ is an example of a slide show authoring program.

3. Click2learn.com's _____ is an example of an authoring program using a book metaphor.

4. Macromedia's _____ is an example of an icon-based authoring program.

5. Macromedia's _____ is an example of a time-based authoring program.

6. Icons are placed on a(n) _____.

7. Lingo is the name of a(n) _____ language.

8. _____ is a programming language specifically designed to add interactivity to Web pages.

9. _____ is a player that can be used to view Director movies on the Web.

10. <A HREF="jazz.wave"><IMG SRC="sax.gif"></A> is an example of _____ code.

INDEPENDENT CHALLENGE 1

Over the years multimedia authoring systems have evolved to meet the complex needs of the multimedia designer. As new technologies become available, multimedia designers must find ways to incorporate them into their titles or adapt their titles to accommodate the new technologies. To do so, they must stay current on industry trends and news.

To complete this independent challenge:

1. Connect to the Internet.

2. Go to *http://www.course.com*; navigate to the Student Online Companion for this book; then click the link for Unit D.

3. The Unit D link contains links to Web sites providing information about authoring programs. Click each link to visit the site, and read about various authoring programs. Write a brief summary of each site, highlighting key points about at least three multimedia authoring systems. Also, discuss how these sites can help you as a multimedia designer stay current on industry trends and news. Develop a report that includes the following information:

  a. The URL for each site.

  b. A discussion of how each site provides information about multimedia authoring programs.

  c. A discussion of resources that are available through these links.

  d. A discussion of which sites you would bookmark for future use and why.

INDEPENDENT CHALLENGE 2

Many multimedia authoring programs are similar, but each has features that make it unique. As you research and work with various multimedia authoring programs, you will become more aware of each program's assets and limitations. To help facilitate your research, many publishers of multimedia authoring programs provide information, including tutorials and sample programs created with the authoring program, on their Web sites.

To complete this independent challenge:

1. Select two of the four program listed in Steps 2–5 to review. Your review might involve using print or electronic reviews, visiting the product Web site, or using the product itself if you have access to it.

2. Review Macromedia's Authorware program, and write a report. Include the following information in your report:

  a. List features of the program. Provide information about three features that are not mentioned in this unit. How do these features add to the usefulness of Authorware?

  b. Study three applications that have been developed with Authorware. (*Hint:* Look for examples at their Web site.) What do you find particularly compelling about the applications and why?

  c. Complete a tour or tutorial of the program. List and explain three features that are presented. (*Hint:* A tour may be available online or via the product CD.)

  d. What other products does the company make? List those products that can be used with the Authorware program (such as an animation program) and indicate how the product would be used to complement or enhance Authorware's capabilities.

e. What are other users saying about Authorware? Visit other sites that are linked to the Authorware site, or pursue reviews by users. What information is available? Which links or reviews do you find most valuable and why?

3. Review Macromedia's Director program, and write a report. Include the following information in your report:

   a. List features of the program. Provide information about three features that are not mentioned in this unit. How do these features add to the usefulness of Director?

   b. Study three applications that have been developed with Director. (*Hint:* Look for examples at their Web site.) What do you find particularly compelling about the applications and why?

   c. Complete a tour or tutorial of the program. List and explain three features that are presented. (*Hint:* A tour may be available online or via the product CD.)

   d. What other products does the company make? List those products that can be used with the Director program (such as an animation program) and indicate how the product would be used to complement or enhance Director's capabilities.

   e. What are others saying about Director? Visit other sites that are linked to the Director site or pursue reviews by users. What information is available? Which links or reviews do you find most valuable and why?

4. Review click2learn.com's Toolbook program, and write a report. Include the following information in your report:

   a. List features of the program. Provide information about three features that are not mentioned in this unit. How do these features add to the usefulness of Toolbook?

   b. Study three applications that have been developed with Toolbook. (*Hint:* Look for examples at their Web site.) What do you find particularly compelling about the applications and why?

   c. Complete a tour or tutorial of the program. List and explain three features that are presented. (*Hint:* A tour may be available online or via the product CD.)

   d. What other products does the company make? List those products that can be used with the Toolbook program (such as an animation program), and indicate how the product would be used to complement or enhance Toolbook's capabilities.

   e. What are others saying about Toolbook? Visit other sites that are linked to the Toolbook site, or pursue reviews by users. What types of information are available? Which links or reviews do you find most valuable and why?

5. Review Microsoft's PowerPoint program, and write a report. Include the following information in your report:

   a. List features of the program. Provide information about three features that are not mentioned in this unit. How do these features add to the usefulness of PowerPoint?

   b. Study three applications that have been developed with PowerPoint. (*Hint:* If you are able to connect to the Web, use your favorite search engine, and search for PowerPoint presentations.) What do you find particularly compelling about the applications and why?

   c. Complete a tour or tutorial of the program. List and explain three features that are presented. (*Hint:* A tour may be available online or via the product CD.)

   d. What other products does the company make? List those products that can be used with the PowerPoint program (such as an animation program), and indicate how the product would be used to complement or enhance PowerPoint's capabilities.

   e. What are others saying about PowerPoint? Visit other sites that are linked to the PowerPoint site or pursue reviews by users. What types of information are available? Which links do you find most valuable and why?

INDEPENDENT CHALLENGE 3

Multimedia applications were available on CDs before they became available on the Internet. One challenge faced by multimedia developers was how to deliver multimedia applications currently on CD efficiently over the Internet. As you learned in the unit, Macromedia's Shockwave is a utility program that lets Internet users play Director movies. Shockwave marked a significant technological breakthrough, because Director is a popular authoring program, and there were thousands of Director movies that had been developed and could now be viewed on the Web. In addition, those having expertise in Director would not have to learn additional skills to develop movies for the Internet market. This independent challenge will help familiarize you with Shockwave.

To complete this independent challenge:

1. Use your favorite search engine to find information on Shockwave. Write a brief summary that includes background information on this program.

2. Search for sites that use Shockwave to display multimedia applications. Run applications on these sites. Then use your review to write a report that includes the following information:

   a. Did you need to download the latest version of Shockwave? If so, what message appeared indicating that you needed the player? How long did it take you to download the player?

b. Which type of applications did you view, and which multimedia elements were used?

c. Which applications did you find most compelling and why?

d. Which applications did you find least compelling and why?

INDEPENDENT CHALLENGE 4

After studying the different authoring programs discussed in this unit, it is important to organize the findings in a manner that will make comparing the programs more efficient. A comparison chart is often a good way to summarize findings. A comparison chart can then be kept for handy reference as well as updated regularly. To determine which program you feel would be the most interesting to work with and why, you must gather all your thoughts and notes together.

To complete this independent challenge:

1. Work in small groups. Be sure that all four of the multimedia authoring programs listed in Independent Challenge 2 have been reviewed by at least one group member.

2. Combine notes to create a comparison chart similar to the one shown in Table D-6. (*Note:* The topics listed in the left column are samples only. The information listed in the left column will differ based on the group's notes.)

3. Prepare an oral report for the class with your findings.

TABLE D-6

	AUTHORWARE	DIRECTOR	TOOLBOOK	POWERPOINT
Basic Info				
Platforms				
Tech support				
Price				
Features				
Animation				
Video				
What others say				
Ease of use				
Compatibility issues				

INDEPENDENT CHALLENGE 5

All commercial-quality multimedia titles will involve programming, using a programming language and/or an authoring program's scripting language. Interviewing a person involved in multimedia development can provide valuable insights into his or her role in the development process

To complete this independent challenge:

1. Contact a programmer who is involved in the development of multimedia.

2. Prepare a report that includes the following information:

a. Name of person

b. Educational background

c. Employment history

d. Name of current employer

e. Projects in which he or she has been involved

f. Other individuals with whom he or she works and their roles in the development process

g. Type of programming experience

h. Programming languages used

i. Authoring program(s) used (if any)

j. Scripting language(s) used (if any)

k. Proudest accomplishment related to multimedia

l. Trends he or she sees in the industry

m. Advice for someone interested in a career in authoring multimedia titles

n. Other

INDEPENDENT CHALLENGE 6

Electronic slide show programs, such as Microsoft PowerPoint, have become increasingly more sophisticated through the use of multimedia elements and hyperlinking. Creating a slide show presentation helps in understanding how multimedia authoring is accomplished without writing programming code.

To complete this independent challenge:

1. Use Microsoft PowerPoint or another electronic slide show program.

2. Create a slide show that includes the following:

a. A template provided by the program

b. At least ten slides

c. At least three graphics

d. At least one sound clip

e. A different transition for each slide

f. A link (using text or a graphic such as a button) to another slide

g. A link (using text) to a Web site

3. Save the slide show

4. Present it to at least three fellow students, and obtain their ideas on how it could be improved.

1. Figure D-17 shows the development environment for which multimedia authoring program?

2. The authoring program shown in Figure D-17 is based on what metaphor?

3. What are the major components of the development environment shown in Figure D-17? Name each, and briefly describe its purpose.

FIGURE D-17

When creating and editing a movie, you typically work in five key windows: the Stage, the Score, the Cast window, the Property Inspector, and the Control Panel.

Development and Design of Multimedia Titles

Like many other processes that require the use of the computer (programming, report writing, computer-aided design), the tendency with multimedia development is to "wing it" or "jump" right into the project—that is, to load a graphics or authoring program and immediately begin to create the title. Because developing multimedia can be extremely complex, costly, and time-consuming, the "wing it" approach invariably results in less effective and more costly titles. The rule of thumb for multimedia development is 80% planning and 20% production. Following a well-defined development process that places the actual production in perspective helps ensure a successful project. This unit focuses on the development process and on design issues related to multimedia development. This unit also discusses the issue of online privacy.

Planning the title–Part 1

The steps in multimedia development can be grouped in several ways such as pre-production, production, and post-production or, as in this case, planning, creating, and testing. In Figure E-1, the steps are presented as a numbered series; in practice, however, there is a great deal of overlap and rework among them. For example, content development may overlap with authoring and testing, which is an ongoing process throughout the project. This lesson provides details about the first three steps in the planning the title phase.

DETAILS

Step 1: Developing the Concept (Idea) — "What, in general, do we want the title to accomplish?"

▶ Companies that develop multimedia titles have a vision for their products. A **vision** is a broad statement of the company's intentions, such as "Be the leader in educational CD-ROM/DVD titles."

▶ A multimedia project starts with an idea that supports the vision. The process for generating ideas can be as unstructured as "brainstorming" sessions or as formal as checklists with evaluation criteria. Companies that rely on providing a continuous stream of products might have a process for generating product ideas that includes team "brainstorming" or asking the development team and users of current titles questions about the company product line, such as those listed in Table E-1.

Step 2: Stating the Purpose (Goals and Objectives) — "What, specifically, do we want to accomplish?"

▶ Once the idea for a multimedia title is agreed upon, then the goals and objectives for the title must be stated. The **goals** support the vision. The **objectives**, which must be clear, measurable, and obtainable, are developed from the goals.

▶ Writing the goals and objectives of a title is perhaps the most critical step in multimedia planning because they guide the development process. The goals and objectives provide a way to evaluate the title both during and after its development. Because multimedia development is a team process, goals and objectives are necessary to keep the team focused, on track, on budget, and on time. The goal for a specific multimedia title must fit within the overall vision of the company or organization. Figure E-2 shows an example of a company's vision, which is supported by a goal for one product and by objectives related to that goal. Notice that the vision and goal provide the development team with an overview of the title, whereas the objectives, which are more precise statements than goals, provide the team with specific direction regarding the title's development.

▶ The multimedia category also helps shape the goals and objectives of a particular title. For example, an instructional title will have very different goals and objectives than an entertainment title.

Step 3: Identifying the Target Audience — "Who will use the title?"

▶ The more information a developer has about the potential users, the more likely a title can be created that will satisfy the user's needs and be successful. For example, because children are likely to respond to the elements of exploration and surprise, using elements of surprise—such as a dog wagging its tail when it is clicked—in a children's title might help the title attract its target audience.

▶ Audiences can be described in many ways such as demographics, lifestyle, and attitudes.

▶ There is a trade-off between a precise definition of your audience and the size of the audience. In other words, if the definition of your audience is very precise, then the size of your audience may be very small. If the definition of the audience is more broad, then the size of your audience will be large. Companies want to identify as large an audience as possible to maximize potential sales. The larger the audience, the more diverse its needs, however, and the more difficult it is to "give them what they want." For example, a company might want to develop a title on earthquakes. The goal of the title is to teach people how to prepare for an earthquake and what to do if caught in one. The target audience for this title is defined, to some degree, by geographical location. Alternatively, the company could consider creating a series of disaster-preparedness titles (earthquakes, hurricanes, tornadoes, floods, and so on) that would have the same basic structure but varying content. Creating a series of titles around the basic goal of disaster preparedness would reach a broader audience, increase the potential market, and hold down the cost of developing each title.

FIGURE E-1: *The phases of multimedia development*

Multimedia Development
Phase 1 – Planning the Title
- Step 1: Developing the concept
- Step 2: Stating the purpose
- Step 3: Identifying the target audience
- Step 4: Determining the treatment
- Step 5: Developing the specifications
- Step 6: Storyboarding and navigation

Phase 2 – Creating and Testing the Title
- Step 7: Developing the content
- Step 8: Authoring the content
- Step 9: Testing the content

FIGURE E-2: *Sample vision, goal, and objectives*

VISION:
Be a leader in educational CD-ROM/DVD titles

GOAL:
Develop an interactive educational title based on one woman's real-world travel experience

OBJECTIVES:
- Include interactive map—trace woman's journey, highlight major events
- Provide audio clips of interview vignettes—specific to places on the interactive map
- Create key vocabulary terms as hyperlinks to glossary
- Ask strategic questions to focus users' attention and comprehension of events

TABLE E-1: *Sample of Focus Questions*

QUESTION TO ASK	ASK DEVELOPERS	ASK MARKETING	ASK USERS
How can we improve our existing titles (add multimedia elements, better-quality graphics)?	√	√	√
How can we take advantage of or adapt our current titles for new technologies (streaming over the Internet, virtual reality, speech recognition)?	√	√	
How can we repackage or repurpose our content (CD-ROM/DVD, Web site)?	√	√	
How can we use the Web to provide feedback on our products, which we can use for future development of titles?	√	√	√
How can we meet our customers' needs? (For example, listen and respond to a professor's comment: "My students have a difficult time visualizing the theory of DNA replication. If they could experience the process through a computer simulation, it might help them understand.")	√	√	√

Planning the title–Part 2

After the concept has been identified, the goals and objectives listed, and the potential audience identified, the developers are ready to plan the "look and feel" of the title as well as the specifications of the title. This lesson looks more closely at the next steps in the process of planning the title: determining the treatment and developing the specifications.

DETAILS

Step 4: Determining the Treatment — "What is the look and feel?"

Treatment. The **treatment** of a title is how the title will be presented to the user. The concept, goals and objectives, and target audience largely determine the treatment. It can include such things as the title's tone, approach, metaphor, and emphasis.

Tone. Will the title be humorous, serious, light, heavy, formal, or informal? The tone of a title can often be used to "make a statement"—for example, projecting a progressive, high-tech, well-funded corporate image.

Approach. How much direction will be provided to the user? Some titles, especially children's games and interactive books, focus on exploration. In the scene from a child's title shown in Figure E-3, for example, the child is presented with few or no instructions. Other titles, especially adult education applications, provide a great deal of direction in the form of menu choices. In such titles, the user typically follows a predetermined path to complete the title.

Another decision related to approach is identifying how much help to provide and what form to offer. Some titles include a "host" or "guide" that is available to assist the user, as shown in Figure E-4. Other titles simply have a Help button that can be used to display a Help screen.

Metaphor. Will a metaphor or a theme be used to provide interest or aid in understanding the title? The Teaching of English for International Communications (TOEIC) test program uses a mountain-climbing metaphor. That is, the user starts at "base camp" and, by answering a set of questions correctly, proceeds to a higher camp until the summit is reached.

Emphasis. How much emphasis will be placed on the various multimedia elements? For example, a company may want to develop an informational title that shows the features of its new product line, including video clip demonstrations of how each product works. The budget might not allow for creating the video segments, so the emphasis would shift to still pictures with text descriptions that might be available in the company's printed catalogs.

Step 5: Developing the Specifications — "What precisely does the title include, and how does it work?"

The specifications of a multimedia title state what will appear on each screen, including the arrangement of each element and the functionality of each object (for example, what happens when you click on the button labeled Next). The specifications include several parts:

Playback System. The specifications should always include the operating systems and the processing speeds for which the title is to be developed.

Elements to be Included. The specifications should include details about the elements to be included in the title. Should sound be recorded at 44 MHz, 16-bit, stereo? Should the resolution for the graphics be 8-bit, 256 colors? Should video be designed to play back at 15 frames per second and at what size? What are the sizes of the objects, such as buttons? What fonts, font sizes, and type styles will be used? What are the colors for the various objects? Questions such as these need to be addressed so that all members of the development team are consistently creating the same quality elements.

Functionality. The specifications should describe how the program reacts to an action, such as a mouse click, by the user. For example, clicking on a door (object) might cause the door to open (an animation), a doorbell to ring (sound), an "exit the program" message to appear (text), or an entirely new screen to be displayed. In addition, the specifications should indicate how the object itself changes based on a user action, such as how a button changes when a user clicks it.

User Interface. The user interface involves designing the appearance—how each object is arranged on the screen—and the interactivity—how the user navigates through the title.

FIGURE E-3: *A children's title with a focus on exploration*

As a child interacts with the title through exploration, an action occurs.

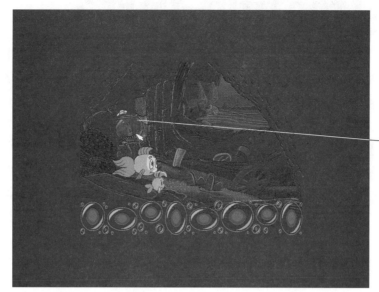

Surprise: Clicking on the fishbowl causes the fish to jump out of the bowl.

FIGURE E-4: *Multimedia title that uses a guide*

The space theme in this children's title reinforces the idea of exploration and adventure

Thaddeus Pole acts as a guide to help the child while he or she uses the mutimedia title

More about specifications

Specifications should be as detailed as possible. The goal in creating the specifications is to be able to give them to the production team and, with few additional instructions, to have the team create the title. In practice, this scenario rarely materializes because unexpected problems or questions often arise as the project progresses. Specifications are important, however, because they provide a starting point for the development team. The team understands that adjustments, additions, and corrections must be made based on input such as quality testing reviews or content reviews.

Planning the title–Part 3

Multimedia borrows many of its development processes from movies, including the use of storyboards. A **storyboard** is a representation of what each screen will look like and how the screens are linked. Its purpose is to provide an overview of the project, to provide a guide (roadmap) for the programmer, to illustrate the links between screens, and to indicate the functionality of the objects. This lesson focuses on the final steps in the process of planning the title: developing the storyboard and the navigation scheme.

DETAILS

Step 6: Storyboard and Navigation — "What do the screens look like and how are they linked?"

▶ Figure E-5 shows a storyboard. Notice that it consists of hand-drawn sketches on 8.5 × 11- inch paper turned sideways to more closely represent the dimensions of a computer screen. Also, notice that each piece of paper represents one screen of the title and shows a rough layout of the elements to be displayed on the screen, their approximate size, and their location on the screen. It is not necessary at this point in the planning process to decide on the exact content (such as a particular photo or graphic) for each screen. It is important, however, to show where text, graphics, photos, buttons, and other elements will be placed. As a consequence, the storyboard includes place-holders for the various elements. The storyboards can be hand-written on paper, as shown in Figure E-5, or created as slides in an electronic slide show authoring program.

▶ An important feature of the storyboard is the navigation scheme. One of the most significant aspects of multimedia is its nonlinear interactivity. The linking of screens through the use of buttons, hypertext, and other hot spots allows the user to jump from one screen to another. The multimedia developer must decide how the various screens will be linked and show this scheme in the storyboard. In this way, problems with the navigation scheme can be identified before the programming begins. Figure E-6 shows some primary links assigned to the screens. The title in the storyboard example is a fairly simple application with all of the screens linked to the main menu. In some titles, however, the linking is quite complex and does not lend itself well to a storyboard display. For these titles, the programmer must implement the navigation scheme based on written specifications.

▶ Navigation schemes can be set up in a variety of ways, including sequential, topical, and exploratory. A **sequential navigation scheme** takes the user through a more or less controlled, linear process. Examples are games with a story line that has a beginning, middle, and end; books that are repurposed as multimedia titles; electronic slide show presentations; and instructional tutorials that require the student to move through the material step by step. Figure E-7 shows a sequential navigation scheme in which the user moves through the screen in a linear way. The only options for the user are to move back and forth in both the addition and subtraction screens before taking a test. Sequential titles often have buttons (Next, Forward, Continue, Previous, Back) or graphics (arrows, pointing fingers) that serve as navigational aids. To keep the user's interest in a linear navigation scheme, the developer could provide interactivity by allowing the user to click on an object to hear a sound, play an animation, or display a graphic.

▶ A **topical navigation scheme** allows the user to select from an array of choices or even to search for specific information. Examples are multimedia encyclopedias, interactive shopping catalogs, and informational kiosks. Topical navigation schemes often include several layers, as shown in Figure E-8. In this example, the user chooses among three options (Education, Employment, Services) and selects links that move through the various screens to display the desired information. This navigation scheme requires the developer to design an interface that ensures that users understand where they are and what their navigation options are on each screen.

▶ An **exploratory navigation scheme** provides little structure or guidance for the user; instead, it relies on user interaction, such as clicking objects displayed on the screen. Many games, directed at both children and adults, use some form of exploration. An example of a title that uses an exploratory navigation scheme was shown in Figure E-3.

▶ While storyboarding remains the method of choice for sequential titles, developers are using other methods, such as mapping structures and flowcharting, to provide the overview for the title.

FIGURE E-5: *A storyboard*

FIGURE E-6: *The linking of various screens*

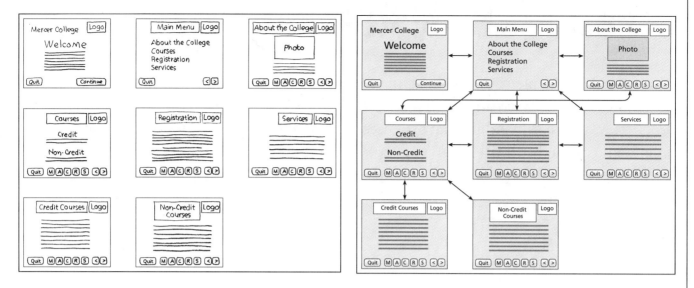

FIGURE E-7: *A sequential navigation scheme*

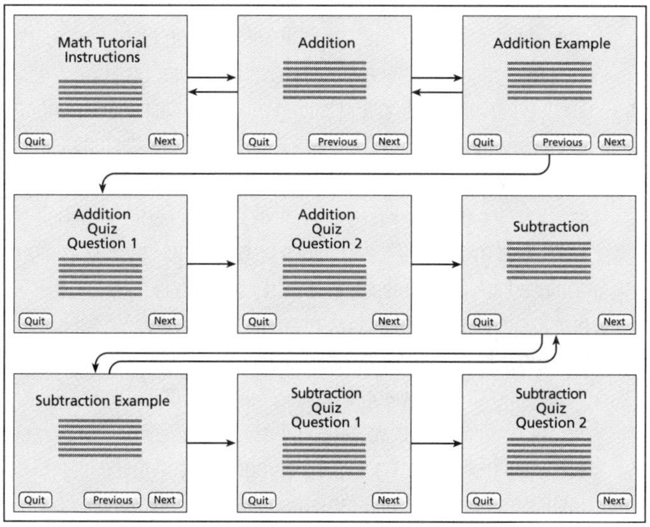

FIGURE E-8: *A topical navigation scheme*

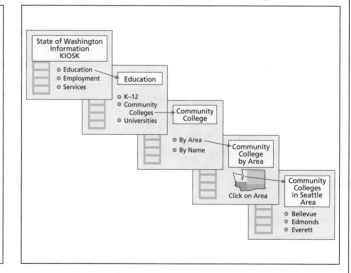

Creating and testing the title

Once the planning phase is complete, the focus turns to the next phases of the development process: creating and testing the title. These phases of the development process are very costly. Additional expenses, such as cost overruns and troubleshooting to handle unexpected surprises, can be kept to a minimum if the groundwork for the title has been properly established in the planning phase. This lesson provides details on creating and testing the title.

DETAILS

Step 7: Developing the Content — "Creating the pieces."
- ▶ Content issues that need to be addressed include the following:"How will the content be generated?" (for example, repurpose existing content, hire content experts to write text, employ a graphic artist, or contract with other professionals) "Who will be responsible for acquiring copyrights and licensing agreements?" "How will the content be archived and documented?"
- ▶ Many sources for content exist, including libraries of clip art, sounds, and video, as well as scanned photos and slides. If particular content is not available or is of low quality, then original content may need to be created. Graphic artists and photographers should be used to create original art work and pictures. Actors should be employed for video production and narration. Musicians should be hired to write and to produce original music and sound effects. Teachers or other content specialists should be contracted to write the text for concepts to be presented. Editors should be hired to review text.
- ▶ A multimedia title can contain hundreds of images and other multimedia elements. An **elements database** is used to keep track of the elements, to determine the overall file size, and to provide a reference for filenames that might be used in scripting. Figure E-9 shows a typical database of images including name, type, and size.

Step 8: Authoring the Title — "Bringing it all together."
- ▶ If the planning—especially the specifications and storyboard—has been completed properly, then the authoring requirements should be fairly straightforward. This statement does not mean that the authoring will be easily or quickly accomplished, but rather that there is a clear indication of what needs to be done.
- ▶ It is critical that the programmer work closely with those team members who are designing the user interface and those who are providing the content to ensure that the specifications are met.
- ▶ Invariably, scripting becomes a focal point to provide the functionality laid out in the specifications. Scripting is needed for such things as checking user input from the keyboard, accessing an external device such as a DVD, determining the configuration of the playback system, and creating an installation program that is used to start the title.

Step 9: Testing — "Does it work the way it was planned?"
- ▶ Although testing is listed as one of the last steps in the development process, it is really an ongoing component of the development process. In fact, testing should start at the very beginning of the process, during the concept step. At this point, small groups (focus groups) of potential users are shown a prototype of the proposed title. The prototype can be as simple as an electronic slide show presentation with enough content (even rough graphics) and interactivity to demonstrate the concept and to determine its feasibility. Conducting this "proof of concept" test can provide valuable information that helps refine the initial idea and prevent costly overruns later on.
- ▶ Throughout the creating and testing phase for the title, it is important to test the design and the function. Testing the design determines how the user interacts with the title. It asks questions such as "Does the user understand the navigation scheme, terminology, icons, and metaphors?" and "Does he or she get stuck, become confused, or lose interest?" **Usability testing** is a formal process in which potential users are filmed as they interact with a title and asked to verbalize what they are thinking. This type of testing allows the developer to see what users do (which objects are clicked and when), why they interact in the way that they do, and what their feelings are as they progress through the title.
- ▶ Testing the function of a multimedia title involves verifying that it works according to the specifications. This type of testing answers questions such as "Does clicking on each button or object cause the appropriate action?", "Can animation, sound, and video clips be controlled by the user?", and "Do graphics, text, and other elements appear in the correct locations?"

Portfolio - Media.fdb

File   Edit   View   Catalog   Item   Scripts   Window   Help

Media.fdb - Untitled

Showing 46 of 46 records

Filename	File Size	Last Modified	Extension Win	Volume
APPLAUSE.WAV	14 K	10/21/1992 4:38	WAV	C:
0050066_LOW.JPG	81 K	11/17/2000 12:2	JPG	C:
0110003.bmp	118 K	11/17/2000 3:05	bmp	C:
0110003.TIF	117 K	12/16/1995 5:38	TIF	C:
0110018.bmp	206 K	11/17/2000 3:05	bmp	C:
0110018.TIF	206 K	12/16/1995 5:39	TIF	C:
0110027.TIF	200 K	12/16/1995 5:07	TIF	C:
0110032.TIF	199 K	12/16/1995 5:08	TIF	C:
0110056.TIF	130 K	12/16/1995 5:40	TIF	C:

Item Details

Thumbnail:

Keywords:

| MediaElements | 46 |
| 0110018.bmp | 1 |

Description:

For Help, press F1

Bug Report

Title tested: _____
Date tested: _____
Tested by: _____
Tested on: _____
       Operating system
       Processor
       Graphics card
       Video card
       Monitor settings
Start time: _____
End time: _____

Type of error:

___ text___ graphic _____ video_____ flow_____ other: _____

Location of error: _____
_____
Description of error: _____
_____
_____
_____

Bug Report continued

Sequence of events immediately prior to error: _____
_____
_____
_____
_____
_____

Observations on what might have caused error: _____
_____
_____
_____

Additional comments: _____
_____
_____
_____
_____
_____
_____
_____
_____

Testing multimedia titles: two processes

While testing the functionality of the title continues throughout the production steps, there are two formal testing processes: alpha and beta testing. **Alpha testing** is usually conducted in-house and is not restricted to the development team. The idea is to "try to make it crash"; thus every conceivable action (point and click) and navigation path should be explored. As testers work through the title, they document any errors they encounter by completing a "bug report," similar to the one shown in Figure E-10. **Beta testing** is the final functional test carried out before the title's release to the general public. It involves selected potential users who could number in the thousands. Users who are not members of the company may be required to sign nondisclosure agreements to prevent them from revealing information about the title before it is released.

Understanding multimedia design guidelines

Over time, principles of multimedia design have been established. Developers use these principles as design guidelines, which are based on the intended audience, content, and type of title, rather than as absolute design rules. Multimedia design guidelines help the developer achieve the overriding design consideration from which the entire title flows. This lesson presents selected multimedia design guidelines in more detail.

DETAILS

▶ **Balance.** Balance in screen design refers to the distribution of optical weight in the layout. **Optical weight** is the ability of an element (such as a graphic, text, headline, or subhead) to attract the user's eye. Each element has optical weight as determined by its nature and size. The **nature of an element** refers to its shape, color, brightness, and type. For example, a stunning color photograph of Mount Everest has more weight than a block of text having an equal size.

Balance is determined by the weight of the elements and their position on the screen. That is, if you divide the screen into two parts, a balanced layout has about the same weight for each part, as shown in Figure E-11. A screen can have symmetrical balance, asymmetrical balance, or no balance. **Symmetrical balance** is achieved by arranging elements as horizontal or vertical mirrored images on both sides of a center line. **Asymmetrical balance** is achieved by arranging nonidentical elements on both sides of a center line, as shown in Figure E-12. A **no balance** design has elements arranged on the screen without regard to the weight on both sides of the center line.

In general, symmetrical design is static and suggests order and formality. It might be appropriate for multimedia titles that highlight the corporate image of conservative organizations such as banks and insurance companies. On the other hand, asymmetrical design is dynamic and suggests diversity and informality. It might be appropriate for entertainment titles for which a feeling of movement and discovery are important.

▶ **Unity.** A multimedia designer must be concerned about two types of unity: inter-screen unity and intra-screen unity.

Intra-screen unity has to do with how the various screen elements relate. That is, do all the elements "fit in"? An element that seems out of place can be disconcerting to the user, and it can prevent the design from achieving the desired effect for a particular screen. Figure E-13 shows an example of a design in which each element complements the other elements, thereby reinforcing the message or theme.

Inter-screen unity is the interactive design that users encounter as they navigate from one screen to another. It provides consistency throughout the title.

Unity is a desirable design goal in many multimedia titles and can be achieved by maintaining consistency in shapes, colors, text styles, and themes. In games and other entertainment titles, however, where exploration and surprise are important considerations, a unified design may be perceived as rather dull.

▶ **Movement.** In general, **movement** relates to how the user's eye moves through the elements on the screen. When a screen appears on the monitor, the viewer's eye is drawn to a particular location. In a balanced design, this point might be the **optical center**—a point somewhat above the physical center of the screen. In Western culture, the tendency is to move through the contents of the screen by going from the upper left to the lower right. As we design for the global community, however, it is critical to include visual clues such as arrows that help direct the viewers' movement on the page.

Movement is especially important in training and educational titles in which the designer wants the user to work through the contents in a more structured way. It is also important in situations wherein the designer wants to convey one primary message or impression. In these cases, the designer will try to affect the movement and emphasize various elements by:
- Controlling where the user starts on the screen—for example, by placing emphasis on a graphic or headline
- Using lines or objects that point the user in a certain direction
- Using color gradients that go from a light shade to a dark shade
- Having people or animals looking in the direction you want the user to look
- Emphasizing an element—for example, making it a different shape or color, surrounding it with white space, using a different font or type style, creating borders, or using different backgrounds for selected objects

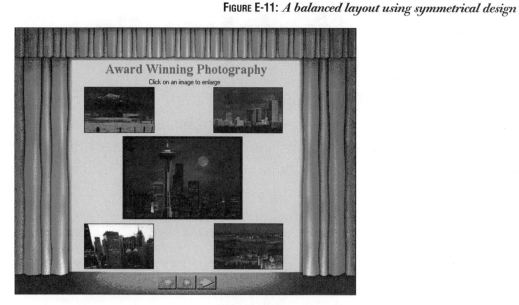

FIGURE E-12: *A balanced layout using asymmetrical design*

FIGURE E-13: *An example of unity in design*

The screen subject, Santa Fe, is complemented by the
- architecture
- food
- Southwestern color scheme
- Indian artifacts
- graphics

The icons used for the links to other parts of the title fit the theme

Designing for interactivity

In addition to designing the appearance of a title, developers must design the title's interactivity. The interactive design needs to be user-centered. The interface must support user control that works with the content while addressing the needs of the user (for example, if a sound is played, the user should be able to adjust the volume). In this lesson you will learn how the audience, type of title, contents, and elements used in a multimedia title affect the interactive design.

DETAILS

▶ **Audience.** Foremost in guiding the interactive design process is the user. As much as possible, the designer must understand the user's needs and the way in which he or she works with the product. The tendency is to approach the design process from our own perspective, reflecting our knowledge and experiences. The challenge for designers is to put themselves in the place of the user.

▶ **Type of Title.** The type of title affects the design, as illustrated in the following examples.

If the title is a corporate annual report and the user wants to quickly access specific information, then the design might include only a main menu with a straightforward navigation scheme based on the user's ability to point and click the mouse.

If the title is a reference work, such as an encyclopedia, the design might become more complex. The user might be given the ability to access a topic in several ways—menu, index, object, or keyword search.

If the title allows transactions, such as a registration kiosk at a college, the designer must consider how users will know which field (box) is active, how they will move from field to field, how users will indicate when they are done with a field, and how they will indicate when they are done with the form.

If the title is a game and the focus is on entertainment, the design might allow random interaction. Users are not as concerned with where they are and what they can do next in such titles, because the focus is on exploration and discovery. Thus the user interface becomes more implicit (with invisible hot spots) rather than explicit (with visible buttons).

▶ **Content.** The content affects the design of the interactivity. Two content concerns are the existence of large amounts of content and the nature of the content.

Large amounts of content. A major consideration in designing interactivity is determining how many levels users must navigate. The tendency is to add more levels as the content increases.

The more levels, however, the greater the chance for confusion and frustration by users as they try to determine where they are, how they got there, and how they can return to the starting point. You can reduce the number of levels by providing shortcuts in the form of hotwords or hot areas that skip several levels; replacing parts of the original screen with new content but leaving the shell of the screen intact so that users have a frame of reference; using pop-up windows that display additional information; using scroll bars (for text-intensive titles); and providing tabs or bookmarks that indicate where the user has been and allow the user to return quickly to a previously viewed screen.

Nature of the content. The nature of the content often suggests a theme that the interactive design needs to complement and reinforce. For example, if the title is a walk-through of a museum, the interactive design might include a virtual reality environment, similar to the one shown in Figure E-14, in which the mouse pointer is used to navigate through the museum and the mouse button is used to zoom in on paintings.

▶ **Elements Used in the Title.** The multimedia elements used in a title also affect the interactive design. For example, if the multimedia element of video (or animation or sound) is used, then decisions that affect interactive design include the following: Who controls the video? Does the video play automatically, or can the user stop and start it? Can the user adjust the sound volume? Where and when does the video image appear on the screen? If the video starts automatically, what controls are needed so that the user can control the video—that is, pause, stop, rewind, and cancel it? If the user has viewed the video previously and does not want to see it again, what controls are needed to allow the user to bypass the video? Finally, what will the video controls look like? While most people are familiar with standard VCR controls, these controls may not fit visually with the rest of the screen. Figure E-15 shows video controls that fit the theme of the title.

FIGURE E-14: *An example of an interactive design that reinforces the theme of the title*

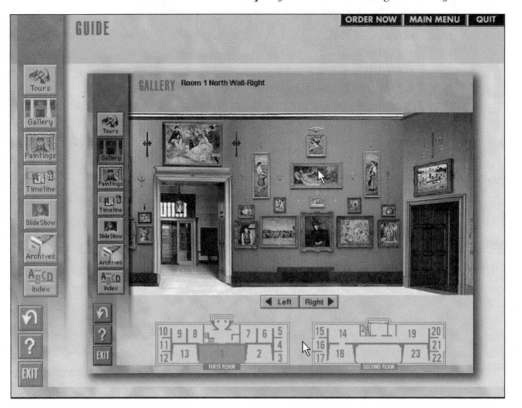

FIGURE E-15: *Video controls that fit the theme of the title*

Video is played inside this screen

Simulated video player with controls

Understanding interactive design guidelines

In addition to guidelines for multimedia design that affect the visual appearance of a title, guidelines for multimedia interactive design that affect the navigation of the title have been established. These guidelines are not absolute interactive design rules, but rather help the developer achieve the overriding interactive design consideration from which the entire title flows. That is, they help the developer design the interactivity of the title so that it is user-friendly while enhancing the overall design of the title. This lesson presents selected multimedia interactive design guidelines in more detail.

DETAILS

▶ **Make it simple, easy to understand, and easy to use.** The entire design process is undertaken for the benefit of the user. The user should not have to be taught how the navigation scheme and media controls work—these components of the multimedia title should be intuitive. From the moment the first screen appears and throughout the interactive process, users should know where they are and where they can go (unless the title is designed to be exploratory, such as a mystery- or adventure- type game). The initial screen should indicate what is contained in the title and how to navigate through it. Metaphors should be within the user's frame of reference and consistent with the content. All of the screen images, including icons and pointer symbols, as well as the navigation process, should complement one another and be consistent with the title's theme.

▶ **Build in consistency.** Consistency is especially important in reference titles wherein the user is searching for specific information. It applies to both the appearance of each screen and how the navigation scheme works. Figure E-16 shows how a consistent look is achieved as the user navigates from one level to another. In this example, the user clicks on the keyboard to move to the second screen. A portion of the graphic in the first screen (the hand on the keyboard) becomes a graphic and the background for the second screen.

▶ **Use design templates.** A template is a precise layout indicating where various elements will appear on the screen. Figure E-17 shows an example of a design template. Notice that the design template dictates the positions of the various elements (graphic, heading, menu, text, and navigation bar). While the actual content will change, the positions of elements on the screen will remain the same throughout the title.

Templates can aid the design process in several ways:

- *Provide consistency:* Each element of the screen will appear in the same location, which aids the user in understanding how the title works and increases the speed at which the user can navigate through the title.
- *Shorten the development time:* Because of the similarity of the screens, templates can reduce the amount of time needed to arrange elements on the various screens.
- *Prevent "object shift":* An object that moves even one pixel as the user navigates through the title causes a noticeable and disconcerting jump. Templates that utilize grids can specify the exact layout, down to a pixel of each screen element, which prevents objects from shifting.

▶ **Provide feedback.** Interactivity is a two-way process. Users need to know when an action, such as clicking a button or a hotword, is completed. This goal can be accomplished by providing user feedback for actions. For example, once a user clicks a button, the feedback might be to show a depressed button, to change the button color, or to play a sound. Figure E-18 shows another form of user feedback. In this example, check marks indicate where the user has been—that is, what sections of the title have been viewed.

▶ **Provide choices and escapes.** One of the guiding principles of interactivity is that the user should have control. With that principle in mind, consider the following: Avoid long introductions of automatically scrolling text, narration, music, or credits. Don't make the user view a video or animation, or listen all the way through sound clips that he or she might already have heard; provide a way for the user to skip or escape viewing these elements. Provide options for a user to quit the title, but build in safety nets so that the user does not completely exit the program without confirming that action.

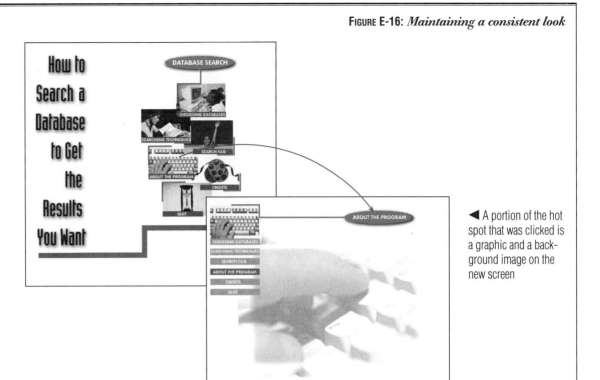

◄ A portion of the hot spot that was clicked is a graphic and a background image on the new screen

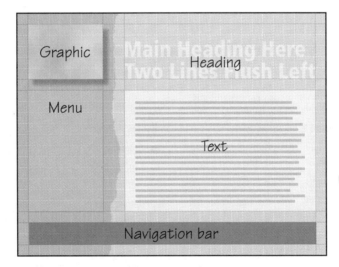

Check mark indicates the user has previously selected this option

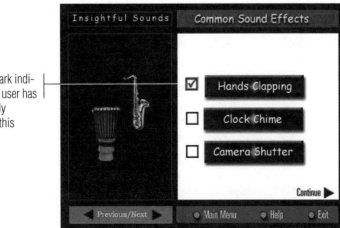

Designing multimedia for the Web

Design considerations for the Web are similar to those for non-Web applications. Guidelines for designing the appearance (for example, unity, movement) and for designing the interactivity (navigation) still apply. Other considerations—especially those related to the constraints of the Web and the commercial nature of many Web sites—also affect the design of multimedia titles delivered through the Web. In this lesson you will learn how to approach the design of multimedia applications delivered through the Web.

DETAILS

▶ The intended audience largely determines the layout of a Web page, including the arrangement of the various elements and the features provided. Some users are primarily interested in getting into a site, quickly obtaining up-to-date information (such as stock quotes), and moving on. In this case, the design should be simple and straightforward. Other users are interested in how the information is presented or in the entertainment value of a Web site and may be willing to wait for large video or 3-D files to be displayed. For this reason, some companies provide Web sites that accommodate different audiences. These Web sites let the user choose what best meets his or her needs. Figure E-19 shows a site that provides two options when viewing a tour of the company's products.

▶ For most designers of multimedia titles to be delivered through the Web, the overriding considerations are how to attract viewer attention, keep viewer interest, and help viewers get what they want out of the site (information, entertainment, and so on). To attract attention, many developers rely on flashy animations, catchy sounds, scrolling text, and lively colors. This strategy may work to attract new viewers, but the experience can become rather irritating for repeat viewers. Therefore, developers often provide a way for the viewer to skip an introduction by merely clicking a button.

▶ Provide quick downloads. Users are impatient when it comes to waiting for Web pages to appear. They become frustrated and may even abort the process after a short time. Techniques to improve download times include the use of compressed graphics, thumbnail graphics, and progressive loading of graphics. After the page appears, it is important to provide ways that the user can control the playing of animations, sound, and video.

▶ Keep it simple. Users do not read a Web page—they simply scan it. They look for keywords and links. Consequently, providing too much information on a page or cluttering it up with too many graphics or animations may hinder the user. First-time visitors to a Web site generally spend less than 60 seconds on the Web page. During that time, the site must capture the visitor's interest, and the visitor must understand what the site is about, how to navigate through it, and how to obtain the desired information. Therefore, a premium is placed on making it easy for the user to find the desired information.

▶ Get to the point. Viewers come to a Web site in many ways, such as through a search engine list, through a link from another site, or through surfing. The Web site must be designed in a way that makes it easy for the viewer to learn the purpose of the Web site. Be sure to use appropriate text fonts and sizes to communicate the Web site's purpose and to use graphics to reinforce the point.

▶ Keep the site fresh. Users want consistency in design and navigation so they don't get lost in a site; yet they don't want the site to be stale. Developers realize they cannot redesign their sites too often, so they rely on updating the content and changing the multimedia elements, especially the graphics and animations, to keep the site fresh. Table E-2 provides additional Web development tips.

TABLE E-2: *Web Development Tips*

√	**Users should be able to display any page within three to five clicks of the mouse button and return to the home page in one click.**
√	**Navigation options (often presented in button or table formats) should be labeled clearly.**
√	**Text links should be color-coded.**
√	**A site map that lists and provides links to the major topical areas is a quick reference for the viewer.**
√	**A search feature is a useful tool for finding desired information.**

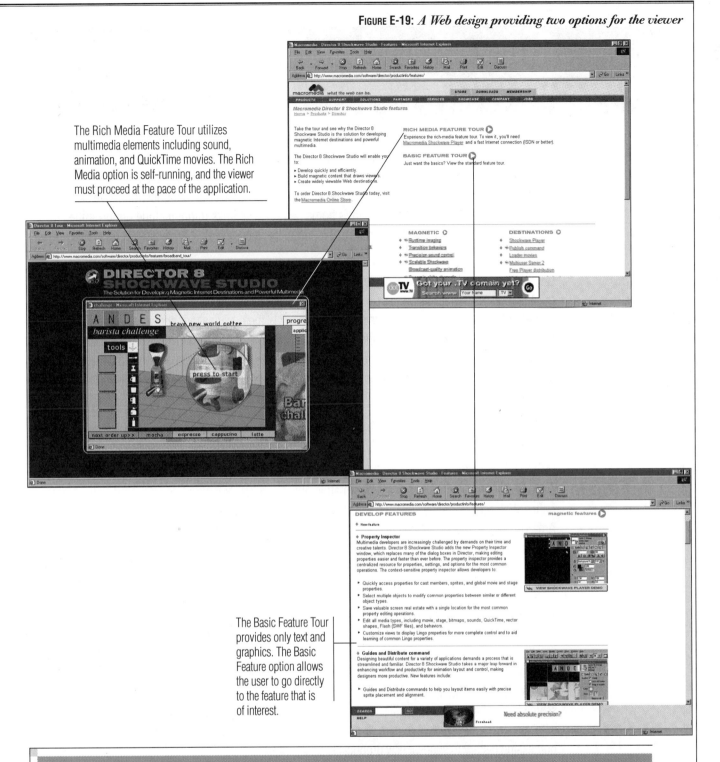

The Rich Media Feature Tour utilizes multimedia elements including sound, animation, and QuickTime movies. The Rich Media option is self-running, and the viewer must proceed at the pace of the application.

The Basic Feature Tour provides only text and graphics. The Basic Feature option allows the user to go directly to the feature that is of interest.

Multimedia and banner ads

Banner ads are the most prevalent form of promotion on the Web. They often include multimedia elements such as sound or animation. Studies show that more than half of all Web users look at banner ads, but less than 1% actually click on them. Banner ads are popular with developers for two reasons.

First, they know that consumers visiting Web sites are more active than consumers watching some other media, such as TV. Second, they know how to include multimedia elements, such as GIF animations, to attract attention. There are standard banner ad sizes, which must be considered when

developing graphics, text, and animations for such ads. The position of a banner ad is also important. Many appear at the top of the page because a Web page is loaded from the top down, and this placement gives the ad the maximum amount of exposure.

This unit discussed ways of soliciting new ideas for products. Some ways to elicit new ideas include customer satisfaction surveys, marketing surveys, in-house research, and stakeholder focus groups. One of the focus questions suggested earlier in the unit asks, "How can we use the Web to provide feedback on our products?" Of course, there is the obvious answer to this question: have customer feedback links available on the company's home page. These links might include opportunities for feedback as informal as the ability to e-mail a comment to customer service or as formal as a survey to be completed and returned.

But do Web technologies lend themselves to other avenues for feedback? Could multimedia developers create programs to track how the user moves through a multimedia title? That is, what path does the user follow? What "surprises" does the user stumble upon? Is there any pattern showing how users navigate through the title? Answers to these and similar questions could be helpful to developers as they strive for continuous improvement. To a certain degree, some of these questions can be answered through usability testing. Usability testing, however, requires gathering willing participants to come to a lab to be filmed while they use the title. It requires the lab to be staffed. It requires the video to be analyzed.

What if multimedia developers could use the power of the Web to gather the same or similar information obtained during usability testing but from a wider, unsuspecting audience? Is this possible? Does the technology already exist? To answer that question, let's take a closer look at cookies.

Cookies are small files containing information about you that are stored on your hard drive. Many online Web sites currently share cookies with you. For example, when you purchase a product from Amazon.com, you provide the company with personal data such as a name, mailing address, e-mail address, and credit card number. The next time you visit Amazon.com, you are presented with a personal greeting, including your first name and suggestions for products you might be interested in purchasing. How does Amazon.com know that the visitor is you and determine which products to suggest?

The answer is cookies. When you visit Amazon.com, its server sends a cookie to your browser and gives it a unique ID number. The same ID number is placed in the Amazon.com database along with information you have provided, such as your name, and data that the company has collected, including the products you have purchased. The cookies are stored on your hard drive. Then, whenever you return to the Amazon.com site, the Amazon.com server reads the cookie on your hard drive and uses the ID number to search its database, which identifies you and your purchasing history. Based on the information in the database, the Amazon.com program displays your first name to "customize" the greeting and uses your purchasing history to suggest new products to you.

Cookies are transparent to the user and are useful to both buyer and seller.

- **Buyer Benefits:** *Site personalization.* The company customizes the site to provide the information you want, often in the form of advertising. *Quicker access.* Because the ID number identifies you, you do not need to provide login information when entering a site.
- **Seller Benefits:** *Target marketing.* Companies can build a user profile by tracking where the user goes and which banner ads he or she chooses. Companies can then tailor advertisements to areas of user interest and track which ads are most effective.

Not everyone agrees that cookies are a good thing. Many groups and individuals who support online privacy are appalled that information about you can be collected and stored—sometimes without your knowledge. Groups who oppose the use of cookies because of online privacy concerns include the following:

- Individuals concerned with keeping their online information and activity private. Studies show that 90% of online consumers want the right to control how their personal information is used. Half are willing to have the government regulate privacy (Forrester Research). In addition, 64% of online consumers are unlikely to trust a Web site, even if it prominently features a privacy policy (Jupiter Communications).
- Consumer advocacy groups concerned with abuse of individuals' profiles.
- Businesses concerned with accumulating information on current and potential customers while avoiding government control. In response to criticism of online profiling, industry guidelines suggest that companies make available their privacy policies as a form of self-regulation, including their adherence to the Federal Trade Commission's (FTC) Fair Information Practice Principles.
- Government agencies concerned with violation of privacy regulations. In 1988, the FTC issued guidelines for industry self-regulation including what should be covered in a company's privacy policy.

While debates continue among these stakeholders, the individual does have control over the use of cookies on his or her computer. First, a browser can be set to either alert the user that a cookie is trying to be sent (and allow the user to refuse it), or the browser can be set to refuse all cookies. Second, users can delete cookie files from their hard drive.

What do cookies have to do with multimedia developers? Earlier, the following question was raised: What if multimedia developers could use the power of the Web to gather the same or similar information obtained during usability testing but from a wider, unsuspecting audience? Cookies can and do gather information from a wide, and sometimes, unsuspecting audience. Multimedia developers could develop cookie-like programs or other advanced tracking programs to track user information about a title. This information could help them improve titles by providing information such as how long a user stays on any given screen, whether the user clicks several "decoys" before clicking the proper button, and so on. As developers analyze such data, they could use their findings to make improvements to the title.

Can such tracking programs be developed? Yes. Can information obtained from such tracking programs be beneficial to both the multimedia developer and the consumer? Yes. But the question remains—Is product improvement at the expense of online privacy acceptable?

EXPAND THE IDEAS

1. In what situations, if any, is it acceptable for companies to engage in online profiling? Provide concrete examples.
2. Research the cookie controversy. What are others saying about cookies? Is the voice in the articles consistent, or do viewpoints on the topic vary? Write a report detailing your findings.
3. Use your research about cookies to answer the following questions: Does the cookie controversy apply to multimedia developers? Explain. What can multimedia developers learn from what has been written about cookies?
4. Should multimedia developers use tracking programs to gather user feedback? Explain your position.
5. If you were to design an online tracking program for a multimedia title, explain what information you would want to track. Would you include personal information about the user, such as age? Would you include the time of day that the title is accessed? What else would you include or not include? Combine your ideas with those of other students while working in a small group. Make a chart detailing information that your group would track and information that your group would not track.

End of Unit Exercises

STUDY TIPS

1. List key terms presented in this unit. Define them in your own words, and then check your definitions against those listed in the glossary. Use additional sources to seek expanded information for any terms that need further clarification.

2. Summarize the steps in the multimedia development process. Refer to Figure E-1 as needed.

3. Pretend you work for an educational company that develops multimedia titles for the K–8 market. Write a vision statement for the company, identify a goal for one project, and list five objectives to support that goal.

4. In the introduction to this unit the following statement is made: "The rule of thumb for multimedia development is 80% planning and 20% production." What does this statement mean? Based on the information presented in this unit, do you agree or disagree with it? Explain.

5. Summarize the multimedia design guidelines outlined in this unit. Devise a system to help you remember key terms associated with each guideline.

6. Explain "balance" as it relates to screen design and the three designs that can be used to achieve balance.

7. Discuss the factors you must take into account when you design for interactivity.

8. Describe common navigation schemes used in multimedia titles. Provide an example of each navigation scheme.

9. Compare the process of designing multimedia titles for the Web with multimedia titles for CD/DVD distribution. How is the design process similar? What special considerations must you take into account when designing multimedia titles for the Web?

SELECT THE BEST ANSWER

1. Which of the following is not part of the planning phase?
   a. Determining the treatment
   b. Stating the purpose
   c. Developing the content
   d. Developing the concept

2. "To be the leader in online training programs" is an example of a(n) _____.
   a. Tactic
   b. Vision
   c. Objective
   d. Strategy

3. Balance is determined by the position of the elements on the screen and their _____.
   a. Weight
   b. Movement
   c. Interactivity
   d. None of the above

4. _____ balance is achieved by arranging mirrored elements horizontally or vertically on a center line.
   a. Interactive
   b. Linear
   c. Asymmetrical
   d. Symmetrical

5. Which of the following is NOT an example of movement?
   a. Using lines or objects that point in a certain direction
   b. A person looking in a certain direction
   c. A dog running
   d. A text heading that is centered

6. Which of the following is NOT part of the treatment?
   a. Metaphor
   b. Approach
   c. Emphasis
   d. Timing

7. Which of the following is NOT part of the specifications of a title?

   a. Tone

   b. Functionality

   c. Elements to be included

   d. User interface

8. Which of the following is NOT a navigation scheme?

   a. Exploratory

   b. Symmetrical

   c. Topical

   d. Sequential

9. _____ testing is the final functional test before release of a title.

   a. Usability

   b. Alpha

   c. Beta

   d. Prototype

10. _____ balance is achieved by arranging nonidentical elements on both sides of a center line.

   a. Symmetrical

   b. Unified

   c. Functional

   d. Asymmetrical

FILL IN THE BEST ANSWER

1. The rule of thumb for multimedia development is that the process should break down into _____ % planning and _____ % production.

2. _____ is the part in the development process that should be performed throughout the process.

3. Brainstorming can be useful in generating _____ for multimedia titles.

4. Step 2 in the planning process is "stating the purpose" which includes listing the _____ and _____.

5. The _____ of a title determines whether it is humorous, serious, formal, or informal.

6. A(n) _____ is a visual representation of what each screen will look like and how the screens are linked.

7. In a(n) _____ navigation scheme, the user proceeds more or less through a controlled linear process.

8. _____ testing is a formal process in which potential users are filmed as they interact with a title and are asked to verbalize what they are thinking.

9. _____ in screen design refers to the distribution of optical weight in the layout.

10. A design _____ is a precise layout indicating where various elements will appear on the screen.

INDEPENDENT CHALLENGE 1

As stated in the unit, planning should be 80% of the multimedia development process. If you have applied care, thought, and attention to detail in the planning phase, then the development of the title should unfold naturally. This statement does not mean that there will not be difficulties to overcome in each phase of development, but rather that you should know what difficulties you will face if you have planned carefully. As you work through this independent challenge, review the multimedia development process presented in Figure E-1. Your instructor will let you know if you should complete this independent challenge on your own or in small groups.

To complete this independent challenge:

1. Identify a topic for a multimedia title

2. Briefly go through the steps in the multimedia development process by completing a report with the following information:

   a. Develop the concept and specify, in general, what you want to do.

   b. State the purpose of the title, including the goals and objectives.

   c. Identify the target audience, including demographics and lifestyle information.

   d. Specify the treatment—the title's "look and feel." Include metaphors and emphasis you will place on various multimedia elements. Support your decision based on the target audience, concept, and objectives.

   e. List the specifications.

3. Specify the target playback system(s), elements to be included, functionality, and user interface.

4. Design the storyboard and the navigation scheme. Include a template design, if appropriate, and specify the links.

5. Indicate how and where the content will be acquired.

6. Specify when in the development process testing will occur and how it will be done.

7. Prepare a brief oral presentation of your report, and be prepared to present it to your class.

INDEPENDENT CHALLENGE 2

Principles of multimedia development have been established as guideposts for multimedia developers. These principles are not hard-and-fast rules, but rather guidelines that help the developer in all phases of the multimedia development process. This unit presented some fundamental multimedia guidelines, but it did not attempt to cover all possible guidelines. This independent challenge is designed to help you broaden your understanding of and familiarity with guidelines for multimedia development.

To complete this independent challenge:

1. Connect to the Internet.

2. Go to *http://www.course.com*, navigate to the Student Online Companion for this book, and then click the link for Unit E.

3. The Unit E link contains links to Web sites offering more information about multimedia design guidelines. Click each link to visit the site. Write a summary of each site. Include the following information in the summary:

  a. Give the name of the resource (URL).

  b. Who is the intended audience for the guidelines (students, experienced multimedia developers, and so on)?

  c. Are all of the guidelines covered in this book also mentioned at the site? If no, list guidelines covered in this book that are not covered on the site.

  d. Does this site provide additional guidelines that are not mentioned in the book? If yes, list these additional guidelines.

  e. Compare the guidelines in the book with the guidelines at the site. Even though the same wording may not be used, do both cover the same global principles of design?

  f. Which of these sites, if any, would you bookmark for future reference? Explain.

INDEPENDENT CHALLENGE 3

As you have learned, balance is important to screen design. The three screen designs include symmetrical, asymmetrical, and no balance. Before designing your screens, it is helpful to analyze how other designers have applied the principle of balance to their screen designs.

To complete this independent challenge:

1. Select several multimedia titles, and study their screen designs on the basis of balance.

2. Find one example of each of the following designs: symmetrical, asymmetrical, no balance. If possible, print a copy of each example, and include it with your report. If it is not possible to print the page, then draw a sketch of the page illustrating how the balance (or lack of balance) was achieved.

3. Prepare a report including the following information:

  a. For a screen that has symmetrical balance:

    1. How are the elements (heading, text, graphics, colors) used to achieve the balance?
    2. How does this design enhance the title?

  b. For a screen that has asymmetrical balance:

    1. How are the elements (heading, text, graphics, colors) used to achieve the balance?
    2. How does this design enhance the title?

  c. For a screen that has no balance:

    1. How are elements (heading, text, graphics, colors) used to achieve no balance?
    2. How does this design enhance the title?

INDEPENDENT CHALLENGE 4

Many factors, such as movement, contribute to the appearance of a multimedia screen. To better understand these factors, it is helpful to analyze how other designers have applied these factors to their screen designs.

To complete this independent challenge:

1. Identify one screen from a multimedia title that exemplifies each of the following: movement, optical center, and unity. You may use one screen if that screen exemplifies all three factors, or you may use a different screen to illustrate each factor.

2. Print each screen or provide a drawing of each screen to include with your report.

3. Analyze the screen(s).

4. Briefly describe how movement, optical center, and unity affect each screen in a written report.

  a. For a screen that has obvious movement:

    1. How is the movement achieved?
    2. How does the movement enhance the design?

  b. For a screen that has an obvious optical center:

    1. Where is the optical center?
    2. How was the screen designed to achieve the optical center?
    3. What purpose does the optical center achieve?

  c. For a screen that has unity:

    1. How is unity achieved?
    2. How is inter-screen unity evident in the design?
    3. How is intra-screen unity evident in the design?

5. In your report, include changes you would make to improve the screens you studied. Explain how these changes would improve the screen.

6. Prepare a brief oral presentation of your written report, and be prepared to present it to your class.

INDEPENDENT CHALLENGE 5

Many multimedia titles are the result of repurposing the content from another medium, such as putting street maps on a DVD.

To complete this independent challenge:

1. Using the development process that you learned in this unit, prepare a plan to repurpose the content from a textbook that you have used.

2. In your report, explain how multimedia and interactivity can be used to enhance the content.

INDEPENDENT CHALLENGE 6

An important aspect of any multimedia title is its interactivity. This unit discussed the following types of interactivity: sequential navigation scheme, topical navigation scheme, and exploratory navigation scheme. Before designing your screens, it is helpful to analyze how other designers have applied the principles of interactivity to their screen designs. Your instructor will let you know if you should work individually or in groups of three to complete this independent challenge. If you work in groups of three, each group member might report on a different type of interactivity.

To complete this independent challenge:

1. Select several multimedia titles, and study their screen designs on the basis of interactivity.

2. Identify a screen that exemplifies each type of interactivity: sequential navigation scheme, topical navigation scheme, and exploratory navigation scheme.

3. Draw sketches of each title to show how the screens exemplify each type of interactivity.

4. Display the sketches on a poster, and prepare an oral report that includes the following information:

   a. How has the interactivity been designed to address the needs of the intended audience?

   b. How has the interactivity been designed to address the type of title?

   c. How has the interactivity been designed to address the type of content?

   d. Is the design of the interactivity intuitive and easy to understand? Explain.

   e. Does the design of the interactivity provide consistency? Explain.

   f. Does the design of the interactivity provide needed feedback and choices for the user? Explain.

   g. What changes would you make to improve the interactivity of the titles you studied, and how would these changes improve the screen?

5. Prepare a brief oral presentation of your report, and be prepared to present it to your class.

VISUAL WORKSHOP

1. What is Figure E-20?

2. Who would have created it? For what purpose?

3. Label the components of Figure E-20.

4. Draw arrows to show a possible navigation scheme for the title in Figure E-20.

FIGURE E-20

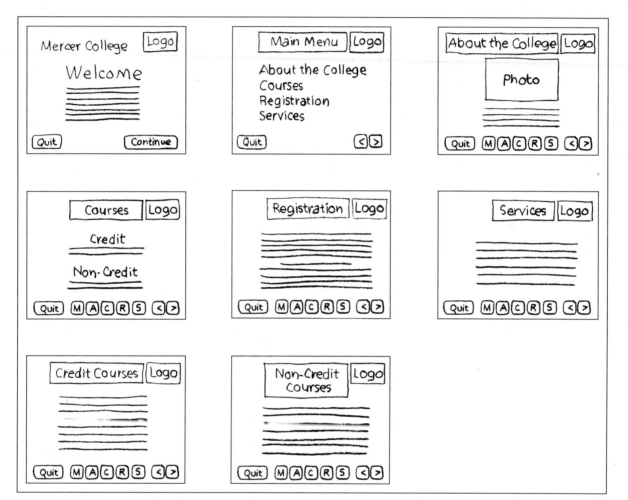

Management and Distribution of Multimedia Titles

OBJECTIVES

Decide who should develop the multimedia title

Outsource multimedia titles

Understand project management: plan the project

Understand project management: identify the team

Understand project management: organize the project

Explore careers in multimedia

Understand mass-market distribution of multimedia titles

Explore online distribution of multimedia titles

There are thousands of multimedia developers creating thousands of applications, many of which compete with one another. No individual multimedia title—even an award-winning one—is assured of commercial success. Nevertheless, those companies that manage their multimedia projects effectively, from planning through marketing and distribution, are more likely to be successful. Because multimedia is so people-intensive, the management of people—their creative talents, experience, and expertise—is a critical skill. In this unit you will learn how companies approach project management, what kinds of multimedia skills are used in the development process, and how to prepare for careers in multimedia. In addition, you will learn how companies market and distribute their titles in a way that helps ensure their success.

Deciding who should develop the multimedia title

After deciding to create a multimedia title, a company needs to determine who will manage the project. Will it be done in-house or will the project be outsourced? A company **outsources** a project when it contracts with a service provider—that is, an organization specializing in developing multimedia applications—to produce the title. In this lesson you will learn what factors a company must consider before determining whether it will create a multimedia title in-house or outsource the title. If a company decides to outsource, then it must identify the criteria it will use to select the service provider.

DETAILS

▶ The decision on whether to produce a multimedia title in-house or to outsource it is affected by the following considerations:

Complexity of project. A simple electronic slide show presentation might easily be produced in-house. Generally, a company has the resources available to create multimedia presentations. Some companies, even though they have the resources to produce a multimedia presentation title, still opt to outsource the title because of the project's complexity. For example, a typical company could not produce an interactive corporate image title including video, sound, and animation, so it would likely outsource this project.

Expertise of current staff. Large companies like AT&T and Boeing often have corporate divisions that produce multimedia applications, such as training titles. In most cases, however, companies do not have the highly specialized talent that is needed to develop multimedia titles as well as manage the development process. When a company does not have employees with the expertise needed to create the multimedia title, it must decide whether to train the current staff, hire the needed personnel, or contract with a multimedia service provider. Management making this decision must determine whether the creation of the multimedia title is a one-time or rare occurrence or if many more multimedia projects are scheduled for the near future.

Training existing personnel or hiring new staff with the needed skills may be an appropriate alternative if a company determines there is an ongoing development need. The expense could be considered an investment that would pay off for years to come. Also, some talented individuals may have existing skills that can be transferred to digital technology. For example, graphic artists could learn interface design and be trained to use image-processing programs such as Photoshop; programmers could be trained on authoring programs such as Director; and technical writers could learn how to edit content for multimedia titles.

Even if a company makes a commitment to establish a comprehensive multimedia development division, there will always be the need for specialized talent. A company is rarely able to support a staff that includes people with such highly specialized skills as sound engineers, video producers, and 3-D animators. Thus even a company that decides to create or that already maintains a multimedia division will contract out to obtain the specialized skills needed to create highly sophisticated multimedia titles.

▶ In addition to their technical expertise, what are some benefits in hiring a service provider?

Service providers know the industry. They keep up on the latest trends and research. They know what is forward-thinking and what is already passé when it comes to creating multimedia titles. They know what has and has not worked for other clients. They can bring this knowledge to the development discussion, which gives the company a wider view of its project.

Service providers have a database of multimedia experts. They can match the appropriate specialists to projects based on clients' needs. Figure F-1 shows two multimedia titles with very different approaches—the "look and feel" for each title is unique and requires different skills. The service provider knows which freelance interface designers have the skills and understanding to create an appropriate title for each project.

▶ What criteria do you use to identify the service provider best suited for the job? A service provider's established niche in the market is a key consideration. The service provider must be able to provide concrete examples of its expertise either by making past projects available for viewing on CDs or by providing testimonials, references, and portfolios. Figure F-2 shows an excerpt from a multimedia provider's promotional packet that lists its philosophy, services, and experience.

FIGURE F-1: *Two multimedia titles requiring different development skills*

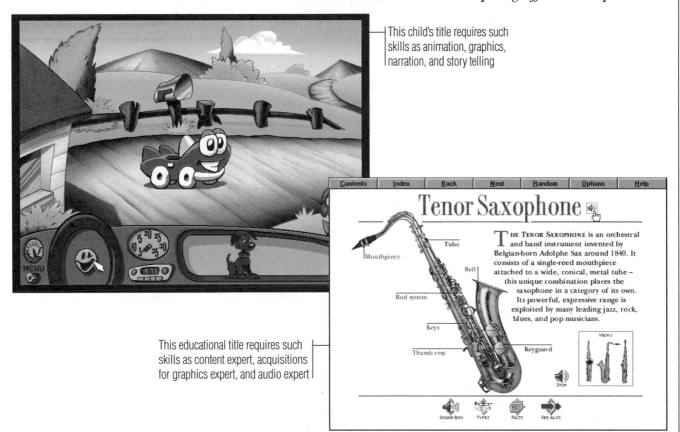

This child's title requires such skills as animation, graphics, narration, and story telling

This educational title requires such skills as content expert, acquisitions for graphics expert, and audio expert

FIGURE F-2: *An excerpt from a multimedia provider's promotional packet*

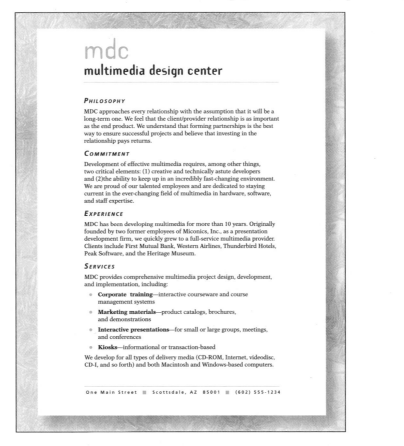

Outsourcing multimedia titles

Once a company decides not to develop multimedia titles in-house but to outsource the entire development process to a comprehensive service provider, it must contract and establish a relationship with a particular service provider. The company then becomes the "client" of the service provider. It is important that the relationship between the client and the service provider be approached as a partnership, because the success of the project depends on close cooperation and effective communication. This lesson looks more closely at the working relationship that must be forged between a client and its multimedia service provider.

DETAILS

▶ Before outsourcing a multimedia project, the company must identify its needs. Often the company will write a **request for proposal (RFP)**, which clearly defines the multimedia project. The RFP is made available in a variety of ways—for example, it might be published in trade magazines or posted on the company's Web site. The originator of the RFP becomes the client. Figure F-3 shows an RFP outline of the content required for a multimedia Web site.

▶ Service providers who are interested in the project respond to the RFP. The depth of detail in the service provider's response depends on the depth of detail requested in the RFP. In addition to specifically addressing the RFP issues, the service provider's response includes such things as references, deliverables, timelines, and a budget. The **references** provide concrete examples that prove the service provider's expertise in creating similar projects or in having the skills necessary to complete the project defined in the RFP. The **deliverables** are the components of the project that will be provided to the client. The **timelines** identify dates for the deliverables and key components of the project. The **budget** outlines the project costs.

▶ After reviewing the responses to the RFP, the company identifies the service provider that will be awarded the project. The client writes a contract that is based on its RFP and the service provider's response, and then submits this contract to the service provider. Once both parties agree to the terms of the contract, the project development can begin. Figure F-4 shows an excerpt from a contract with a service provider for a multimedia project.

The contract generally identifies who is responsible for what tasks in the development of the multimedia title. Table F-1 outlines the responsibilities typically assigned to the client and the service provider. While all of the responsibilities are important, the two primary considerations are agreement on the specifications and agreement on who makes the final decisions.

Specifications. Who creates them? Who has the final say? Until what point can the specifications be changed? Who is responsible for costs incurred because of changes in the specifications? These critical questions must be answered before the project even begins. Specifications to a multimedia developer are like house blueprints to a building contractor. They help in determining the tasks that are required, the types of subcontractors needed, the project costs, and the schedule. Changes in the specifications often result in additional costs. For example, during the development process, product testing might indicate that users prefer to have the ability to adjust the volume and turn off a segment of audio. Adding this new feature would require changes to the screen design so that a control (audio on/off and volume adjustment) is available and to the programming so that user input is acknowledged.

Decision maker. A related consideration is who in the client's company makes the final decisions concerning the project. As the saying goes, "Too many cooks in the kitchen spoil the stew." The same is true with too many decision makers on a multimedia project. There needs to be one person who makes final decisions. This person can and should consult others in the company before making a decision, but the project will become confusing and expensive if the service provider is receiving directions and decisions from a variety of sources. The goal is to avoid a situation in which substantial work has been done and then a "new player" (such as a corporate executive in another state) sees the title for the first time and suggests significant changes. To prevent such situations from happening, it is important that the client determine who is involved in the decision-making process and keep them "in the loop" from the beginning.

Figure F-3: *An excerpt from a request for proposal*

Figure F-4: *An excerpt from a service provider's contract for a multimedia project*

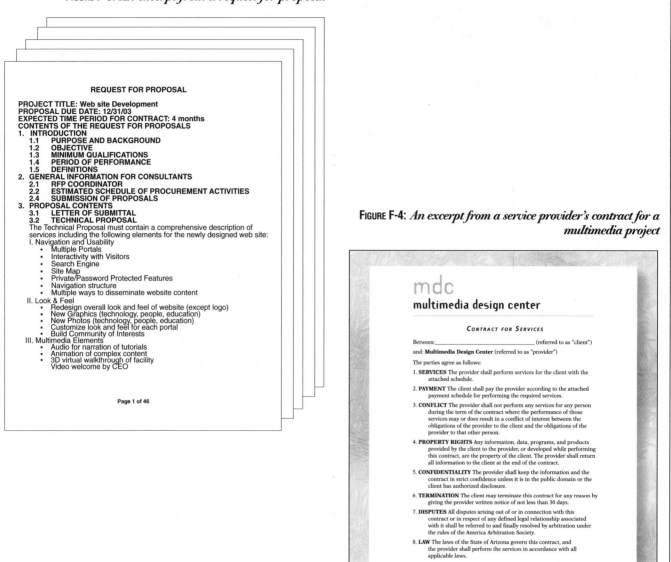

Table F-1: *Project responsibilities for the client and the service provider*

CLIENT	SERVICE PROVIDER	CLIENT	SERVICE PROVIDER
providing idea	helping refine idea	providing the budget	providing cost estimates
stating objectives	helping clarify objectives	determining initial timeline	establishing schedules and meeting timelines
developing specifications	clarifying and meeting specifications	identifying company liaison	identifying company liaison
providing content as appropriate	generating content as appropriate	identifying the decision maker	managing the project

Understanding project management: planning the project

Whether a project is managed in-house or through a multimedia service provider, project management—which identifies certain activities that must be carried out—is critical to the success of the project. Project management includes planning the project, forming the team, and organizing the resources. In this lesson, you will learn about the process involved in planning the multimedia project. Planning the project is different from planning the title, which was discussed in an earlier unit and which is actually one of the many components of planning the project. In this lesson, you will learn about project planning as it relates to the management of an entire multimedia project. Three important project-planning areas are task analysis, budget development, and schedule development.

DETAILS

▶ From a corporate standpoint, planning involves determining where the company is and where it wants to be. This type of planning is known as **strategic planning**. A company's strategic plan reflects its corporate vision. Often a five-year plan, it is reviewed regularly to see whether the objectives of the plan remain valid and whether the company is meeting those objectives. A strategic plan is one tool that a company uses for developing continuous-improvement plans. The company starts with an as-is analysis. That is, if the firm determines that it has a 5% share of the market and the market leader has a 25% share, then the company knows where it stands in the market and what it must achieve to become the market leader. As part of its strategic plan, a company identifies projects that will help it meet its long-range goals. Each project has measurable attributes so that the company can analyze all of its projects to determine whether it is attaining its strategic plan. Project planning, including task analysis, budget development, and schedule development, is a key factor in the success of a project.

▶ Tasks Analysis. The **task analysis** identifies who is responsible for what in the project development. It is based on the client's RFP, the service provider's proposal, and the specifications for the multimedia title.

   The project manager uses the task analysis to determine the resources needed as well as the budget. Table F-2 lists some questions that might be answered as part of the task analysis.

▶ Budget Development. The **project budget** provides the financial plan that affects project decisions. For example, it determines whether it is feasible to create original music, license commercially available music, or settle for sound clips. The budget provides a control mechanism that is used to evaluate the status of a project. If a comparison of the planned budget with the actual expenditures shows a discrepancy during the project (for example, more money has been spent than has been budgeted to this point in the development), then a decision needs to be made either to adjust the original budget to accommodate the increased spending or to align the budget dollars by

reducing monies allocated (for example, cut monies for components not yet expensed or eliminate other planned expenditures). The project manager must carefully track the budget to ensure that money does not run out before the project is completed. Figure F-5 shows a budget for a multimedia title and a chart indicating how the funds are allocated. Although the cost of developing titles will vary (depending on the content, features, and quality), it is unlikely that a company or a service provider can produce a commercially viable title for less than $100,000.

▶ Schedule Development. A **schedule** specifies the project's beginning and ending dates, as well as milestones along the way. If a project misses the targeted completion date, the company may suffer in two ways. First, there inevitably will be cost overruns because multimedia development is so people-intensive, and the budget may be partly based on the number of person-hours used. Second, missing the targeted completion date could cause the company to lose sales because of a delay in shipping the product. **Milestones** are significant accomplishments, such as the development of a prototype for usability testing. Whether a milestone is achieved on schedule is critical to management control of the project.

   A schedule is useful in coordinating the efforts of team members by showing how the various activities relate to one another. It also can indicate where potential bottlenecks might occur and where additional resources might be needed. Figure F-6 shows a project schedule with various tasks and their planned beginning and ending dates. The schedule includes the sequence of activities and the way in which they overlap, as well as what has been completed to date.

   Avoiding **"feature creep"** is critical to keeping a project on schedule. Feature creep occurs when new features are added, which changes the original specifications and therefore the development time. This common phenomenon is seen most often when a company tries to enhance a product as it is being produced. Unfortunately, feature creep often results in additional costs and missed deadlines.

mdc
multimedia design center

PROPOSED BUDGET

Project Title: **Museum Tour**

In-house development

Art	$ 180,000
Programming	$ 150,000
Testing	$ 40,000
Total estimated cost for in-house development	$ 370,000

Outside development

Studio	$ 6,000
Actors	$ 20,000
Writers	$ 25,000
Marketing	$ 100,000
Contracted art	$ 80,000
Contracted testing	$ 35,000
Total estimated cost for outside development	$ 266,000
Total proposed budget	$ 636,000

One Main Street ■ Scottsdale, AZ 85001 ■ (602) 555-1234

mdc
multimedia design center

PROJECT SCHEDULE

Project Title:_____ Date:_____

Project Director:_____

ID	Task	Duration	Start Date	Finish Date
1	Refineconcept and develop initial budget	1 week	2/1	2/7
2	Conduct planning session	4 days	2/7	2/10
3	Determine objectives, audience, treatment	5 days	2/10	2/14
4	Approve initial design	1 week	2/15	2/21
5	Develop specifications	2 weeks	2/21	3/6
6	Create storyboard	2 weeks	2/21	3/6
7	Approve final design	5 days	3/6	3/10
8	Approve final budget	5 days	3/10	3/14
9	Acquire content, create graphics and animations	3 months	3/10	6/10
10	Create prototype	1 month	3/10	4/10
11	Conduct feasibility testing	5 days	4/10	4/14
12	Programming	6 months	3/10	9/10
13	Conduct usability testing	1 week	8/1	8/7
14	Design package and label	2 weeks	6/15	6/28
15	Create graphics for packaging	1 month	6/29	7/29
16	Create premastered CD	5 days	9/10	9/14
17	CD mastering	15 days	9/16	9/30
18	Ship	0 days	10/1	

On Main Street ■ Scottsdale, AZ 85001 ■ (602) 555-1234

TABLE F-2: *Some questions a task analysis will answer in detail*

► How much and what kind of video, audio, animation, and so on are required?

► What content will be provided by the client, and what will be created from scratch by the service provider?

► How many illustrations will be necessary? What type are needed? How are they generated? What is the budget for illustrations?

► What features will affect programming? User input? Access to databases? User testing?

► Will the title involve external media or hardware? Will it require HTML servers, kiosks, or printers?

► How many and what type of usability tests are planned? Who will interpret the results?

► What licensing and copyright considerations apply?

Understanding project management: identifying the team

Multimedia development, especially for interactive titles, is not a "one-person show." Because of the specialized skills required, a team approach is used. At the minimum, the team needs design and programming expertise as well as content providers. Depending on the type, features, and content of the multimedia title, the team might include several specialists. Team member selection is based on the type, features, and content of the multimedia title. This lesson provides a brief description of selected multimedia team members.

DETAILS

► A critical aspect for multimedia development is forming the development team. (See Figure F-7.) This step involves assessing the current talent in light of the requirements for a particular project. Whether shooting photos, scanning artwork, digitizing video, recording music, programming the interactivity, or testing the end product, people are the key to the success of the project. The challenge for managers is to bring together an often diverse group (for example, designers with creative visions and programmers who must turn the visions into products) and keep them focused on the objectives of the project. Although the exact job titles and descriptions may vary from project to project, the list that follows provides a general overview of the key people who are so critical to the development of multimedia titles.

- *Project or Program Manager.* This person oversees the project; he or she must have outstanding management skills and expert knowledge of the multimedia development process

- *Content (Subject Matter) Expert.* This person provides content and is considered to be knowledgeable about the subject matter; he or she might be an author, editor, teacher, engineer, scholar, and so on

- *Instructional Designer.* This person has a solid understanding of learning theory and can apply that knowledge to multimedia design

- *Interface Designer.* This person has expert understanding of how users work with computers and how screen layout affects user interactivity

- *Programmer.* This person brings all the pieces together and makes it work; he or she utilizes programming languages and/or authoring tools; this individual should be involved in the development discussions from the very beginning for two reasons: (1) the programmer can provide expertise to other team members regarding if and how certain objectives might be met, and (2) hearing all of the preliminary discussions will help the programmer understand the anticipated end results

- *Media Professionals (Photographer, Videographer, Audio Engineer).* These team members create photos, video, and audio content

- *Graphic Artist (Illustrator, Image Editor).* This person creates and manipulates graphic images (see Figure F-8)

- *Animator.* This person creates 2-D and/or 3-D animations

- *Acquisitions Specialist.* This person acquires existing content for the title, especially content involving licensing or copyright issues; for example, if a company wants to use a stock photo, this specialist would pursue the terms of use and contracts necessary to acquire the rights to use the stock photo

- *Usability Tester.* This person designs and conducts product testing

► Depending on the scope of the project, a multimedia team will often include more than one of the team members previously named. For example, a team will often have more than one content expert and more than one programmer. The exception to this statement is the project manager—it would be unusual to have more than one project manager.

► Depending on the skills of each team member, an individual might have multiple skills. For example, a graphic artist might also be an animator.

► The important thing is to determine which functions are needed and how to acquire the necessary talent.

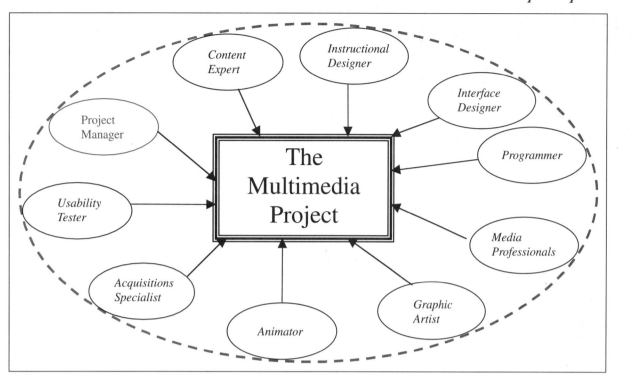

FIGURE F-8: *A graphic artist at work*

Understanding project management: organizing the project

A critical component to project management is organizing the project. Organizing involves making sure the necessary resources, including personnel for the project team, are available. The project team was described in Lesson 4. Organizing the project also means making sure the lines of communication are clear, the procedures for exchanging project pieces are well defined, and the work environment supports creativity and cooperation. A strong team leader is the key to solid project organization. In this lesson, you will learn more about ways to organize a multimedia project and the role the project manager plays in this endeavor.

DETAILS

▶ Organize resources. During the task analysis, a list of resource needs should have been generated. These resource needs include personnel as well as processes to be used. Organizing the project to deal with resource needs addresses questions such as those listed in Figure F-9. Answering such questions helps to ensure that all aspects of the project are covered and that team members are following the same procedures, schedules, and so on. The project manager (also known as the team leader) is responsible for these tasks.

▶ Project manager. Making sure the team is organized and motivated is a critical part of organizing the project. The project manager must have good leadership skills and establish an environment that fosters teamwork. Some important characteristics of a good project manager include the following:

Lead by example. Other team members will take their cue from the project manager, who will want to be viewed as part of the group instead of above the group. If the project manager is organized, other team members will more likely be organized as well. If the project manager provides avenues for being organized, then the team members will have the resources they need to stay organized.

Be straightforward and sincere. It is important to establish a sense of trust among the team members. This mutual trust will lead to more open and effective communication between the project manager and the team members as well as among team members.

Recognize accomplishments. People are encouraged and motivated when they feel that their contributions have been noticed. The project manager provides positive reinforcement through praise and rewards.

Listen. Because of the diverse nature of a multimedia development team, each member provides a unique perspective that needs to be heard. The project manager must listen carefully to what team members are saying to be sure that the project stays on track.

▶ Work environment. Making sure the work environment is organized and promotes teamwork is critical to a successful project. Addressing the physical and psychological needs of the work environment is instrumental in organizing a project.

Physical work environment. The physical work environment can help keep a project organized. Some ideas for creating an organized work environment include the following: Provide proper lighting and work space. Provide plenty of storage space—filing cabinets for hard copies and disk/server space for backups of work files. Provide an area where personnel can meet informally to talk over project-related problems or touch base with other team members.

Team building. The psychological work environment is centered on team building. A team that works well together can help keep a project organized. Team building is an ongoing process. The following are some examples of ways to encourage team building: If possible, set up the project so that the team has the task of creating the complete multimedia title. This approach helps the team take ownership of the project and instills pride in their work. Involve the team as early as possible in the development process. Hold periodic meetings to review the project's status, and encourage involvement by all team members. Set up an e-mail folder for the team to facilitate communications. Give public recognition for the hard work of each team member by including a Credits screen (as an option for the user to view) listing the team members and their roles. Figure F-10 provides an example of a credits screen.

o   Do we have the needed skills on our staff?

o   Can we train current staff for skills we don't have?

o   What do we need to contract out?

o   What are the specific assignments?

o   What physical resources are needed (new or specialized computer equipment, memory, or storage capacity upgrades, new or specialized software or upgrades, slide scanner, digital camera)?

o   What is the communication process for team members (e-mail with shared folders, electronic project postings, periodic team meetings, off-site planning sessions, conference calls)?

o   How is project content shared (company intranet, external storage devices such as Syquest or Zip drives)?

FIGURE F-10: *A credits screen*

MANAGEMENT AND DISTRIBUTION OF MULTIMEDIA TITLES ◄ **131**

Exploring careers in multimedia

Being part of a multimedia team for a company usually requires three things: education in a specialty area, soft skills, and experience. Educational programs are available through public and private institutions, often online, and experience is acquired through internships, volunteer efforts, and entry-level positions. Some individuals entering the world of multimedia concentrate their area of study in one specialized field such as graphic arts design or video production. Others take a broader approach by studying a variety of areas and becoming proficient at each. This lesson takes a closer look at how a person can gain the necessary education and experience when pursuing a career in multimedia.

DETAILS

▶ Education. Thousands of schools offer educational programs related to multimedia. The education required after high school depends on the type of degree you plan to pursue.

College or University. These schools offer four-year undergraduate degrees as well as advanced degrees. Individuals who are interested in project management and advanced computer science programs are attracted to these schools. Many of these institutions are establishing certificate programs in technical areas through what are often called Extension Services.

Community Colleges. These schools provide one-year certificate programs and two-year degrees in professional and technical fields, such as Web design, as well as transfer programs. They attract many people who already have degrees and desire to obtain marketable skills in a technology-related area.

Technical and Specialty Schools. These schools often offer programs lasting from six months to four years, depending on the area of study. The programs offered are highly specialized and focus on an area of interest such as computer networking or art design. These schools pride themselves on the practical application of the area of study.

Information regarding the types of programs available at colleges and universities is available through college counseling services, at libraries, and online. Specific program offerings can often be found through the Web page of an institution, as shown in Figure F-11. When evaluating schools you need to look for, among other things, the placement of graduates, the reputation of the school in the business community, the credentials and work experience of the faculty, availability of internships, and the facilities (lab equipment and software).

▶ Areas of study. As described earlier, the multimedia team are individuals with diverse skills. Each team member has pursued different areas of study to obtain expert knowledge in that field.

The areas of study range from the precise, such as 3-D animation and Web authoring that are directly related to multimedia, to the general, such as business administration (useful in project management) and education (useful in instructional design).

Because of the team environment and the frequent need to work with clients, those pursuing a career in multimedia need to have "soft skills." These skills include people skills, communications (oral and written) skills, and problem-solving and critical thinking skills.

▶ Experience. Popular methods for obtaining experience include internships, entry-level positions, and personal portfolios.

Internships. Multimedia development companies often offer internships to promising students. Students who participate in internship programs often move on to full-time employment with the sponsoring company after the internship ends.

Entry-level positions. Once a job is secured, using it to take advantage of learning from coworkers is a critical part of gaining experience. Always be willing to ask questions and learn.

Personal portfolio. In addition to work-related experience, you should build a personal portfolio that showcases your areas of expertise. This portfolio can be shared with prospective employers by writing the projects to CD or posting them on a Web site. Creating a personal portfolio not only underlines your abilities, but also speaks highly of your personal drive and motivation—key characteristics employers look for when forming a multimedia team.

How do you find jobs in multimedia? Newspaper advertisements, networking, school bulletin boards, and online job-search Web sites are all ways of identifying such positions. If you are fairly mobile (that is, able to relocate), or if the job itself allows for **telecommuting** (that is, working remotely), then searching for jobs online provides valuable resources. Figure F-12 shows an example of a job description posted online.

FIGURE F-11: *Course requirements for a multimedia degree*

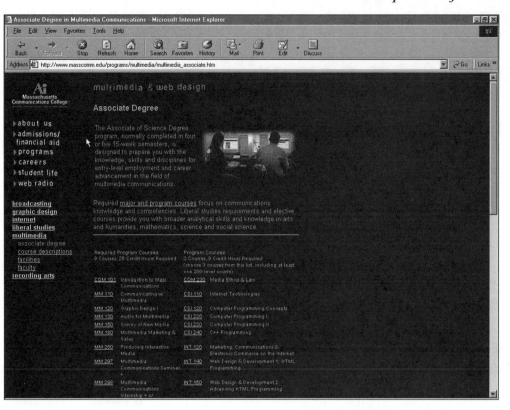

FIGURE F-12: *Job description online*

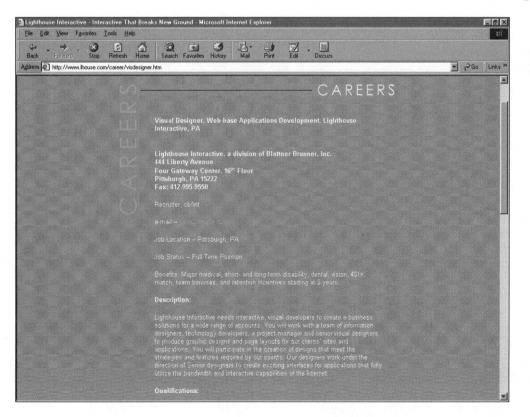

Understanding mass-market distribution of multimedia titles

Once a multimedia title is complete, the development team's job is finished. But the success or failure of the title is not determined until the title is delivered and used by its intended audience. Because multimedia is an industry that affects many fields (such as entertainment, video, music, computer, education, and e-commerce) and involves many players (such as book publishers, film producers, software companies, and multimedia developers), it is not surprising that several distribution models are being tried with varying degrees of success. In theory, a multimedia publisher has several options when determining how to distribute consumer multimedia titles. In practice, the resources of the publisher, especially in terms of promotional support, restrict these choices. The ultimate test of a title is its demand, which is influenced heavily by retail exposure, advertising, and point-of-purchase display materials. In this lesson you will learn about various distribution models.

DETAILS

► Figure F-13 shows three traditional distribution models or channels that have been used for delivering multimedia titles to the consumer market. The decision facing the multimedia publisher is which channel or channels to use. Traditionally, companies that make consumer goods that are ultimately purchased in a retail store sell their products to a wholesaler, which in turn sells to retailers. In some cases, the company sells directly to retailers. Regardless of which model is used, there needs to be some "value added" as the product moves through the distribution channel. The "value added" accounts for the profits to each entity that handles the title as it is transferred along the channel. A discussion regarding various distribution models follows.

► **Wholesalers.** Wholesalers buy from multimedia publishers and resell to other entities, including retailers, catalog companies, and corporate and education markets. Wholesalers can provide services such as controlling inventory, processing returns, and giving technical support. A primary benefit for multimedia publishers is that wholesalers offer access to a worldwide network of retailers. Because wholesalers carry thousands of products, however, they are unlikely to actively promote any particular multimedia title or work to obtain retail shelf space. Rather, the wholesaler just lists the title in its catalog along with related products; it is up to the retailer to select which products to purchase from the wholesaler. Also, publishers need to discount the list price of their products by 50% or more for wholesalers.

► **Retailers.** Traditionally, retailers have provided one of the best ways to reach the consumer market and take advantage of consumer impulse purchasing. Consumers like retail because they can purchase the title immediately. However, a typical retail outlet may stock only 100–200 titles out of the thousands that are published each year. Because of the tremendous demand for shelf space (only 1 in 15 titles finds its way to a retailer's shelf), retailers often obtain market development funds, called slotting fees, from publishers to stock a title. In other words, the publisher pays to have the product carried by the retailer. The publisher's pricing structure has to allow for a 35%–50% margin for the retailer market.

Originally, multimedia titles were sold through computer superstores such as CompUSA and Computer City, or specialty retailers. Computer owners tended to shop at these outlets for software. Eventually, mass merchandisers such as Wal-Mart and Costco began carrying multimedia titles. Now book, toy, video, and music stores as well as other specialty retailers are selling titles. Most national bookstore chains such as Barnes and Noble and Borders stock reference titles that they feel fit their other product lines and their customer base. Toys R Us signed an exclusive contract to have New Media Express, a distributor, provide nearly 150 multimedia children's titles to its 600-plus stores. Children's titles are distributed through early-learning superstores such as Zany Brainy, which has more than 30 outlets. Hardware, sporting goods, and grocery stores are stocking multimedia titles relevant to their product lines and clientele. Thus, while superstores and specialty retailers remain an active avenue for CD-ROM distribution, they are no longer the only option.

► **Catalog sales.** Several companies, such as MicroWarehouse, PC Connect, and Multiple Zones International, publish monthly catalogs listing computer hardware, software, and multimedia titles and distribute these to selected markets. For example, Multiple Zones publishes the Mac Zone for Macintosh users, the PC Zone for Windows users, as well as corporate, education, home, and international catalogs.

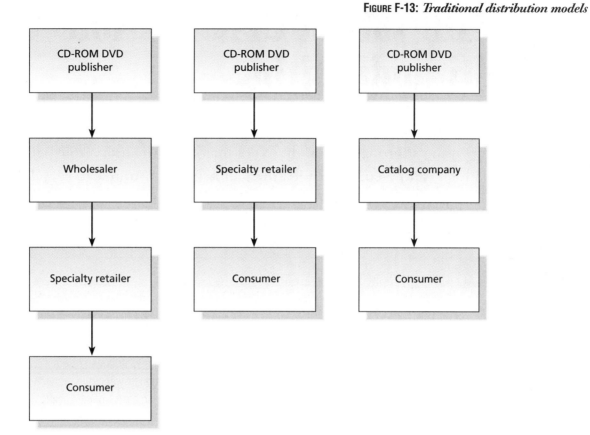

Distribution alternatives

Given the highly competitive nature of the consumer multimedia market and the difficulty of obtaining retail shelf space, several other distribution models are being used. They include the following:

Direct mail. Publishers may find that mail-order sales are a cost-effective way to enter the market, especially if mailing lists are available for their target audience. For example, a company that creates an interactive golf title could purchase the names and addresses of people who subscribe to Golf Digest magazine.

Bundling. Bundling involves distribution of the multimedia title with some other product, such as a new computer or upgrade kit. For example, top-selling titles such as Myst, Rebel Assault, Magic Carpet, and SimCity 2000 have been bundled with computer equipment. This tactic offers a quick way to launch a product in a new market in hopes of establishing brand identification and follow-up sales of new versions. However, the distributor that chooses to bundle a title must expect to discount its title by as much as 70%–80% of the selling price.

Online sales. Many commercial multimedia titles are available on the Web. Lesson 8 explores this distribution option.

Exploring online distribution of multimedia titles

The online distribution of multimedia titles has exploded as more and more consumers are purchasing products through the Web. Every major multimedia publisher has a Web site (see Figure F-14) and e-commerce features allowing a customer to search for various titles, to put them in an electronic shopping cart, to fill out an order form (including credit card and shipping information), and to wait for the product delivery. In this lesson, you will learn how companies are using the Internet to distribute their multimedia titles.

DETAILS

▶ While the Internet allows multimedia publishers to deal directly with the end user, some companies act as distributors, usually specializing in specific product categories such as educational titles or adventure games. It is not unusual for the same product to be found on several Web sites and at various prices. For example, a search on the Internet for a specific children's title typically results in dozens of sellers, including the publisher (such as MattelInteractive.com), and a variety of alternative Web sites (such as KidZone, Parson's Technology, SQC, Shoplet, and Amazon.com). The prices for the same title might range from $14.95 to $25.95 plus shipping.

Whereas some of these sites specialize in children's products, others offer broad product lines of which multimedia titles are only one part. For example, Amazon.com sells hundreds of thousands of products; one of its product categories is software, which is where a consumer can find multimedia titles.

Often Web sites provide reviews of their products, including a summary of their features or storyline, a rating for age appropriateness, and a rating for their overall effectiveness or customer satisfaction. Consumers can purchase the multimedia title online and then have it shipped to them.

▶ Downloading from the Internet is another form of distribution for multimedia titles. Some companies allow you to purchase their products online and then download them directly to your computer. This process has several advantages. First, the buyer does not have to pay for shipping or wait for delivery of the product. Second, the buyer may be more inclined to order the product because he or she can start using it right away. Third, the seller can reduce the costs of manufacturing (no CD-ROM or DVD to produce), storage (no inventory to maintain), and handling. Fourth, the seller can concentrate its promotional efforts on appealing to the buyer's need for instant gratification (impulse buying). A major disadvantage is that downloading works best for programs that are relatively small in size because of the time needed to transfer the files. Online distributors often provide free demos of their products and/or shareware copies that allow the user to "try it before you buy it."

▶ Another common distribution practice combines traditional multimedia products with online versions and updates. For example, purchasers of the Encarta Reference Suite (CD-ROM/DVD) can register to receive a free subscription to Encarta Online that allows access to the Encarta Encyclopedia through the Internet. In addition, the user can receive annual updates at a discount. This subscription process is valuable to the seller because the user remains linked to the seller. It is valuable to consumers because it keeps their programs current and up-to-date.

▶ A major challenge in marketing products on the Web is attracting potential buyers to a site. Millions of Web pages already exist, with new ones being added each day. To sift through all of this information, users rely on search engines to find sites that have the products they want to purchase. When users enter a word or phrase for which to search, the search engine compares the word or phrase with keywords obtained from various sites. It then displays a list of sites that have keywords matching the search word(s). Once the search has identified potential products, consumers can purchase the multimedia titles using a distribution method that suits their needs.

▶ Some search engines, such as AltaVista as shown in Figure F-15 allow you to search for multimedia elements. For example, using the Video option under the Multimedia Search category, a search for "Neil Armstrong + moon" would display several Web sites that have video clips or multimedia titles with video clips of the Apollo 11 moon landing, including Armstrong's famous words "One small step for man, one giant leap for mankind." Once the video clip or multimedia is identified using the search engine, the consumer can decide what to do next—view it online or purchase it.

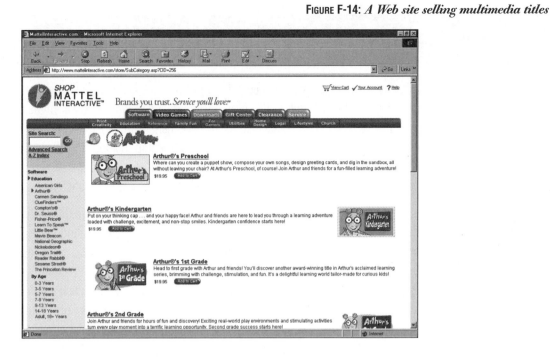

FIGURE F-15: *Searching for multimedia elements*

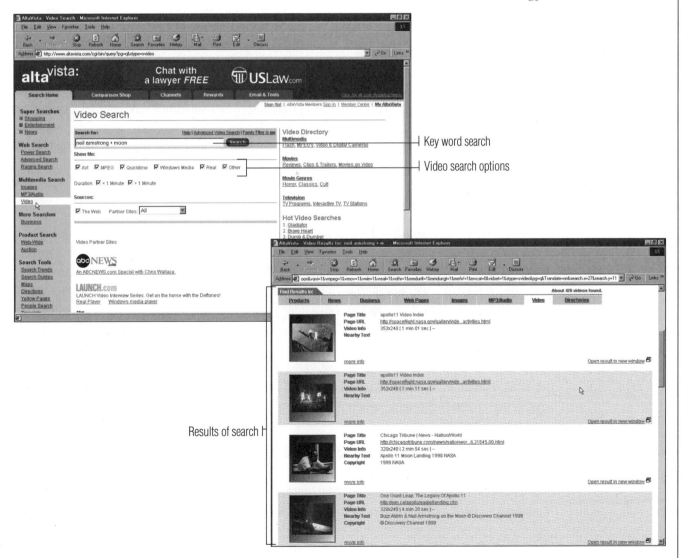

Key word search

Video search options

Results of search

A critical member of any multimedia development team is the marketing expert. This team member needs to understand the multimedia title from the company's viewpoint and from the perspective of the consumers' needs. He or she must help the development team understand how to include elements in the multimedia title that will aid the marketing department in "selling" the title to the public. Because of the intensely competitive atmosphere, a multimedia title that is not properly marketed to the intended user is doomed to fail. Marketing includes marketing strategies, publicity strategies, and pricing strategies.

In a highly competitive field, a company's multimedia titles must be differentiated from those of its rivals. Creating a way to differentiate a product is part of the marketing strategy. One way to distinguish a product from its competitors is to create a character that is used in a series of multimedia titles. For example, a car named Putt-Putt is the main character in a series of children's titles published by Humongous Entertainment. Each Putt-Putt title has a similar "look and feel," objectives, main character, and theme. What changes is the setting and the type of adventures Putt-Putt experiences. Another way to differentiate a product is by creating high-quality graphical images, rich content, or expensive elements such as 3-D animation and video. Another product strategy is to develop brand-name recognition by the target market, as Microsoft and Mattel have done.

Product strategy influences and is influenced by promotion strategies (for example, should advertising be focused on brand recognition or individual titles?), by pricing strategies (for example, higher prices usually connote quality), and by distribution channels strategies (for example, should the titles be sold directly to the consumer or through specialty retailers?). Retailers are more inclined to stock a title that is associated with an aggressive promotional plan, including an advertising campaign, point-of-purchase material, and publicity. Retailers are interested in advertising that will stimulate demand for a product and pull the customer into their stores. The question is, Who pays for the advertising? One option is for the retailer and the publisher to share the cost through a cooperative advertising program. This effort involves promoting both the multimedia title and the retailer in the same advertisement to generate demand for the title and traffic for the store. Advertising is very expensive, and even this type of shared-cost advertising is too expensive for all but the larger publishers.

Publicity comes from stories that appear in various news media. For multimedia titles, this type of recognition usually involves magazines, newspapers, and trade publications. The stories often appear as reviews of new products. Publicity—assuming it is favorable—can be extremely valuable to a publisher for several reasons. First, it is unbiased and therefore lends credibility to the reviewer's conclusions. Second, the publicity can be leveraged by including quotes from the reviews in product advertising, in point-of-purchase displays, and on packaging. Third, publicity is free. One strategy aimed at generating publicity is for multimedia publishers to prepare and distribute "press kits" containing product information and a full version (not a demonstration version) of the title to selected reviewers. For example, a company that has created a multimedia title called "The Castles of Scotland" might send review copies of its title to travel magazines. Reviews in the travel magazines would then be directed toward the intended audience.

With an increasing number of multimedia titles being produced, prices are becoming extremely competitive. Prices for CD-ROM/DVD titles for the home market have steadily declined from the $70–$90 range to $15–$45. Pricing is heavily influenced by cost and competition. Traditionally, companies have determined a suggested retail price and provided discounts to different categories of buyers. For example, publishing companies might provide wholesalers a 50% discount and retailers a 35% discount off of the suggested retail price. Wholesalers and retailers then set their prices to the consumer based on their discount prices from the publisher, which accounts for the varying price tags for the same multimedia title within the different distribution channels. The suggested retail prices usually exceed the price actually paid by the consumer, because retailers lower these prices to increase sales. This fact puts pressure on the retailer to make up in sales volume what it loses through a lower markup. Consequently, many retailers stock only the best selling titles. Initially, a publisher may decide to price a title to cover only development and production costs as a way to keep its price competitive and to obtain a share of the market. Eventually, however, the title must be priced to cover all costs and provide for a profit. One way to keep the price low and return more to the publisher is to follow one of the distribution models that eliminates the wholesaler and goes directly to the retailer or the user.

This issue explains current marketing strategies. Do new and innovative marketing strategies need to be developed? With the proliferation of e-commerce Web sites and advances in providing secure Web sites, will consumers see new distribution models? How will marketing strategies change to accommodate new technologies and consumer needs? The marketing team member of a multimedia team must focus on these forward-thinking questions to keep ahead of market needs.

EXPAND THE IDEAS

1. Reflect on the information presented in this issue. Should the marketing function be part of the duties of the multimedia team? Explain your position.
2. Make a poster that identifies factors influencing marketing strategies.
3. Work in small groups. Brainstorm marketing strategies you might use to introduce a new multimedia title. Provide a brief description of the fictitious title you plan to market, and then explain the strategies you would implement to market the title.
4. How familiar should other team members be with the field of marketing? Should a marketing course be required in programs preparing students for careers in multimedia? Explain why or why not.
5. Following is an alphabetical list of marketing-related activities that influence the success of a new multimedia title. Rearrange the list starting with the activity you feel is most influential in the success of a title. Explain your prioritization.

Advertisements

Brand name

Magazine reviews

Price

Publicity

Testimonials

End of Unit Exercises

STUDY TIPS

1. List key terms mentioned in this unit. Define them in your own words, and then check your definitions against those listed in the glossary. Use additional sources to seek expanded information for any terms that need further clarification.

2. Summarize the criteria used to determine whether to outsource the development of a multimedia title.

3. Summarize the benefits of using a service provider, and give an example of how one could be used.

4. List the information that you feel is important to ask for on a request for proposal.

5. Explain the concept of "feature creep," and give an example.

6. This unit provides a list of the project responsibilities for both the client and the service provider. List the three areas in which you think the service provider can be the most help to the client, and explain why.

7. Summarize the three main activities involved in project planning.

8. Explain the difference between planning the project and planning the title.

9. Explain what is meant by "team development." Why is it so critical to project management?

10. Choose the job (title) in which you are most interested, and explain why it appeals to you.

11. Explain the concept of "value added." Use an example in your explanation.

SELECT THE BEST ANSWER

1. Which of the following is NOT a major activity when managing a multimedia project?
   a. Planning the project
   b. Organizing the resources
   c. Forming and leading the team
   d. All are major activities

2. A(n) _____ understands how users work with computers and how screen layout affects user interactivity.
   a. Usability tester
   b. Instructional designer
   c. Interface designer
   d. Programmer

3. Which of the following is NOT a consideration when deciding whether to produce a multimedia title in-house?
   a. Complexity of the project
   b. Expertise of current staff
   c. Ability to train current staff
   d. All are considerations

4. The originator of a request for proposal is the
   _____.
   a. Client
   b. Service provider
   c. Either of the above
   d. None of the above

5. A(n) _____ is used to showcase your expertise.
   a. Vitae
   b. Resume
   c. Portfolio
   d. Internship

6. Which of the following is NOT a soft skill?
   a. Writing
   b. Critical thinking
   c. Problem solving
   d. Programming

7. Which of the following is considered free advertising?

   a. Promotion

   b. Publicity

   c. Point-of-purchase displays

   d. Poster displays

8. Which of the following is NOT an alternative for distributing CD titles?

   a. Direct mail

   b. Bundling

   c. Online sales

   d. All are considered alternatives.

9. Which of the following is NOT an advantage of downloading products from the Internet?

   a. No shipping charges

   b. No inventory

   c. Easy transfer of large files

   d. No waiting for delivery

10. A (n) _____ _____ identifies who is responsible for what jobs in project development.

   a. Project schedule

   b. Task analysis

   c. Project budget

   d. Strategic plan

FILL IN THE BEST ANSWER

1. If a company does not have the resources to develop multimedia titles, management might decide to _____ the title.

2. The decision on whether to develop a multimedia title in-house is affected by the expertise of the current staff and the _____ of the project.

3. _____ to a multimedia developer are like blueprints to a building contractor.

4. The two primary considerations when a company is working with a multimedia service provider are agreement on the specifications and agreement on the _____.

5. A(n) _____ is a critical part of project management because it provides the financial plan that affects a number of decisions

6. Feature _____ occurs when new features are added to the specifications during the development process.

7. A schedule specifies the project's beginning and ending dates, and _____.

8. When a company outsources a multimedia project, a(n) _____ _____ _____ is used to define the project.

9. The job title for a person who knows learning theory and can apply it to multimedia design is _____ _____.

10. One of the main tasks of the _____ is to influence others to achieve the project goals.

INDEPENDENT CHALLENGE 1

Multimedia providers range from small companies (only a few full-time employees) that contract with specialists as a job requires, to large companies that employ full-time specialists. Both types of companies have one thing in common: they are able to effectively manage a multimedia project. They know how to work with clients to determine the project specifications and required resources, including the personnel needs, and they work to bring the project in on-time and on-budget.

To complete this independent project:

1. Make a three-column table: Column 1 = Question, Column 2 = My Idea, and Column 3 = Researched Response.

2. Write the questions that follow Step 4 in Column 1.

3. Before doing any research, write your answers to the questions in Column 2.

4. Contact a company providing multimedia development services. Write responses to the questions in Column 3.

   a. What is the company name and address (or URL)?

   b. What is the name and title of the contact person?

   c. What is the company mission statement?

   d. How long has the company been in business?

   e. Who are some of the company's current clients?

   f. How does the company acquire new clients?

   g. What services does the company provide?

   h. Of which projects is the company most proud and why?

   i. How does the company promote itself?

   j. What is the length of time required for a typical project?

   k. Who are the company's major competitors?

   l. How many employees does the company have?

   m. What is the company's range of expertise?

   n. What type of talent normally needs to be hired on a contract basis?

(continues on next page)

5. Obtain the following: a sample of the company's work, a rate card, a sample contract (if possible), and promotional materials. Attach these documents to your table.

6. Compare your initial responses with your research findings. Does the information match your preconceived ideas regarding the services a multimedia development service provides? Explain.

INDEPENDENT CHALLENGE 2

Often companies cannot afford or do not have enough work to keep full-time employees with multimedia-related skills on staff. One option is to train current employees to handle these duties. Another option is to work with employment agencies to provide contract workers as the need arises. Employment agencies can match the job requirement with the skills of those they represent. Many individuals choose to pursue contract work because of the freedom it allows them in deciding which jobs to take and which companies to work with. In addition, the employment agencies may provide benefits such as health care to these workers.

To complete this independent challenge:

1. Make a three-column table: Column 1 = Question, Column 2 = My Idea, and Column 3 = Researched Response.

2. Write the questions that follow Step 4 in Column 1.

3. Before doing any research, write your answers to the questions in Column 2.

4. Contact an employment agency that specializes in (or has provided) contract employees. Write responses to the questions in Column 3.

   a. What is the name and address (or URL) of the company?

   b. What is the name and title of the contact person?

   c. What is the company mission statement?

   d. What are the benefits for the hiring company in using the employment agency?

   e. What are the benefits for the employee in using the employment agency?

   f. What does the employment agreement say about the responsibilities of the three parties (agency, employee, company)?

   g. What type of expertise (related to multimedia) is most in demand?

   h. Who are some of the company's clients?

   i. How does the company acquire new clients?

   j. What is the average length of time for a contract position?

   k. What is the pay rate, including benefits?

   l. What is the evaluation process?

m. What is the recruitment and screening process for potential employees?

n. What skills does the company look for in potential employees?

5. Compare your initial responses with your research findings. Does the information match your preconceived ideas regarding an employment agency? Explain.

INDEPENDENT CHALLENGE 3   WEB WORKS

Multimedia is an exciting career choice. With the high demand for multimedia titles, careers in multimedia-related fields are plentiful. The term *multimedia*, however, is very broad and encompasses a variety of career options in diverse fields of study. Whether you have already decided on one particular career path in multimedia or you are exploring the many options available in the area of multimedia, the Web is a great source of information regarding careers in multimedia.

To complete this independent challenge:

1. Connect to the Internet.

2. Go to *http://www.course.com/*, navigate to the Student Online Companion for this book, and then click the link for Unit F.

3. The Unit F link contains links to Web sites with information about careers in multimedia or to education programs with information about course requirements. Click each link to visit the site. Write a summary of each site. Answer the following questions for each Web site:

   a. What is the Web site name and URL?

   b. How easy is it to navigate the site?

   c. Do you have to search the site? If yes, what keywords did you use to search the site? How effective were the search results?

   d. What careers were described? What type of information was provided?

4. Use your favorite search engine to look for information about a multimedia career in which you are particularly interested. After completing your search, answer the following questions:

   a. What search engine did you use?

   b. Were the results of your search satisfactory?

   c. Visit three links. Comment on the following regarding each link. Does the link provide pertinent information about the career? If yes, briefly describe the information provided.

   d. Compare your findings with those of several classmates who searched for information about the same career. Is the information you all collected consistent? If not, how does it vary?

INDEPENDENT CHALLENGE 4

Publicity can be beneficial in selling a multimedia title because consumers view it as being more objective than a company's advertising and promotional material. Developers consider publicity to be "free" advertising. But is that always a good thing? As a consumer, it is important to be aware of publicity about a product. In some cases, product reviewers rely on promotional materials sent to them by the companies that developed the product, rather than conducting their own product evaluations. If a report seems particularly biased, then it is important to find additional reviews or stories for comparison purposes.

To complete this independent challenge:

1. Research three articles (magazine, newspaper, online) that review the same multimedia title.

2. Develop a report that includes the following information for each article:

   a. What is the publication, its date, and the reviewer's name?

   b. What is the name of the product being reviewed?

   c. What type of multimedia title is being reviewed, and who is the intended audience?

   d. What favorable comments were made in the review?

   e. What unfavorable comments were made in the review?

   f. What is the overall rating or opinion of the reviewer?

   g. Was the media voice consistent? Did all the reviewers have a similar opinion? If not, what might account for their varying reactions to the title?

INDEPENDENT CHALLENGE 5

The ease with which products can be purchased over the Internet and the acceptance by consumers of this distribution process have caused companies to focus on online sales.

To complete this independent challenge:

1. Search the Web for three companies selling CD-ROM titles online.

2. Develop a report that includes the following information:

   a. Company name and URL for the site

   b. How you located the site

   c. The process for searching for a particular CD-ROM title

   d. The type of information provided for each title (descriptions, reviews, ratings, and so on)

   e. The process for ordering a title

   f. The method(s) of payment that can be used

   g. Price of the title online compared to the retail store price

3. Evaluate the sites in terms of their ease of use in finding and ordering titles. Which site do you feel is the most effective and why? From which sites would you buy? Why?

1. What does Figure F-16 visualize?

2. Briefly describe a project this figure might be centered around, and explain how these players might interact to accomplish the project.

FIGURE F-16

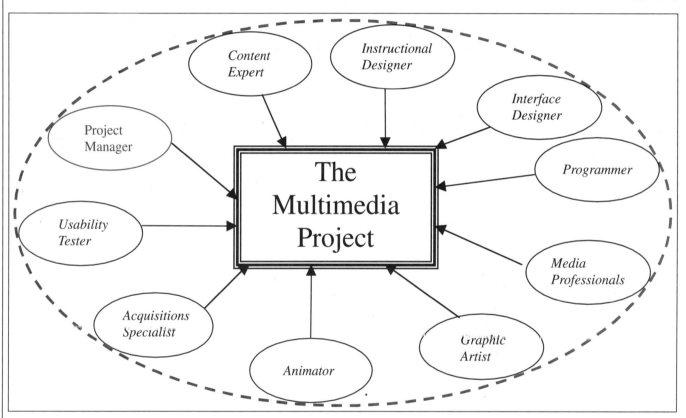

Case Study: Incorporating Multimedia into a Web Site

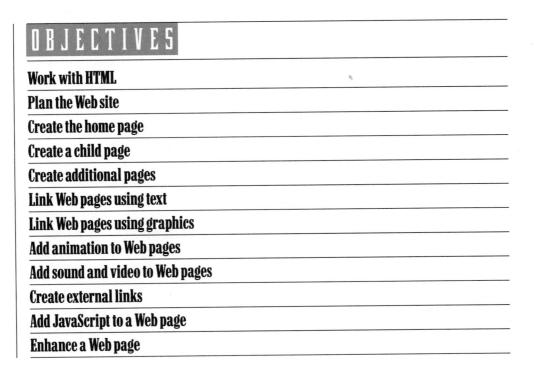

OBJECTIVES

Work with HTML

Plan the Web site

Create the home page

Create a child page

Create additional pages

Link Web pages using text

Link Web pages using graphics

Add animation to Web pages

Add sound and video to Web pages

Create external links

Add JavaScript to a Web page

Enhance a Web page

The use of multimedia on the Internet has greatly enhanced commercial Web sites. Companies use graphics, animation, sound, video, and virtual reality to attract attention, to provide information, and to sell their services and products. This unit provides a case study allowing you to develop a basic Web site for Travel Northwest, a company that has several resorts and bed-and-breakfast accommodations. You will use HTML coding to create a basic Web site and then incorporate various multimedia elements, including sound, animation, and video into this Web site.

Working with HTML

A Web site is made up of Web pages linked together. HyperText Markup Language (HTML) is used to create the Web pages and the links, as well as to specify how the pages appear in a browser. There are three basic ways to work with HTML to create Web pages. First, you can use any of several Web authoring programs, such as Dreamweaver or FrontPage, that are designed to create entire Web sites. Second, you can use office applications such as Microsoft Word or Claris Works that include built-in Web page design features. These types of programs create the HTML coding as you enter the text and graphics, and they help you specify the links. Also, they allow you to create Web pages without extensive knowledge of HTML. Third, you can use a text editor, such as Notepad (shown in Figure G-1) or SimpleEdit, and enter the HTML coding yourself. The advantage of using a text editor is the simplicity of the coding, which allows you to more easily edit it. In this lesson you will become familiar with basic HTML codes and Web page structure. You will also learn about file structures and ways to save and view HTML files.

DETAILS

▶ HTML codes or tags are used to format the appearance of a Web page and to specify functions such as linking one page to another. Generally, the tags are used in pairs, known as container tags. That is, each pair includes an opening tag and a closing tag. Whatever falls between the tags is affected by them. For example, to center the words "My Web Page," the HTML coding would be:
My Web Page
Notice that the tags are enclosed in <> and that the closing tag includes a /. Not all HTML tags need a closing tag. For example, the <br> tag creates a line break and does not use a closing tag. Table G-1 shows some HTML tags that you will use in this unit.

▶ Tips when using HTML: The tags are not case sensitive, so they can be written in either uppercase or lowercase. Whichever you choose, be consistent. Maintaining consistency helps in readability. Indenting tag lines (such as table tags) also helps in readability. Note, however, that when a browser displays the page, any blank spaces are ignored unless they appear within a string of text and any blank lines are ignored unless they are created using the <br> tag. HTML does not allow the use of the spacebar, Tab key, or [Enter] key for aligning or formatting text.

▶ The structure of a Web page is commonly divided into two sections: the Head and the Body. The Head section contains information used to display the page in the browser. The Head section is where, among other things, you can include information used by search engines, write scripts, and specify a title for your page. The title appears in the title bar of the browser and in the list of Favorites when the user bookmarks the site. In addition, some search engines use the title to index the page. The title is the only part of the Head section visible to the user.

The Body includes the contents of the Web page that are visible to the user.

▶ In this unit, you will use a text editor to create a Web page. A text editor does not have the features of a word processing program. Thus, the way a document appears in the text editor may not be the way it appears in a browser. You rely on the HTML coding to format the appearance of the document. *Hints*: Save your document often, and be sure to use the .htm file extension. Open two windows on your computer—one for the text editor and the other for your browser. Then as you are developing the Web page, you can switch between each window to see your progress.

▶ Directory structure. A Web site consists of many files including .htm pages as well as multimedia elements such as graphics, audio, and video. When these elements are used within a page or links are created to them, the file location must be determined. For small sites, you might use a directory with a single folder. For large sites, you might use several folders, such as an images folder and a sounds folder. If only one folder is used, you do not need to specify the path when indicating the location of the file. Figure G-2 shows the directory structure for the Travel Northwest Web site. In this case all of the files appear in one folder called Mysite.

In addition to supporting a folder structure, Web sites follow a file structure hierarchy. The home page is the **parent page** for the Web site. A Web page that has a direct link to its parent page is called a **child page**. A Web page can be a child page to one Web page in the site and a parent page to a different page in the same site. The file structure determines whether a Web page is a parent page or a child page.

My Computer
 C:Drive
  Mysite (folder)
   bgtecture.gif
   resort-lg.jpg
   roche2-lg.jpg
   roche-lg.jpg
   roche-sm.jpg
   star.gif
   sunmtn-sm.jpg
   view.avi
   warm-sm.jpg
   whale-snd.wav

TABLE G-1: *Some basic HTML tags*

HTML TAG	PURPOSE
<html>…</html>	Begin and end an HTML document (also called a page); required as the first and last tags in an HTML document
<head>…</head>	Enclose document information, including scripts, font information, style information, and title tags for the page
<title>…</title>	Used to identify the page; the title appears in the title bar of the browser and in the list when the user bookmarks the site; the title is used by some search engines to index the page
<body>…</body>	Identify the body section of the page, indicating that whatever falls between these tags is available to be viewed by the user
<background="Name">	Specifies an image (graphic) for the page background; *Name* is replaced by the location and filename of the background graphic
<p>	Starts a new paragraph (line); use to create a blank line in a Web page

	Creates a line break; use to force text to the next line; use <br> two times to create a blank line or use additional <br> tags to create additional blank lines
<hr>	Inserts a horizontal rule line
<center>…</center>	Center the content between the tags
<h1>…</h1>	Apply a type style (font and size) to text within the tags. Note: there are 6 HTML styles (h1–h6); h1 uses the largest type size.
<img src="Name">	Inserts an object, such as a graphic, into the page; *Name* is replaced by the location and filename for the object
<a href="Destination">QUIZ</a>	Creates a link allowing the user to click on the word *QUIZ* and go to the link destination; *Destination* is replaced by the link location

<table>
 <tr>
  <td> … </td>
  <td> … </td>
 </tr>
</table>
	The <table>…</table> tags create a table; each pair of row tags <tr>…</tr> creates a row within the table; each pair of data tags <td>…</td> creates a column; any content within the table data tags is placed in that row and column

Planning the Web site

Planning is the first step in developing a Web site. Planning includes determining the concept, goals, target audience, treatment, and specifications, and creating the storyboard and navigation scheme. In this lesson, you will learn how Travel Northwest has approached the planning of its Web site.

DETAILS

▶ *The Concept.* Travel Northwest owns a group of B&Bs (bed and breakfasts) as well as inns and resorts in the Pacific Northwest. The company's mission is to provide a unique vacation experience for people who are traveling to the Northwest. Each of its facilities has a character of its own. Management at Travel Northwest wants to create a Web site that provides potential customers with information about the individual features of each facility as well as contact information.

▶ *The Goal.* The goal of the Web site is to increase the occupancy rate by increasing potential customers' awareness of each Travel Northwest B&B, inn, and resort as well as the uniqueness of individual facilities.

▶ *The Target Audience.* The primary audience is middle- and upper-income couples who are interested in staying at resorts that offer a more personalized experience than provided at "chain"-type hotels.

▶ *The Treatment.* The "look and feel" of the Web site will focus on simplicity and ease of use while providing photographic-quality images. Animation will be used to reinforce important points. Sound and video will be used to enhance the user's experience.

▶ *The Specifications.* The target playback system will try to account for a large portion of the installed market: Windows 95 or later, Pentium, Macintosh G3, OS7, 56K modem with Internet Explorer 3.0 or later, Netscape 3.0 or later, sound card; Multimedia elements: Graphics—high resolution (16-bit) JPEG photos; Animation—animated GIFs; Text: Page headings—Times New Roman Font, 24-point; Subheadings and body text—Times New Roman 12-point; Video: Embedded AVI clips with default controls for start, pause, and stop; Audio: Embedded WAV files with default controls for start, pause, and stop.

▶ *The Storyboard.* Figure G-3 shows a sketch of the Web site, including the home page and the links to the other pages, the e-mail function, and an external Web site. In the lessons that follow, you will create three pages: Home, Bed & Breakfast, and Roche Harbor B&B. To provide consistency in design, the background, rule lines, headings, subheadings, body text, and navigation links will be the same for all pages.

▶ *The Navigation.* Figure G-3 shows the navigation options. Users will be able to click on text and graphics that link with other pages. Every page except the home page will have a [Home] button that enables the user to jump to the home page from any other page in the Web site.

STEPS

> **Trouble?**
>
> Ask your technical support person or instructor if you need help completing these steps.

1. Set your computer settings as follows:

Screen resolution: **800 x 600**; Colors: **16 bit**; Browser: **Internet Explorer version 5**

These are the computer settings used in developing this tutorial. Your screen display may differ somewhat from the figures in this unit if you are not able to set your computer settings to match these settings.

2. Create a folder on your destination drive named **mysite[insert your name here]**

3. Navigate to the drive and location where your Project Files are stored, and copy the files for this unit to the mysite[your name] folder: **bgtexture.gif, resort-lg.jpg, roche2-lg.jpg, roche-lg.jpg, roche-sm.jpg, star.gif, sunmtn-sm.jpg, view.avi, warm-sm.jpg, whale-snd.wav**

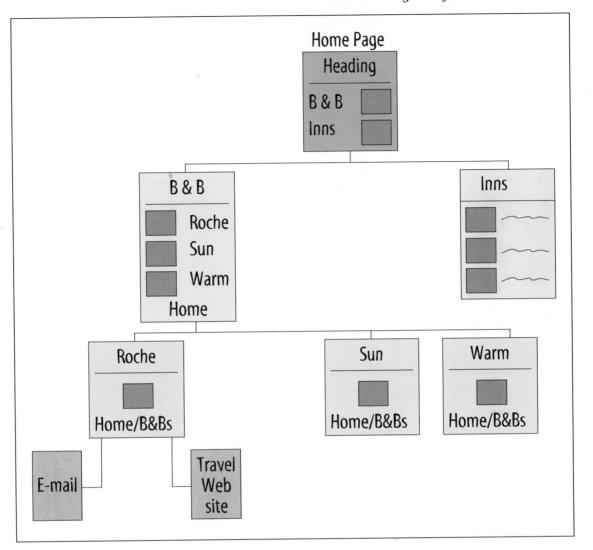

Creating the home page

The first step in coding the Web site is to create the home page. This is the first page that the user sees and it sets the tone for the other pages in the site. Home pages vary considerably in their "look and feel," the amount of information they provide, and their use of multimedia. The Travel Northwest Home Page will have a straightforward design focusing on the company's two primary categories of accommodations, Bed & Breakfast and Inns & Resorts. In this lesson you will create the Travel Northwest Home Page, as shown in Figure G-4. Figure G-5 shows the HTML code used to create the home page.

STEPS

QuickTip

Notepad is the text editor used in this unit. You can use any text editor or word processing program.

1. Start your text editor, type **<html>**, press **[Enter]** two times, type **<head>**, press **[Enter]** two times, type **<title> Travel Northwest Home Page </title>**, press **[Enter]** two times, type **</head>**, then press **[Enter]** two times

   The Head section of the home page is complete.

2. Be sure the insertion point is below the </head> tag, type **<body background="bgtexture.gif'>**, press **[Enter]** two times, type **<h2> UNIQUE PLACES TO STAY IN THE NORTHWEST </h2>**, press **[Enter]** two times, type **<hr>**, press **[Enter]** three times, then type **</html>**

3. Save the file with the name **Index.htm** to your mysite[your name] folder

   Index is a standard name used for home pages.

Trouble?

If the top of your page does not appear as shown in Figure G-4, be sure your code matches exactly the code in Figure G-5

4. Start Internet Explorer or your browser, then open the file **Index.htm**

   The home page appears with the title, Travel Northwest Home Page, displayed at the top of the browser window. The page includes the background texture, the heading, and the horizontal rule based on the HTML code.

QuickTip

To make your code easier to read, press [Enter] at the end of each line that you type in your text editor.

5. Switch to your text editor, position the insertion point on the blank line directly below the <hr> tag, press **[Enter]**, type **<table>**, press **[Enter]** two times, then type the following:

   <tr>
   <td width=60%><h2>Bed & Breakfast</h2>
   Enjoy the personal attention of a home away from home!</td>
   <td><img src="roche-lg.jpg"></td>
   </tr>

Trouble?

If you are using Netscape, the information will not appear in your browser until you type the closing table tag.

6. Press **[Enter]**, save the file, switch to your browser, then refresh the browser to view the table

   Information about the Travel Northwest's Bed & Breakfast facilities appears in your browser window

7. Switch to your text editor, be sure the insertion point is on the blank line directly below the </tr> tag, press **[Enter]**, then type the highlighted code exactly as it is shown in Figure G-5

8. Save the file, switch to your browser, then refresh the browser to view the table

   Compare the Web page on your screen to Figure G-4. Return to your text editor and make changes, if necessary. Be sure your code matches exactly the code in Figure G-5.

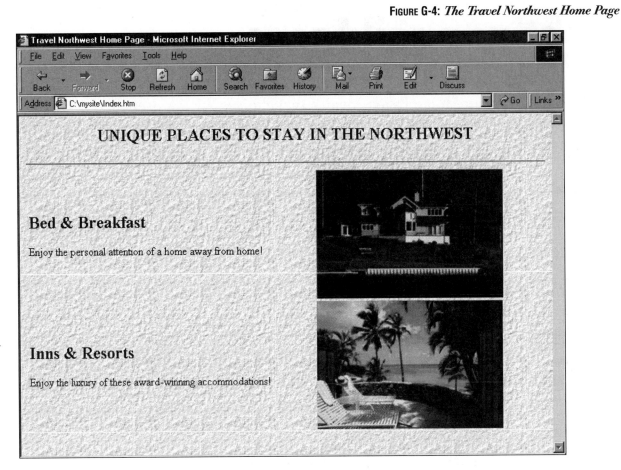

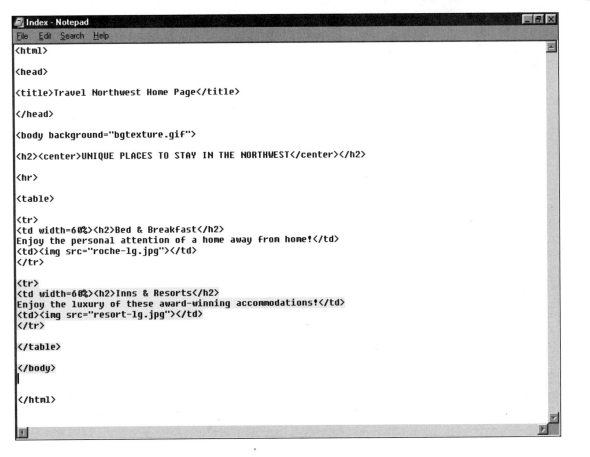

Creating a child page

The Travel Northwest Home Page provides two choices for the user: Bed & Breakfast and Inns & Resorts. In this lesson you will create the Bed & Breakfast page (B&Bpage.htm). Figure G-6 shows the Bed & Breakfast page in the browser. Figure G-7 shows the Bed & Breakfast page in the text editor. In addition to the background texture, page heading, and rule line, the page includes three subheadings with body text and graphics.

QuickTip

When you create a new file in Notepad, any open file automatically closes. Be sure to save the open file before creating a new one.

STEPS

1. Switch to your text editor, create a new file, type **<html>,** press **[Enter]** two times, type **<head>**, press **[Enter]** two times, type **<title>Travel Northwest Bed & Breakfast</title>**, press **[Enter]** two times, type **</head>**, then press **[Enter]** two times

2. Type **<body background="bgtexture.gif">**, press **[Enter]** two times, type **<h2> BED & BREAK-FAST </h2>**, press **[Enter]** two times, type **<hr>**, press **[Enter]** three times, then type **</html>**

3. Save the file with the name **B&Bpage.htm** to the mysite[insert your name here] folder

4. Switch to your browser, then open the file **B&Bpage.htm**

   The B&Bpage.htm page appears, including the background texture, heading, and rule line.

5. Switch to your text editor, position the insertion point on a blank line directly below the <hr> tag, press **[Enter]**, type **Roche Harbor B&B<p>**, press **[Enter]**, type **<img src="roche-sm.jpg">
, press **[Enter], type **Located in the picturesque setting of the San Juan Islands north of Puget Sound...<p>**, then press **[Enter]** two times

6. Type **Sun Mountain B&B<p>**, press **[Enter]**, refer to Figure G-7, then continue to type the information for the two remaining B&Bs (Sun Mountain and Warm Springs)

   The information must be typed exactly as it appears in Figure G-7.

7. Press **[Enter]** two times, type **</body>**, then press **[Enter]**

8. Save the B&Bpage.htm file, switch to your browser, then refresh your browser to view the page
   Compare the Web page on your monitor with Figure G-6. Return to your text editor and make changes, if necessary. Be sure your code matches exactly the code in Figure G-7.

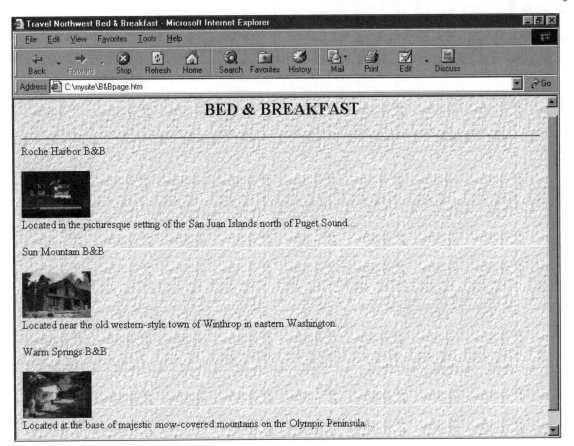

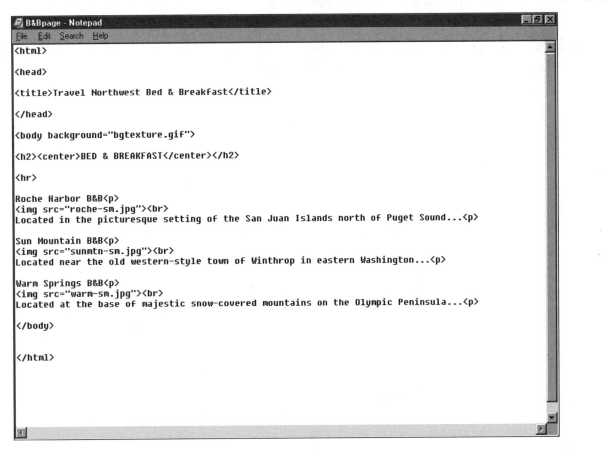

Creating additional pages

So far, you have created the Travel Northwest Home Page and the Bed & Breakfast page. Next, you will create the Roche Harbor B&B page (RHpage.htm). The Roche Harbor B&B page is one of the Bed & Breakfast choices. That is, it is a child page of the Bed & Breakfast page. Figure G-8 shows the file structure for this Web site. Notice that the Bed & Breakfast page is a child page of the Travel Northwest Home Page as well as a parent of the Roche Harbor B&B page. Figure G-9 shows the Roche Harbor page in the browser. Figure G-10 shows the Roche Harbor B&B page in the text editor. In addition to the background texture, page heading, and rule line, you will include a large graphic and body text on the page.

STEPS

1. Switch to your text editor, create a new file, type **<html>**, press **[Enter]** two times, type **<head>**, press **[Enter]** two times, type **<title>Roche Harbor B&B</title>**, press **[Enter]** two times, type **</head>**, then press **[Enter]** two times

2. Be sure the insertion point is below the </head> tag, type **<body background="bgtexture.gif">**, press **[Enter]** two times, type **<h2> Roche Harbor B&B </h2>**, press **[Enter]** two times, type **<hr>**, then press **[Enter]** two times

3. Type ** <img src="roche-lg.jpg">
<p>**, then press **[Enter]**

4. Type **Located in the picturesque setting of the San Juan Islands, this turn-of-the-century home was built for a descendant of one of the original settlers of Spieden Island. Sweeping views of the Straits of Juan de Fuca and the lights of Victoria, British Columbia are available from every room. Listen for the sound of whales on their annual migration to and from Alaska.<p>
**

5. Press **[Enter]** two times, type **</body>**, press **[Enter]** three times, then type **</html>**

6. Save the file with the name **RHpage.htm** to the mysite[insert your name here] folder

7. Switch to your browser, then open the file RHpage.htm to view the page

   Compare the Web page on your monitor with Figure G-9. Return to your text editor and make changes, if necessary. You would use the steps in this lesson to create additional Web pages for this Web site.

Trouble?

If your text editor does not support line wrap, press [Enter] each time you want to force the text to the next line in your text editor. The browser does not recognize [Enter] as a line break, so the text displayed in the browser will wrap based on the resolution setting of your monitor.

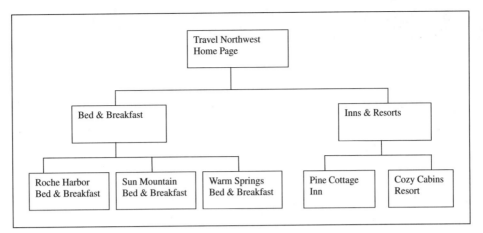

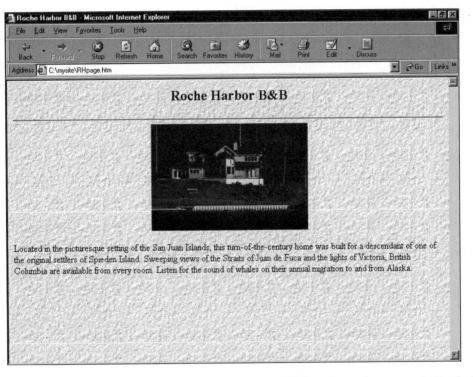

FIGURE **G-10**: *The HTML code used to create the Roche Harbor Web page*

```
<html>

<head>

<title>Roche Harbor B&B</title>

</head>

<body background="bgtexture.gif">

<h2><center>Roche Harbor B&B</center></h2>

<hr>

<center><img src="roche-lg.jpg"></center><br><p>
Located in the picturesque setting of the San Juan Islands, this turn-of-the-century home was
built for a descendant of one of the original settlers of Spieden Island. Sweeping views of
the Straits of Juan de Fuca and the lights of Victoria, British Columbia are available from
every room. Listen for the sound of whales on their annual migration to and from Alaska. <p><br>

</body>

</html>
```

Linking Web pages using text

Now that the Web site has three pages, you can link those pages as shown in the original storyboard in Figure G-3. On the home page, you will create a link from the Bed & Breakfast subheading to the Bed & Breakfast page. On the Bed & Breakfast page, you will create a link from the Roche Harbor subheading to the Roche Harbor page. You will also create a [Home] button on the Bed & Breakfast page so that a user can click [Home] and return to the Travel Northwest Home Page. On the Roche Harbor page, you will create links to both the Bed & Breakfast page and the home page. In this lesson you will use the <a href>…</a> HTML tags to create these links.

STEPS

Trouble?

If you do not see the file listed in the mysite[your name] folder, then be sure All files [*.*] appears in the File of type list box.

1. Switch to your text editor, then open the file Index.htm

2. Position the insertion point after the first <td width= 60%>, then type **<a href="B&Bpage.htm">**

3. Position the insertion point after Breakfast </h2>, then type **</a>**
    Figure G-11 shows the changes made to the home page to create the desired links. The <a href>…</a> HTML tags are used to specify the page to link to and the text to click on to activate the link. The HTML tag <a href="B&Bpage.htm"><h2>Bed & Breakfast</h2></a> indicates that when the user clicks on Bed & Breakfast, then the B&Bpage.htm page will appear.

4. Save the file, switch to your browser, open the file **Index.htm**, then click **Bed & Breakfast**
    The Bed & Breakfast page appears in your browser window.

5. Switch to your text editor, open the file **B&Bpage.htm**, position the insertion point before Roche Harbor B&B<p>, type **<a href="RHpage.htm">,** position the insertion point after Roche Harbor B&B, then type **</a>**

6. Position the insertion point on the line directly above the </html> tag, type **
    <a href="Index.htm">[HOME]</a> **, then press **[Enter]** two times
    Figure G-12 shows the changes to the B&Bpage.htm page.

Trouble?

You may need to scroll to see [HOME].

7. Save the file, switch to your browser, refresh the page, then click **[HOME]**
    The Travel Northwest Home Page appears in your browser window.

8. Switch to the text editor, open the file **RHpage.htm**, position the insertion point one line above the </html> tag, press **[Enter]**, type ** <a href="Index.htm">[HOME]**
    <a href="B&Bpage.htm">[B&Bs]</a> **, then press **[Enter]
    Figure G-13 shows the changes to the RHpage.htm page.

9. Save the file, switch to your browser, open the file **RHpage.htm**, then check your links
    When you click on [B&Bs], the Bed & Breakfast page appears. When you click on Roche Harbor B&B, the Roche Harbor B&B page appears. When you click on [Home], the home page appears. Switch between your text editor and your browser to make corrections as necessary. Remember that your code must be typed exactly as it appears in the steps and the figures.

```
Index - Notepad
File  Edit  Search  Help

<html>

<head>

<title>Travel Northwest Home Page</title>

</head>

<body background="bgtexture.gif">

<h2><center>UNIQUE PLACES TO STAY IN THE NORTHWEST</center></h2>

<hr>

<table>

<tr>
<td width=60%><a href="B&Bpage.htm"><h2>Bed & Breakfast</h2></a>
Enjoy the personal attention of a home away from home!</td>
<td><img src="roche-lg.jpg"></td>
</tr>

<tr>
<td width=60%><h2>Inns & Resorts</h2>Enjoy the luxury of these award-winning accommodations!</td>
<td><img src="resort-lg.jpg"></td>
</tr>

</table>

</body>

</html>
```

FIGURE **G-12**: *The HTML code used to create text links in B&Bpage.htm*

```
B&Bpage - Notepad
File  Edit  Search  Help

<html>

<head>

<title>Travel Northwest Bed & Breakfast</title>

</head>

<body background="bgtexture.gif">

<h2><center>BED & BREAKFAST</center></h2>

<hr>

<a href="RHpage.htm">Roche Harbor B&B</a><p>
<img src="roche-sm.jpg"><br>
Located in the picturesque setting of the San Juan Islands north of Puget Sound...<p>

Sun Mountain B&B<p>
<img src="sunmtn-sm.jpg"><br>
Located near the old western-style town of Winthrop in eastern Washington...<p>

Warm Springs B&B<p>
<img src="warm-sm.jpg"><br>
Located at the base of majestic snow-covered mountains on the Olympic Peninsula...<p>

</body>

<center><a href="Index.htm">[HOME]</a></center>

</html>
```

FIGURE **G-13**: *The HTML code used to create text links in RHpage.htm*

```
RHpage - Notepad
File  Edit  Search  Help

<html>

<head>

<title>Roche Harbor B&B</title>

</head>

<body background="bgtexture.gif">

<h2><center>Roche Harbor B&B</center></h2>

<hr>

<center><img src="roche-lg.jpg"></center><br><p>
Located in the picturesque setting of the San Juan Islands, this turn-of-the-century home was
built for a descendant of one of the original settlers of Spieden Island. Sweeping  views of
the Straits of Juan de Fuca and the lights of Victoria, British Columbia are available from
every room. Listen for the sound of whales on their annual migration to and from Alaska. <p><br>

</body>

<center><a href="Index.htm">[Home]<a href="B&Bpage.htm">[B&Bs]</a></center>

</html>
```

Linking Web pages using graphics

So far, you have created links among the pages using text. You can also create links using other objects on pages, such as graphics. You can often tell visually whether text or images are linked because by default they appear blue and underlined if text or with a blue border if graphic. These default settings can be changed to other colors or non-visible borders. Also by default, the pointing hand icon is visible when the pointer moves over a linked object. This default indicator can also be changed. Finally, the path to the linked object may appear in the lower-left corner of the browser when the pointer moves over a linked object. In this lesson you will learn how to link pages using graphics.

STEPS

1. Switch to your text editor, then open the file **Index.htm**

2. Position the insertion point between <td> and <img src="roche-lg.jpg", then type **<a href="B&Bpage.htm">**

3. Position the insertion point between …roche-lg.jpg"> and </td>, then type **</a>**

4. Save the file, switch to your browser, open the file **Index.htm**, then move your pointer over the graphic to the right of Bed & Breakfast

   Figure G-14 shows changes made to the HTML code to create a graphic link to a Web page. Notice that the pointer changes to a pointing hand, as shown in Figure G-15. The pointing hand icon is a visual indication that the object the pointer is over—whether it is text, a graphic, or some other object—is linked to another page.

5. Click the graphic to the right of the Bed & Breakfast heading

   The Bed & Breakfast page appears in your browser window.

6. Switch to your text editor, open the file **B&Bpage.htm**, position the insertion point before <img src= "roche-sm.jpg">
, type **<a href="RHpage.htm">**, position the insertion point after <img src= "roche-sm.jpg">, then type **</a>**

7. Save the file, switch to your browser, refresh the page, then click the image under the Roche Harbor B&B subhead

   The Roche Harbor page appears in your browser window.

FIGURE G-14: *The HTML code used to create a graphic link in Index.htm*

```
Index - Notepad
File  Edit  Search  Help
<html>

<head>

<title>Travel Northwest Home Page</title>

</head>

<body background="bgtexture.gif">

<h2><center>UNIQUE PLACES TO STAY IN THE NORTHWEST</center></h2>

<hr>

<table>

<tr>
<td width=60%><a href="B&Bpage.htm"><h2>Bed & Breakfast</h2></a>
Enjoy the personal attention of a home away from home!</td>
<td><a href="B&Bpage.htm"><img src="roche-lg.jpg"></a></td>
</tr>

<tr>
<td width=60%><h2>Inns & Resorts</h2>Enjoy the luxury of these award-winning accommodations!</td>
<td><img src="resort-lg.jpg"></td>
</tr>

</table>

</body>

</html>
```

FIGURE G-15: *Web pages linked using a graphic*

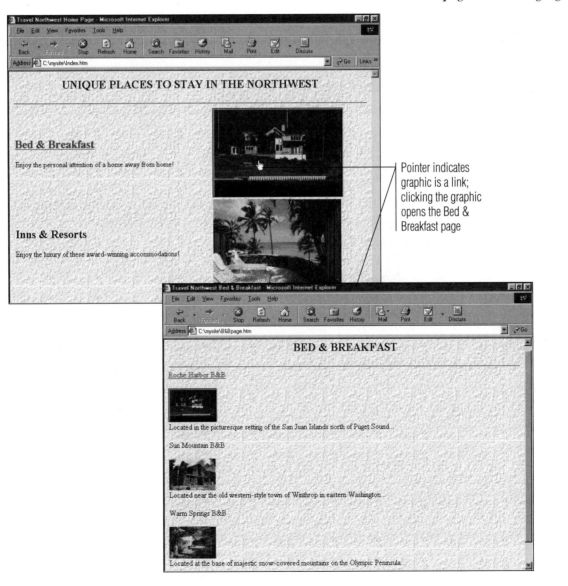

Pointer indicates graphic is a link; clicking the graphic opens the Bed & Breakfast page

Adding animation to Web pages

In this lesson you will add animations to the Web site. On the home page, you will add a marquee to bring attention to Travel Northwest's holiday specials. The marquee tag causes text to scroll across the screen when the visitor is using the Internet Explorer browser. This text can be made to scroll either from the right or from the left. On the Bed & Breakfast page, you will add an animation that promotes the five-star ratings of the company's accommodations. You will cause a GIF animation to appear on the bottom of the Bed & Breakfast page. The file for the animation is named star.gif. The star.gif will be repeated five times to give a five-star animation effect.

STEPS

Trouble?

The marquee tag causes text to scroll when using the Internet Explorer browser. In the Netscape browser, the marquee tag causes text to appear in quotation marks, but the text does not scroll.

1. Switch to your text editor, then open the file **Index.htm**

2. Position the insertion point above the </body> tag, press **[Enter]**, then type **<p><marquee direction=right bgcolor="silver"><b>"Book now for our Holiday Specials"</b></marquee>**

3. Save the Index.htm file, switch to your browser, open the file **Index.htm**, then scroll to the bottom of the screen, if necessary, to view the marquee

   Figure G-16 shows the marquee animation in the browser and the changes that must be made to the HTML code to create this marquee. The <p> tag creates a new paragraph so that the marquee text appears on a new line just at the end of the document.

4. Switch to your text editor, then open the file **B&Bpage.htm**

QuickTip

To make the code easier to read, press [Enter] after each line (See Figure G-17).

5. Position the insertion point on the blank line directly below </body>, press **[Enter]**, type
   <center>We are proud of our <img src="star.gif" align="middle">
   <img src="star.gif" align="middle">
   <img src="star.gif" align="middle">
   <img src="star.gif" align="middle">
   <img src="star.gif" align="middle"> rating by the Puget Sound B&B Association!
   </center><p>, then press **[Enter]**

QuickTip

If you change the background color of the Web page to match the background color of the star graphic, then the animation will blend in with the page. You will learn how to make that change in Lesson 12.

6. Save the file, switch to your browser, open the file B&Bpage.htm, then scroll to the bottom of the screen, if necessary, to view the animation

   The animation appears at the bottom of the page. Figure G-17 shows the GIF animation in the browser and the changes that must be made to the HTML coding to create it. Typing the img src code five times causes the star-gif to appear five times in a row. Having the new image appear in the middle forces the existing images to the left and creates an animation.

   Switch between your text editor and your browser to make changes as needed if the animation does not work as expected.

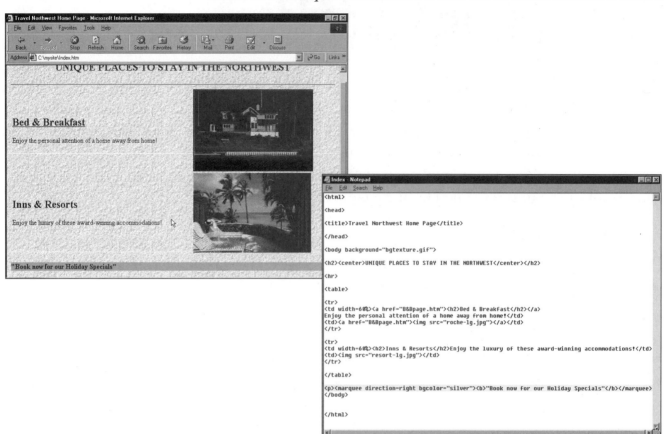

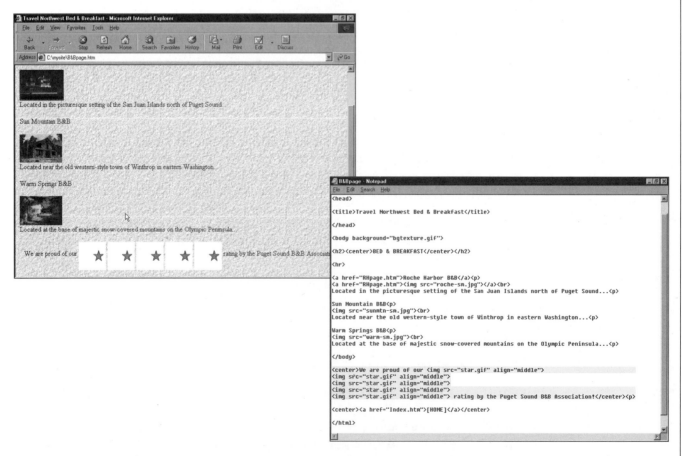

Adding sound and video to Web pages

The Travel Northwest Home Page now has text and graphics that link to other pages in the Web. It also includes animation in the form of both animated text and animated graphics. Next, you will add the multimedia elements of video and sound. You will embed video and sound clips in the Roche Harbor page. You will specify the HTML code that allows the user to click on a word to play a video and to click on a word to play a sound clip. As with graphics files, when you add sound or video elements, you must specify the path that tells where the file is stored. For the Travel Northwest Web site, all graphic, sound, and video files are stored in the mysite[insert your name here] folder.

STEPS

1. Switch to your text editor, then open the file **RHpage.htm**

2. Position the insertion point directly to the left of the *v* in *views*, type **<a href="view.avi">**, position the insertion point after *views*, then type **</a>**

   Figure G-18 shows the updated HTML code in the RHpage.htm file. The <a href> tags create a link from the word *views* to the .avi file named "view." Because the .avi file is stored in the same folder as the Web page, the href includes only the name of the file. If the .avi file were stored in a different folder, then the href information would need to include the path to that file, such as D:\movies\"view.avi". This path identifies a folder named "movies" on the D drive and a specific movie "views.avi" within the movies folder.

3. Save the RHpage.htm file, switch to your browser, then open the file **RHpage.htm** to view the page

   Notice that the word *views* is a hyperlink.

4. Click the word **views**

   Figure G-19 shows the video playing in a media player. Depending on the configuration of your computer and the installed players, a control panel will appear allowing you to start, pause, and stop the video, as well as adjust the volume. Note: This lesson assumes that Windows Media Player is the default media player. If the video does not play, check to be sure Windows Media Player is installed.

5. Close the Media Player window, switch to your text editor, position the insertion point before the word *whales*, type **<a href="whale-snd.wav">**, position the insertion point after the word *whales*, then type **</a>**

   The word *whales* is now linked to a sound file named whale-snd.wav. Because the .wav file is stored in the same folder as the Web page, the href includes only the name of the file.

6. Save the RHpage.htm file, switch to your browser, then refresh the page

   Notice that the word *whales* is a hyperlink.

7. Click the word **whales**

   Depending on the configuration of your computer and the installed players, a control panel will appear allowing you to start, pause, and stop the sound, as well as adjust the volume. Use your controls to play the sound. Also, depending on the configuration of your computer, a dialog box may appear asking if you want to download the file to a disk or open it from the current location. If you see this dialog box, select open it from the current location.

Trouble?

If you are using Netscape as your browser, the movie will appear in a new window. Click the picture to start the movie. Click the Back button at the top of the browser window to return to the Roche Harbor page.

Trouble?

If you are using Netscape, click the Back button to return to the Roche Harbor page.

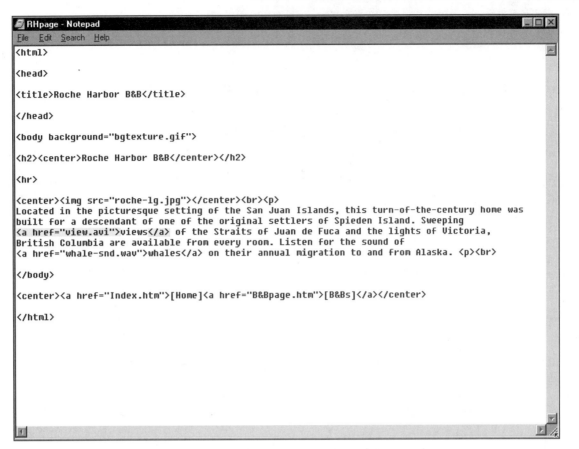

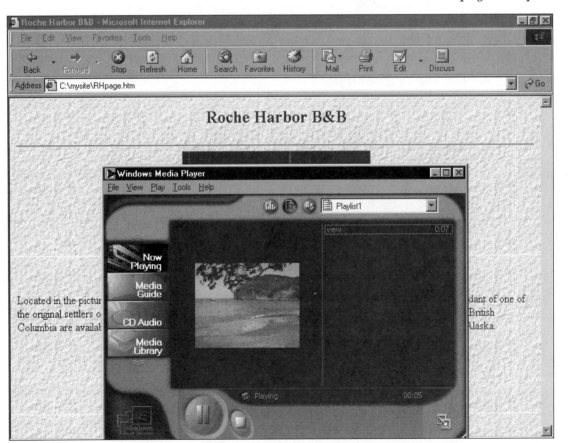

Creating external links

Until now, you have been working with files on your hard drive to simulate a server. It is often useful, however, to allow the user to access files that do not reside on your hard drive. Examples of when you might want to link to files not on your hard drive include links to other Web sites or files on a CD. For the browser to display the correct file, it needs to know the type and location of the file. A uniform resource locator (URL) provides this information. A URL has two primary parts. The first part is the scheme, which tells the browser how to deal with the file. HTTP (HyperText Transfer Protocol) is a scheme telling the browser that the file is a Web page. The second part of the URL indicates the location of the server where the file resides. Table G-2 lists three common URL formats, identifying the scheme, location, and purpose of each. In this lesson you will create two external links within your Web site as shown in Figure G-20. The first link displays an e-mail form that users can complete to send a message to the company. The second link connects to a travel Web site, Travelocity, that allows users to make travel arrangements such as booking airline flights. Both of these external links will be placed on the Roche Harbor page.

STEPS

1. Switch to your text editor, then make sure that the file **RHpage.htm** is open

2. Position the insertion point on the line directly below </body>, press **[Enter]**, type **<p> <a href="mailto:rocheharbor@mymail">Contact [insert your name here]</a>**, then press **[Enter]**

3. Save the Web page, switch to your browser, then refresh the Roche Harbor page
   Notice that the words *Contact [your name]* appear as a link at the bottom of the Web page.

4. Click **Contact [your name]**
   An e-mail window opens with the To: address filled in. A user could complete the e-mail form and send it to Roche Harbor. (Note: This example is not a working address. If this form is completed and sent, the sender will receive a message stating that the mail is undeliverable.)

5. Close the e-mail window, then switch to your text editor

QuickTip

To make the |, press [shift] and \.

6. Position the insertion point below the mailto line, type **<a href="http://www.travelocity.com "target=_blank>| Make your travel arrangements</a> <p>**, then press **[Enter]**
   Figure G-21 shows the changes to the Roche Harbor page that create the external links. The target=_blank command is used to open a new browser window. This is useful when you are linking to an external site and you don't want your current site to be replaced.

7. Save the Web page, switch to your browser, then refresh the page
   Notice the words *Make your travel arrangements* appear as a link at the bottom of the page.

QuickTip

Links to external Web sites must be checked periodically. Companies may discontinue a Web site or change the URL. Users may become irritated if your Web site contains an external link that is invalid.

8. Click **Make your travel arrangements**
   Another browser window appears that contains the Travelocity site. A visitor could use this Web site to make travel arrangements to any of Travel Northwest's properties.

9. Close the browser window with the Travelocity site

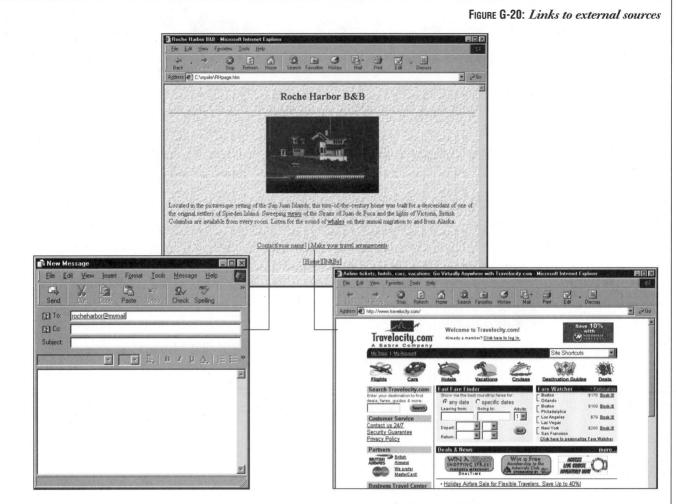

TABLE G-2: *Common URL formats*

URL	SCHEME	LOCATION	PURPOSE
http://www.nasa.gov	http:// (HyperText Transfer Protocol)	www.nasa.gov	Display the NASA Web site
mailto:bvdyke.mymail.com	mailto:	bvdyke.mymail.com	Send an e-mail
file:///d:images/mycat.jpg	file:///	d:images/ (note that: d: could be a CD drive)	Display an image from a specific drive

Adding JavaScript to a Web page

HTML is essentially a formatting language. Programming languages are needed to extend the functionality of HTML when creating Web pages. For example, you can use the programming language Java to create animations, such as the banner ads that are so prevalent on commercial Web sites. You can use the programming language JavaScript to add interactivity to a Web page, such as checking for a password or displaying a counter of visits to a Web site. In this lesson, you will use JavaScript to create a rollover that allows the user to point to a graphic and have another graphic appear. The following steps will create the rollover for the graphic on the Roche Harbor page.

STEPS

1. Switch to your text editor, then make sure that the file **RHpage.htm** is open

2. Position the insertion point below the <head> tag, press **[Enter]**

3. Type **<script language="javascript" type="text/javascript"></script>**, then press **[Enter]**
   The <script language> tag tells the browser which programming language will be used within the HTML document. The browser can then appropriately interpret the scripting language.

QuickTip

To make the code easier to read, press [Enter] after each line (See Figure G-22).

4. Select ** <img src="roche-lg.jpg">
<p>**, press **[Delete]**, then type
   ** <a href="RHpage.htm"**
   OnMouseOver="document.bbimage.src='roche2-lg.jpg'"
   OnMouseOut="document.bbimage.src='roche-lg.jpg'"><img src="roche-lg.jpg"
   **name="bbimage" width=274 height=181></a>
<p>**

   Figure G-22 shows the coding that creates the rollover. Table G-3 discusses the purpose of this code. The OnMouseOver command tells the program that when the user's mouse is over the picture on the RHpage, the user will see one image (a terrace at the Roche Harbor B&B facility). The OnMouseOut command tells the program that when the user's mouse is not on the picture, the user will see a different image (an outside view of the Roche Harbor facility).

5. Save the Roche Harbor page, switch to your browser, then refresh the page

6. Move the mouse over the graphic

   The image changes from the Roche Harbor graphic to a balcony view.

7. Move the mouse so that it is no longer over the graphic

   The image changes back to the Roche Harbor graphic. Make adjustments as needed until the mouse rollover is working as expected. Remember that your HTML code must match exactly the HTML code in the steps and the figure.

```
RHpage - Notepad
File  Edit  Search  Help
<html>

<head>

<script language="javascript" type="text/javascript"></script>

<title>Roche Harbor B&B</title>

</head>

<body background="bgtexture.gif">

<h2><center>Roche Harbor B&B</center></h2>

<hr>

<center><a href="RHpage.htm" OnMouseOver="document.bbimage.src='roche2-lg.jpg'"
OnMouseOut="document.bbimage.src='roche-lg.jpg'"><img src="roche-lg.jpg"
name="bbimage" width=274 height=181></a></center><br><p>
Located in the picturesque setting of the San Juan Islands, this turn-of-the-century home was
built for a descendant of one of the original settlers of Spieden Island. Sweeping
<a href="view.avi">views</a> of the Straits of Juan de Fuca and the lights of Victoria,
British Columbia are available from every room. Listen for the sound of
<a href="whale-snd.wav">whales</a> on their annual migration to and from Alaska. <p><br>

</body>

<p><center><a href="mailto:rocheharbor@mymail">Contact[your name]</a>
<a href="http://www.travelocity.com"target=_blank>| Make your travel arrangements</a></center><p>


<center><a href="Index.htm">[Home]<a href="B&Bpage.htm">[B&Bs]</a></center>

</html>
```

TABLE G-3: *The purpose for each part of the JavaScript code for a rollover*

CODE	PURPOSE
<script language="javascript" type="text/javascript">	Indicates to the browser that the type of scripting language is JavaScript (Note: there are other scripting languages such as VBScript)
<a href="RHpage.htm"	Indicates that the RHpage.htm file will be affected by the JavaScript
OnMouseOver="document.bbimage.src='roche2-lg.jpg'"	Indicates that when the user's mouse pointer is over the image, the roche2-lg.jpg file appears
OnMouseOut="document.bbimage.src='roche-lg.jpg'">	Indicates that when the user's mouse pointer is not over the image, the roche-lg.jpg file appears
<img src="roche-lg.jpg"	Indicates that the image to display when the page first appears in the browser is roche-lg.jpg
name="bbimage"	Identifies the space for the images that will be loaded
width=274 height=181>	Specifies the width and height for the space for the image
</a>	Closes the <a href tag

Enhancing a Web page

Now that the Web site has taken shape, you can experiment with making changes to it. In this lesson you will learn how easy it is to modify and enhance the Web site. The enhancements include changes to the text and background. In this lesson, you will make changes to the heading, subheading, body text, and background of the Bed & Breakfast page as shown in Figure G-23. Table G-4 identifies the HTML tags that you will use.

STEPS

1. Switch to your text editor, then open the file **B&Bpage.htm**
Figure G-24 shows the HTML code used to enhance the Web page.

2. Position the insertion point after <h2><center> and before BED & BREAKFAST</center></h2>, then type **<font color="purple">**
The <font is an opening tag and color is used to specify the color attribute assigned to the text. For this Web page, it specifies that the text following this opening tag will appear in the color purple.

3. Position the insertion point after BED & BREAKFAST and before </center></h2>, then type **</font>**
The </font> tag closes the opening tag entered in Step 2. You need the closing tag so that only the text between the opening and closing tags—in this case, BED & BREAKFAST—appears in the color purple. If you did not include the closing tag, all text following the opening tag would appear in purple.

4. Save the file, switch to your browser, then open the file **B&Bpage.htm**
Notice that the heading appears in the color purple.

5. Switch to your text editor, place the insertion point after <a href="RHpage.htm"> and before Roche Harbor B&B, type **<i><font size=4 face="arial">**, place the insertion point after Roche Harbor B&B, then type **</font></i>**
These tags close the opening tags for the font and italic.

6. Save the file, switch to your browser, then refresh the B&B page
Notice that the subheading Roche Harbor B&B is displayed in italics, size 4, Arial font. The size 4 font is larger than the other text.

7. Switch to your text editor, place the insertion point before Located in the picturesque..., type **<b>**, place the insertion point after Sound... and before <p>, then type **</b>**
All text between the <b> tags will appear as bold text in the browser window.

8. Save the file, switch to your browser, then refresh the B&B page
The body text appears in bold.

9. Switch to your text editor, select **<body background="bgtexture.gif">**, press **[Delete]**, then type **<body bgcolor="#FFFFFF">**
The code to display a background image is replaced with the code to use the background color #FFFFFF, which is white.

10. Save the file, switch to your browser, then refresh the B&B page
Figure G-23 shows the enhanced Web page. Notice that the background for this page is white. You will have the opportunity in Independent Challenge 1 to continue to enhance the Travel Northwest Web site so that the pages in the Web site are consistent.

11. Print each page of your Web from your browser, print each page from your text editor, place each page of code behind its Web page, then place the Roche Harbor B&B page on top and staple the pages together

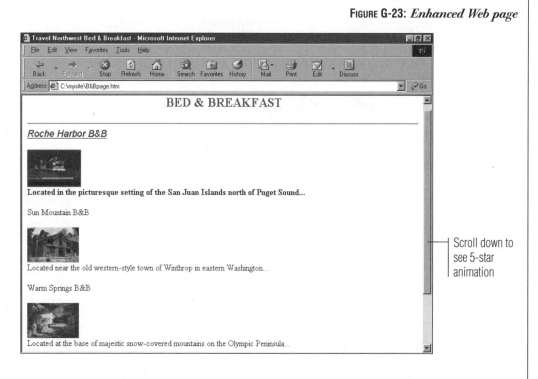

Scroll down to see 5-star animation

```
B&Bpage - Notepad
File  Edit  Search  Help

<html>

<head>

<title>Travel Northwest Bed & Breakfast</title>

</head>

<body bgcolor="FFFFFF">

<h2><center><font color="purple">BED & BREAKFAST</font></center></h2>

<hr>

<a href="RHpage.htm"><i><font size=4 face="arial">Roche Harbor B&B</font></i></a><p>
<a href="RHpage.htm"><img src="roche-sm.jpg"></a><br>
<b>Located in the picturesque setting of the San Juan Islands north of Puget Sound...</b><p>

Sun Mountain B&B<p>
<img src="sunmtn-sm.jpg"><br>
Located near the old western-style town of Winthrop in eastern Washington...<p>

Warm Springs B&B<p>
<img src="warm-sm.jpg"><br>
Located at the base of majestic snow-covered mountains on the Olympic Peninsula...<p>

</body>

<center>We are proud of our <img src="star.gif" align="middle">
<img src="star.gif" align="middle">
<img src="star.gif" align="middle">
<img src="star.gif" align="middle">
<img src="star.gif" align="middle"> rating by the Puget Sound B&B Association!</center><p>

<center><a href="Index.htm">[HOME]</a></center>
```

HTML TAG	EXAMPLE	RESULT
`<font>...</font>`	`<font face="arial">Travel</font>`	The word *Travel* displays in Arial
	`<font size="4">Travel</font>`	The word *Travel* displays in a size larger than the browser default
	`<font color="green">Travel</font>`	The word *Travel* displays in green
	`<font face="arial" size="4" color="green">Travel</font>`	All of the above
`<b>...</b>`	`<b>Travel</b>`	The word *Travel* displays in bold
`<i>...</i>`	`<i>Travel</i>`	The word *Travel* displays in italic
`<body bgcolor...>`	`<body bgcolor="red">`	The page background displays in red

End of Unit Exercises

CONCEPT REVIEW

Label each of the formatting elements shown in Figure G-25.

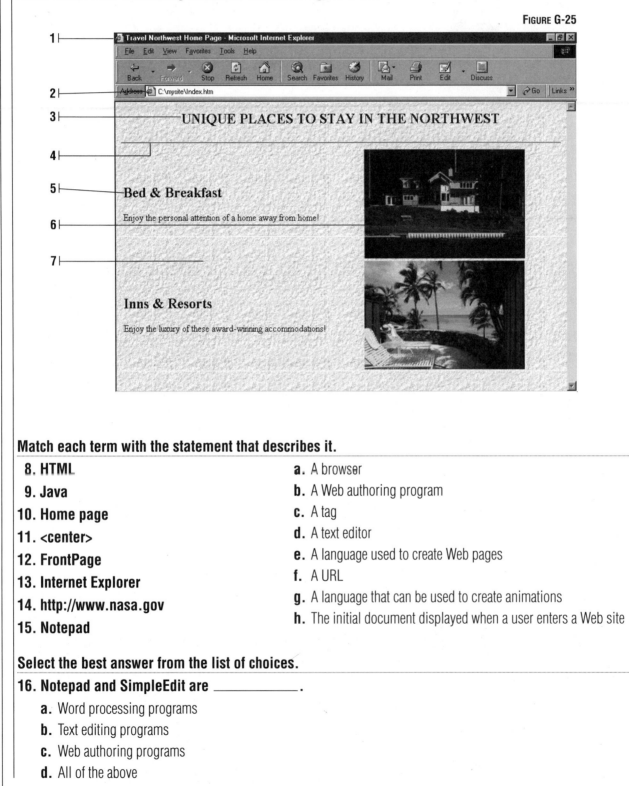

Match each term with the statement that describes it.

8. HTML
9. Java
10. Home page
11. `<center>`
12. FrontPage
13. Internet Explorer
14. http://www.nasa.gov
15. Notepad

a. A browser
b. A Web authoring program
c. A tag
d. A text editor
e. A language used to create Web pages
f. A URL
g. A language that can be used to create animations
h. The initial document displayed when a user enters a Web site

Select the best answer from the list of choices.

16. Notepad and SimpleEdit are _____.

  a. Word processing programs

  b. Text editing programs

  c. Web authoring programs

  d. All of the above

17. Dreamweaver and FrontPage are _____.

a. Scripting programs

b. Text editing programs

c. Web authoring programs

d. Word processing programs

18. _____ are HTML codes used to format a Web page.

a. Tags

b. Languages

c. Scripts

d. None of the above

19. Which of the following is NOT true regarding <title>Travel Tours</title>:

a. Travel Tours appears in the title bar of the browser.

b. Travel Tours appears at the top of the Web page.

c. Travel Tours appears in the list when the user bookmarks the Web site.

d. All of the above are true.

20. When aligning text in a Web page, HTML does NOT allow the use of the _____.

a. Spacebar

b. Tab key

c. [Enter] key

d. All of the above are not allowed.

21. The structure of a Web page is generally divided into _____ and _____.

a. Introduction, Documentation

b. Head, Body

c. Introduction, Body

d. Title, Body

22. The structure of a Web site includes _____ pages and _____ pages.

a. Home, destination

b. Home, linked

c. Home, child

d. Parent, child

23. What is the purpose of the following tag: <a href="Index.htm">HOME</a> ?

a. Centers the word *Index* on the Web page

b. Allows the user to click on the word *HOME* to display the Index.htm page

c. Allows the user to click on the Index.htm page to go to the HOME page

d. None of the above

24. Which of the following is NOT an external link?

a. <a href="mailto:nwcet.org@mailit">Click Here</a>

b. <a href="http://www.apple.com" target=_blank> Click Here</a>

c. <a href="Index.htm"><img src="Click Here.jpg"></a>

d. ALL are external links

25. OnMouseOver would be used in _____ code used to create a rollover.

a. JavaScript

b. Java

c. HTML

d. FrontPage

1. Plan the Web site.

a. Use Figures G-26 and G-27 to list the goal and target audience for the Web site.

b. Sketch the storyboard with the navigation options that might have been used to develop the Web site in the figures.

c. Create a folder on your destination drive named UGSR[insert your name here].

d. Copy the files from the drive and folder (UGSR) where your Project Files are stored to your UGSR[your name] folder. (*Note:* Eight files should be copied.)

2. Create the home page.

a. Create a new file in your text editor.

b. Specify the Web page title as Fun Test Home Page.

c. Specify the background texture as bluetexture.jpg.

d. Include the following heading: Which of the following reminds you of the Fourth of July? Specify the h2 heading, which is a large font size, and be sure to center it.

e. Add a horizontal rule line.

f. Create a table, and add the body text as shown in Figure G-26 (*Hint:* Row 1: table data width=60%; text—Fireworks as a heading 3; Lots of excitement with exploding missiles and loud sounds! as body text, graphic—fireworks.jpg; Row 2: table data width–60%; text—Healthy Food as a heading 3; Fresh and healthy fruits and vegetables in a quiet setting. —as body text, graphic—fruits.jpg. The graphics are stored in your UGSR[yourname] folder).

g. Save the file as Index.htm to your UGSR[yourname] folder.

h. Start your browser, open the file Index.htm, then switch to your text editor to make and save changes as needed.

FIGURE G-26

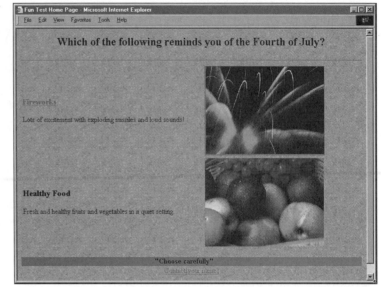

FIGURE G-27

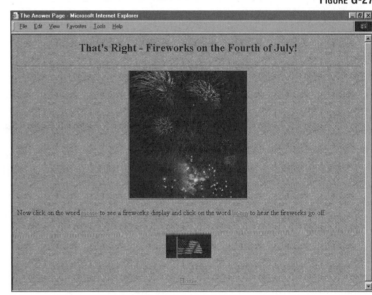

3. Create a child page.

a. Create a new file in your text editor.

b. Specify the Web page title as The Answer Page.

c. Specify a background texture as bluetexture.jpg.

d. Include a centered heading, That's Right – Fireworks on the Fourth of July! in a large font.

e. Add a horizontal rule line.

f. Add a graphic named fireworks1.jpg and center it. (*Hint:* width=259, height=273.)

g. Type this statement under the figure: Now click on the word movie to see a fireworks display and click on the word boom to hear the fireworks go off. (*Hint:* Refer to Figure G-27.)

h. Save the file as Answer.htm to your UGSR[your name] folder.

i. Start your browser, open the file Answer.htm, and be sure that the page closely resembles Figure G-27. Switch to your text editor to make and save changes as needed.

4. Link Web pages using text.

a. Open the file Index.htm in your text editor. Use the <a href tag to link the subheading Fireworks on the home page to the child page.

b. Save the file, switch to your browser, open the file Index.htm, and test your link. Return to your text editor and make corrections as needed.

c. Open the file Answer.htm in your text editor. Center the word Home at the bottom of the child page and use the <a href tag to link Home to the home page.

d. Save the file, switch to your browser, open the file Answer.htm, and test your links. Return to your text editor and make corrections as needed.

5. Link Web pages using a graphic.

a. Open the file Index.htm in your text editor. Use the <a href tag to link the graphic fireworks.jpg on the home page to the child page.

b. Save the file, switch to your browser, open the file Index.htm, and test the graphic link. Return to your text editor and make corrections as needed.

6. Add animation to a Web page.

a. Make sure that the file Index.htm is open in your text editor. Create a marquee that scrolls from right to left on the bottom of the home page. (*Note:* The background color for the marquee is blue. The wording for the marquee is "Choose carefully.")

b. Save the file, switch to your browser (Internet Explorer if possible), refresh the page, and verify that the marquee appears as expected. Return to your text editor and make changes as needed.

c. Open the file Answer.htm. Add the following image as a centered GIF animation to the child page: usflag.gif. (*Note:* Place the animation above [Home].)

d. Save the file, switch to your browser, open the file Answer.htm, and verify that the GIF animation appears as expected. Return to your text editor and make changes as needed.

7. Add sound and video to a Web page.

a. Make sure that file Answer.htm is open in your text editor. Use the word movie to create a link to the fireworks.avi video clip.

b. Save the file, switch to your browser, refresh the page, and verify that clicking on the word movie starts the video clip as expected. Return to your text editor and make changes as needed.

c. Use the word boom to create a link to the boom.wav sound file.

d. Save the file, switch to your browser, refresh the page, and verify that clicking on the word boom starts the sound file as expected. Return to your text editor and make changes as needed.

8. Create external links.

a. Open the file Index.htm in your text editor. Add an e-mail link centered under the marquee text from the words Contact [your name] to your e-mail address. (If you do not have an e-mail account or prefer not to use yours, use this e-mail address: *Webmaster@mymail.*)

b. Save your file, switch to your browser, open the file Index.htm, and test the link. Return to your text editor and make changes as needed. (*Note:* If you used your e-mail address, you can send an e-mail message to your account.)

9. Add JavaScript to a Web page.

a. Open the file Answer.htm in your text editor. In the head section of your Web page, identify the script language to be used to create a rollover for the graphic image on this page. (*Note:* The language to use is JavaScript and the type to use is text/javascript.)

b. In the body of your Web page, create the rollover script based on the following:

```
<a href="Answer.htm" OnMouseOver="document.bbimage.src='fireworks2.jpg'"
OnMouseOut="document.bbimage.src='fireworks1.jpg'"><img src="fireworks1.jpg"name="bbimage" width=259
height=273>
```

c. Save your file, switch to your browser, open the file Answer.htm, and test the rollover. Return to your text editor and make changes as needed.

10. Enhance a Web site.

a. Open the file Index.htm. Change the background color of the home page to #BFBFBF.

b. Use the font tag to change the size of the heading to 4 and the color of the heading to purple.

c. Specify that both subheadings (Fireworks and Healthy Foods) on the home page be in italic type.

d. Specify that the body text for both subheadings in the home page be in bold type.

e. Save your file, switch to your browser, open the file Index.htm, and make sure that your enhancements appear as expected. Return to your text editor and make changes as needed.

f. Print the page from your browser, and then use a link to open the child page and print it from the browser. Switch to your text editor, and then open and print each file used to create the Web pages. Place the printout of the HTML code behind the relevant Web page. Place the Index.htm file on top and staple all pages together.

INDEPENDENT CHALLENGE 1

You have completed the basic Web site for Travel Northwest, and you are satisfied with its overall structure. Now it is time to add two more child pages to the Bed & Breakfast parent page. After creating those pages, you will go through the Web site to ensure that the same enhancements are made to all pages. These changes will give the Web site a consistent "look and feel" for the user. (*Note:* More sophisticated ways for providing a consistent "look and feel" to a Web site exist, such as applying a theme or using Cascading Style Sheets. These techniques are outside the scope of this book.) For the purposes of this independent challenge, you will complete the Bed & Breakfast thread of the Travel Northwest Web site. Your instructor will advise you whether you will create additional pages for the Inns & Resorts thread.

To complete this independent challenge:

a. Create a folder on your destination drive titled UGIC1[insert your name here]. Copy all files from the drive and folder (UGIC1) where your Project Files are stored to UGIC1[your name]. Copy three files—Index.htm, B&Bpage.htm, and RHpage.htm— from the folder mysite[your name] to UGIC1[your name]. (*Note:* Ask your technical support person for help as needed.)

b. Start your text editor. Refer to and modify the steps in Lesson 5 to create two new child pages as follows:

CREATE FILE NAMED	PAGE TITLE	GRAPHIC	TEXT
Sun-mtn.htm	Sun Mountain B&B	sunmtn-lg.jpg	Create your own body text
Warm-spr.htm	Warm Springs B&B	warm-lg.jpg	Create your own body text

After creating each page, save the page, switch to your browser, then open the page to make sure that the page appears as expected. Switch to your text editor and make changes as needed.

c. Refer to and modify the steps in Lesson 6 as noted in the table to add the following text links:

USE FILE NAMED	STEPS TO USE	TEXT TO LINK	FILE TO LINK TO
B&Bpage.htm	Step 5	Sun Mountain B&B	Sun-mtn.htm
B&Bpage.htm	Step 5	Warm Spring B&B	Warm-spr.htm
Sun-mtn.htm	Step 8	[HOME]; [B&Bs]	Index.htm; B&Bpage.htm
Warm-spr.htm	Step 8	[HOME], [B&Bs]	Index.htm; B&Bpage.htm

After creating each text link, save the page, switch to your browser, then open the page to make sure that the text link functions as expected. Switch to your text editor and make changes as needed.

d. Refer to and modify Step 6 in Lesson 7 to add the following graphic links:

USE FILE NAMED	GRAPHIC TO LINK	FILE TO LINK TO
B&Bpage.htm	sunmtn-sm.jpg	Sun-mtn.htm
B&Bpage.htm	warm-sm.jpg	Warm-spr.htm

After creating the graphic links, save the page, switch to your browser, then open the page to make sure the graphic links function as expected. Switch to your text editor and make changes as needed.

e. Refer to and modify the steps in Lessons 8 and 9 as noted in the table to add multimedia elements to the pages as follows:

USE FILE NAMED	STEPS TO USE	TEXT TO LINK	MULTIMEDIA ELEMENT TO LINK TO
Sun-mtn.htm	Lesson 8, Step 2; no background color for the marquee	None; create new text as Bold	Add a marquee that says "Enjoy the beautiful hikes"
Warm-spr.htm	Lesson 9, Step 5	Warm Springs B&B	Audio file: warm-sprsnd.wav

After adding the multimedia element, save the page, switch to your browser, then open the page to make sure that the multimedia element functions as expected. Switch to your text editor and make changes as needed.

f. Refer to and modify the steps in Lesson 12 to make all subheadings and body text on the Bed & Breakfast page consistent:

USE FILE NAMED	ELEMENT TO MODIFY	STEPS TO USE	CHANGE TO MAKE
B&Bpage.htm	Subheadings (Sun Mountain B&B and Warm Springs B&B)	Lesson 12, Step 5	Italic, font size 4, Arial
B&Bpage.htm	Body text (Located near.. and Located at...)	Lesson 12, Step 7	Bold

After enhancing the Web page, save the page, switch to your browser, then open the page to make sure that the enhancements appear as expected. Switch to your text editor and make changes as needed.

INDEPENDENT CHALLENGE 2

You have been asked to create a Web site for a prominent artist. Initially, the site will have two pages: a home page and a gallery page. After creating the home page and a child page named gallery.htm, you will create text and graphic links from the home page to the gallery page. You will also create a text link from the child page to the home page. These links will help the user navigate through the Web.

To complete this independent challenge:

a. Create a folder on your destination drive titled UGIC2[insert your name here]. Copy all files from the drive and folder (UGIC2) where your Project Files are stored to UGIC2[your name]. (*Note:* Ask your technical support person for help as needed.)

b. Use your text editor to create the home page. Use the details in the following table to construct the home page.

File name	Index.htm
Page title	Barbara VanDyke Home Page
Page background color	Aqua (<body bgcolor="aqua">)
Heading	Barbara VanDyke - Artist
Horizontal rule line	Below heading
Body Text	Copy and paste text from file named UGIC2-info.txt (*Note:* Format the text so that the contact information appears centered on the page and the paragraph appears under the centered text. Refer to Figure G-28.)
Graphic image (centered at the bottom of the page)	gallery.jpg

Save the page, then switch to your browser to make sure that the page appears as expected. Switch to your text editor to make corrections as needed.

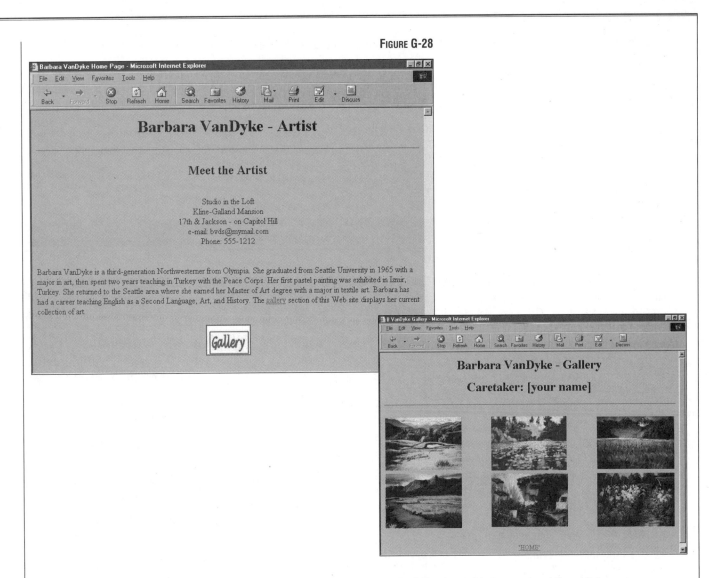

c. Use your text editor to create the child page. Use the details in the following table to construct the child page.

File name	gallery.htm
Page title	B VanDyke Gallery
Page background color	Aqua
Heading	Barbara VanDyke – Gallery Caretaker: [your name]
Horizontal rule line	Below heading
Body text	None
Graphic images (*hint:* use a 2-row, 3-column table and set the column width to 40%.)	art1.jpg art2.jpg art3.jpg art4.jpg art5.jpg art6.jpg

Save the page, then switch to your browser to make sure that the page appears as expected. Switch to your text editor to make corrections as needed.

d. Create a link from the gallery page to the home page using the word "HOME" at the bottom of the page. Save the page.

e. Create a link from the home page to the gallery page using the word gallery in the body text.

f. Create another link from the home page to the gallery page using the gallery.jpg graphic. Save the page.

g. After creating your links, save each page, switch to your browser, and test the links to make sure that they function as expected. Switch to the text editor and make corrections as needed.

h. Print your pages from your browser and your text editor.

INDEPENDENT CHALLENGE 3

You have been asked to create a Web page to announce a hot-air balloon festival. The site will have a single page, which will include a graphic, a video, and an external link to an e-mail address. The site will also have background sound so that the user will hear the sound of a hot-air balloon when first arriving at the site. The background sound will loop three times, which means that the sound will be heard three times and then stop.

To complete this independent challenge:

a. Create a folder on your destination drive titled UGIC3[insert your name here]. Copy all files from the drive and folder (UGIC3) where your Project Files are stored to UGIC3[your name]. (*Note:* Ask your technical support person for help as needed.)

b. Use your text editor to create the home page. Use the details in the following table to construct it.

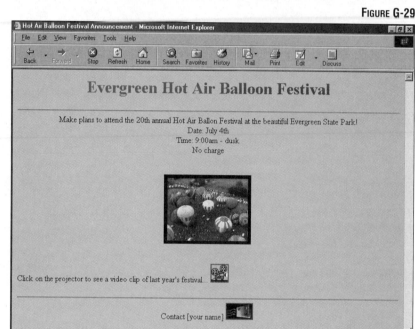

File name	Index.htm
Page title	Hot Air Balloon Festival Announcement
Page background	Your choice of texture or color
Background sound	Add a sound that will play automatically when the page is opened in the browser (*Hint:* Use <bgsound src="filename" loop=#> where "filename" is the name of the sound filename "introsnd.wav" and # identifies how many times the sound file should loop. The tag should be on its own line after the body tag. *Note:* bgsound only works in Internet Explorer.)
Heading (with large font and colored text)	Evergreen Hot Air Balloon Festival
Horizontal rule line	Below heading
Body text (default font size; Centered below the rule line)	See UGIC3-info.txt (*Hint:* Use the text beginning Make... and ending with No charge. Center the text. Place each idea on its own line.)
Graphic image (centered below the body text)	balloon.jpg
Text with video icon linked to the video clip	See UGIC3-info.txt for the text for these lines. [*Type:* Click on the projector to see a video clip of last year's festival. Then insert the video icon after the ellipsis. The video icon is a GIF animation ("movie-icon.gif") that the user will click to play the video. The video clip is "balloon.avi." Be sure Windows Media Player is installed and set as the default media player.]
Horizontal rule line below the text	
"Contact [your name]" text followed by an animation, centered below the rule line; when user clicks on the animation, the e-mail program starts.	Animation file: "mail.gif"

INDEPENDENT CHALLENGE 4

WEB WORKS

Now that you have studied how multimedia can be incorporated into a Web document, you can more effectively evaluate the use of multimedia on the Web. In this independent challenge, you will study several Web sites and complete a table to identify the different ways in which multimedia is used and to describe how interactivity (especially links) is developed.

To complete this independent challenge:

a. Connect to the Internet.

b. Go to *http://www.course.com/*, navigate to the Student Online Companion for this book, and then click the link for Unit G.

c. The Unit G link contains links to Web sites with multimedia elements. Click each link to visit the site. Complete a table like the one that follows.

d. Write a summary of how multimedia is used on the sites, and describe one innovative use of multimedia.

Web site URL	How are the links developed (e.g., text, graphics, buttons)?	How do you know a link is available (e.g.,color, wording)?	What animation, sound, and video are used? What triggers them (e.g., controls, links, automatic)?
URL:			
URL:			
URL:			
URL:			
URL:			
Your choice:			
Your choice:			

Create the HTML document shown in Figure G-30. To create the document, which includes a rollover, create a folder named UGVW[insert your name here] on your destination drive. Copy the files from the drive and folder where your Project Files are stored to your UGVW[your name] folder. Create a new document in your text editor. Name the document Capitol.htm. Navigate to UGVW[your name] and use the figures Capitol-east.jpg and Capitol-west.jpg. Use the callouts to help determine the other specifications for the page.

FIGURE G-30

Title

Heading:
Size: h1
Font color: white
Centered

Size: default
Font color: white
Align: center

Blue background
color

Rule Lines

Graphic size:
width=524
height=350

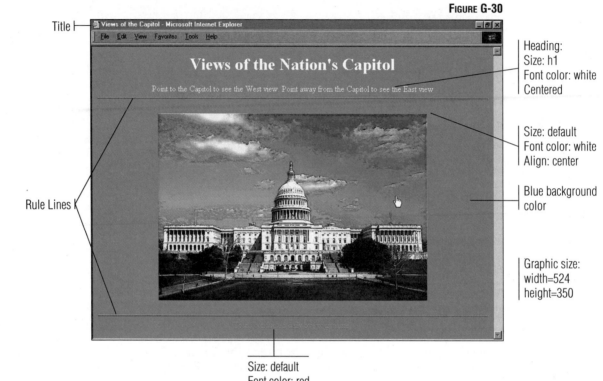

Size: default
Font color: red
Align: center

Case Study: Using Macromedia Director

Throughout this book you have been studying multimedia concepts, including the authoring programs used to develop applications. In this unit you will use Macromedia Director, a popular authoring program, to create an interactive movie complete with text, graphics, animation, and sound. In addition, you will learn how to save the movie for distribution on media such as CD/DVD as well as through the Web. The case study in this unit focuses on Multimedia Design Center (MDC), a service provider that creates multimedia applications for clients such as Learning R Us. Learning R Us develops short children's animations that can be viewed and downloaded from its Web site or distributed on CDs. MDC has asked you to create a short opening movie to be part of the FunTimes series.

Planning the movie

Planning is the first step in developing a Director movie. As you learned earlier, planning includes determining the concept, goals, target audience, treatment, and specifications, as well as creating the storyboard and navigation scheme. In this lesson you will learn how MDC and its client, Learning R Us, approached the planning of this movie.

DETAILS

▶ *The Concept.* Learning R Us distributes a series of children's educational titles on various subjects. Its mission is to provide both educational and entertaining experiences for its audience. The company is creating a new series called FunTimes, which focuses on the user having fun by choosing the "adventure." While it is transparent to the user, each adventure follows a different educational path.

▶ *The Goal.* The goal of the FunTimes series is for the primary audience to have an entertaining experience while encountering educational objectives based on user input. In addition, Learning R Us is hoping that the FunTime series will increase users' awareness of the company and, as a result, increase sales of its educational titles.

▶ *The Target Audience.* The primary audience consists of children ages 4–8 who use the computer for entertainment and education. The primary audience may or may not have access to the Web.

▶ *The Treatment.* The "look and feel" of the application will focus on simplicity and ease of use with large, cartoon-type graphics. Animation with sound will be used to provide entertainment. The user will use buttons to control the animation.

The button selection also will determine which educational adventure is presented—that is, which navigation scheme is followed. An element of surprise will help create excitement.

▶ *The Specifications.* The target playback system will account for a strong portion of the installed market: Windows 95 or later, Pentium, Macintosh G3, OS7, 56K modem with Internet Explorer 3.0 (or later) or Netscape 3.0 (or later), sound card; Multimedia elements: Graphics—GIFs and BMPs; Animation— Path animation with GIF graphics; Text—screen headings in Arial font, 18 point, bold, red; button controls for starting and stopping the animation; Audio—WAV files synchronized to the animation.

▶ *The Storyboard.* Figure H-1 shows a sketch of the application (movie).

▶ *The Navigation.* Figure H-1 also shows the navigation options. Users will be able to click the Plane button to start one animation, the Fun button to start a different animation, the Stop button to stop the animation, and the Next button to continue the title without running the animations. The opening movie gives clues to the educational "adventures." After playing the movie animations, the user can click the Next button to read more about the two possible adventures.

STEPS...

Trouble?

Ask your technical support person or instructor if you need help completing these steps.

1. Set your computer settings as follows: Screen resolution—**800 × 600**; Colors—**16 bit**; Browser—**Internet Explorer version 5**

   These are the computer settings used in developing this tutorial. Your screen display may differ somewhat from the figures in this unit if you are not able to set your computer settings to match these settings.

2. Create a folder on your destination drive named **mymovie[insert your name here]**

QuickTip

The order of your files may differ.

3. Navigate to the drive and location where your Project Files are stored and copy the files for this unit to the mymovie[your name] folder: **cloud1.gif, cloud2.gif, hotair.gif, hotair-snd.wav, plane.bmp, plane-snd.wav**

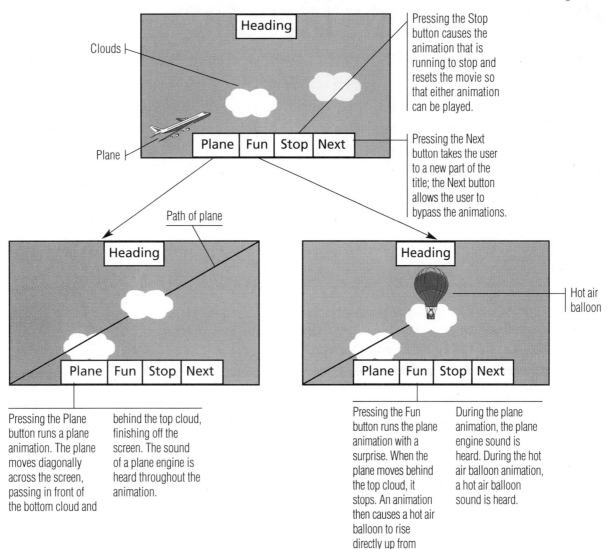

Clouds

Heading

Plane

Plane | Fun | Stop | Next

Pressing the Stop button causes the animation that is running to stop and resets the movie so that either animation can be played.

Pressing the Next button takes the user to a new part of the title; the Next button allows the user to bypass the animations.

Path of plane

Heading

Plane | Fun | Stop | Next

Heading

Hot air balloon

Plane | Fun | Stop | Next

Pressing the Plane button runs a plane animation. The plane moves diagonally across the screen, passing in front of the bottom cloud and behind the top cloud, finishing off the screen. The sound of a plane engine is heard throughout the animation.

Pressing the Fun button runs the plane animation with a surprise. When the plane moves behind the top cloud, it stops. An animation then causes a hot air balloon to rise directly up from behind the top cloud.

During the plane animation, the plane engine sound is heard. During the hot air balloon animation, a hot air balloon sound is heard.

Understanding Director

As you learned earlier, Director uses a movie metaphor that is made up of a series of frames. Cast members (graphics, text, sounds, and so on) are placed on a stage and controlled by a score. The score indicates in which frame(s) of the movie each cast member appears. Figure H-2 shows frame 1 of the completed movie that you will be creating in this unit. Refer to Figure H-2 as you read the following description of the various parts of the Director environment.

DETAILS

▶ *Stage*—The Stage window shows a background (blue color) and the following cast members:
- Plane Fun from Learning R Us—a heading created using the Director Text tool
- cloud1—the cloud in the lower-left corner of the stage, a GIF graphic imported into Director
- cloud2—the cloud in the center of the stage, a GIF graphic imported into Director
- Plane button—created using the Director Button tool
- Fun button—created using the Director Button tool
- Stop button—created using the Director Button tool
- Next button—created using the Director Button tool (*Note:* This button will branch to another part of the title; it will be placed on the stage as a placeholder in this unit.)

▶ *Cast*—The Cast window shows thumbnails of the cast members and their names or cast numbers. Cast members that are imported into Director from a folder such as **mymovie** on the C drive are automatically placed in the Cast window. They can then be dragged from the Cast window to the desired location on the stage. When you drag a cast member to the stage, it becomes a sprite. A **sprite** is one instance of a cast member. This approach allows you to use the same cast member more than once. For example, to place two planes on the stage, you would drag the plane cast member from the Cast window onto the stage twice; each time a different sprite would be created. You could then change the planes to make them look or behave differently. For example, the plane sprites might move in different directions. Some changes to sprites are made using the Properties Inspector window.

▶ Score—The Score window consists of frames and channels. Each channel is made up of frames, and each channel can have one or more cast members. When cast members are placed on the stage, they are automatically inserted into a channel in the score. You can specify the channel and the frame where a cast member will be inserted. When the movie plays, the playback head starts in frame 1 and moves sequentially to frames 2, 3, 4, and so on through all of the channels. Those cast members that appear in a frame as the playback head passes over it will be displayed on the stage. To alter the sequential playback of the frames, you can insert scripts into the score or assign scripts to cast members.

▶ *Property Inspector* (not shown in Figure H-2)—You use the Property Inspector window to change the properties of a sprite, such as displaying or not displaying a background of a sprite.

▶ *Tool palette*—The Tool palette is used to create headings, such as "Plane Fun from Learning R Us." (It is used for many other tasks as well.) You use the Text tool to create text boxes for headings. You use the Button tool to create buttons for user interaction.

▶ Figure H-3 shows the stage displaying frame 2. Notice the following changes from frame 1 to frame 2:
- The Plane and Fun buttons do not appear on the stage (these buttons appear only in frame 1 of the score).
- A plane appears on the stage (the plane starts in frame 2 of the score and continues to frame 28 of the score); the plane is a graphic imported into Director.

▶ Figure H-4 shows the stage displaying frame 10. In this frame the plane has moved to a position between the clouds. This change in the plane location from frame to frame will create an animation that continues through frame 28.

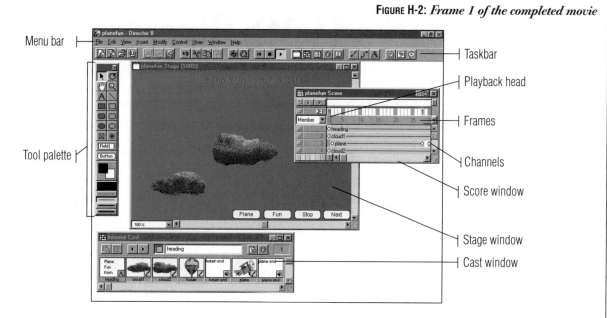

Menu bar

Tool palette

Taskbar

Playback head

Frames

Channels

Score window

Stage window

Cast window

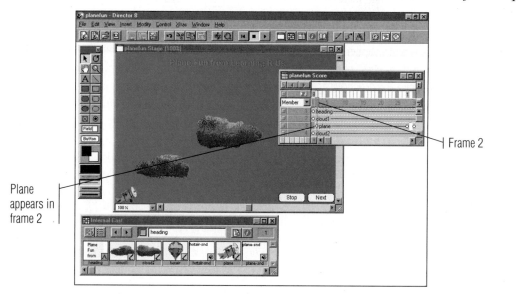
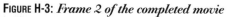

Plane appears in frame 2

Frame 2

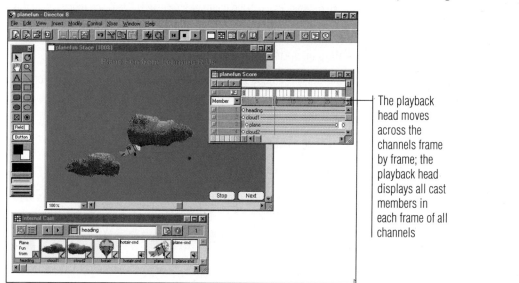
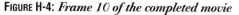

The playback head moves across the channels frame by frame; the playback head displays all cast members in each frame of all channels

Getting started with Director

Now that you understand how Director works, you are ready to set up the Director environment for your use. In this lesson, you will start the program, learn how to open and manipulate Director windows, and save the movie. Figure H-5 shows the Director screen and the windows you will need to open.

STEPS

QuickTip

If you need help, ask your technical support person for assistance. Your Director environment might differ from that in Figure H-5 depending on the Director properties set at last use.

1. Start Director, then click **Window** on the menu bar

Figure H-5 shows the Window menu, which lists the Window options available.

2. Be sure that **Toolbar, Tool Palette, Stage, Score**, and **Cast** are selected

A check mark to the left of an option indicates it is selected. Notice in Figure H-5 that Cast is marked with a circle instead of a check mark. The circle indicates that Cast is the active window. In Figure H-5, you know that Cast is the active window because the title bar changes color and a circle appears to the left of Cast in the Window menu. (Macintosh users will see a triangle Next to the active window and the window will not be dimmed.)

3. Click the title bar of the Stage window

Notice that the color of the title bar changes to indicate the active window. Whenever possible you should click the title bar of a window to make it active so that you do not inadvertently change a frame.

QuickTip

When you work with Director, you will find it useful to move the windows (Stage, Score, Cast, and so on) around the screen so that you can better view and work with the active window. You can drag and resize Director windows just as you do windows in other applications.

4. Drag the Stage, Score, and Cast windows to position them, as shown in Figure H-5, then resize the Stage and Cast windows as needed

5. Point to the right side border of the score window; when the pointer changes to ↔, hold down the mouse button, then drag the border to enlarge the score to **85** frames as shown in Figure H-6

6. Click **frame 10 of channel 2** in the Score window

Figure H-7 shows frame 10 in channel 2 selected. The black rectangle in this frame indicates that the frame is selected. The playback head moves to the selected frame, which is frame 10.

7. Click **Help** on the menu bar, then click **Director Help**

The Director Help window opens. You can use this window to search for help on Director topics. You can perform a keyword search by entering a keyword or phrase in the text box in the Index tab. The Help window is a useful tool as you learn to use Director.

8. Close the Help window, click **File** on the menu bar, then click **Save**

The Save Movie dialog box appears.

9. Navigate to the destination drive and folder named **mymovie[your name]**, type **planefun** in the File name text box, then click **Save**

The movie is saved to the mymovie[your name] folder.

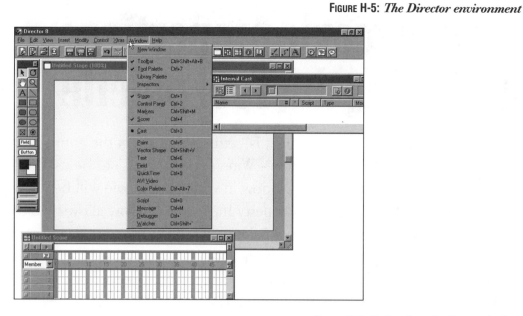

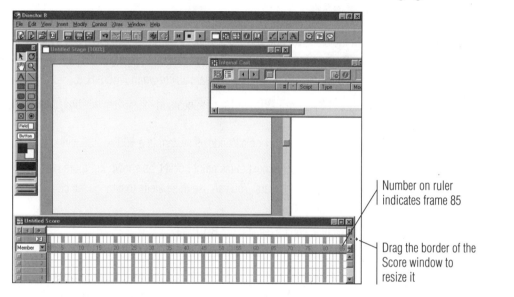
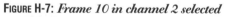

Number on ruler indicates frame 85

Drag the border of the Score window to resize it

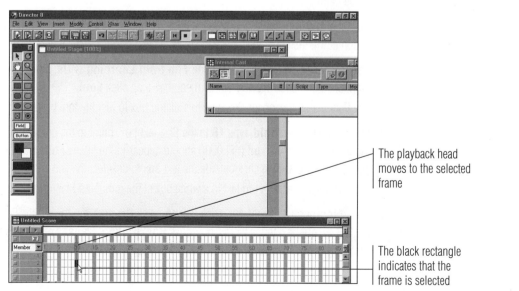

The playback head moves to the selected frame

The black rectangle indicates that the frame is selected

Setting movie properties and using the Tool palette

Director movies have properties—that is, settings that affect the entire movie. For example, you can specify the color palette (System - Win, Mac, or others) to be used when working with graphics, the dimensions for the window in which the movie will be displayed, and the background color for the movie. The Property Inspector window allows you to quickly view and set the properties for a movie. The Tool palette provides various tools for creating line drawings, a Text tool for inserting text on the screen, and a Button tool for creating buttons that control the playing of the movie. In this lesson, you will use the Property Inspector to set movie properties and the Tool palette to create the heading text.

STEPS

Trouble?

If the Property Inspector window is not completely visible, point to the title bar and drag the Property Inspector window into full view.

1. Click the Stage window title bar to make it the active window, click **Modify** on the menu bar, click **Movie**, click **Properties**, then click the **Movie** tab, if necessary
   The Property Inspector window appears as shown in Figure H-8.

2. Verify that **System - Win** (or **Mac**) appears in the system text box, then change the stage size to 500 × 330, if necessary
   The movie is set to play on a Windows system in a 500 × 330 window.

3. Point to the color chip next to the paint bucket, as shown in Figure H-9, then hold down the mouse pointer
   The Color palette appears. You can use this palette to change the color of a sprite and to select a color for the stage background.

4. Click the blue square (see Figure H-9)
   The Color palette closes and the stage background appears blue.

5. Close the Property Inspector window, then click **frame 1 of channel 1** in the Score window (see Figure H-10)
   The movie properties are defined. Frame 1 in channel 1 is the active frame. Cast members are added to the active frame.

6. Click the **Text tool button** [A] in the Tool palette, position the pointer in the Stage window, hold the mouse button down, then drag the mouse to create the text box as shown in Figure H-10

7. Release the mouse button, type **Plane Fun from Learning R Us**, drag the pointer across the words to highlight them, click **Modify** on the menu bar, then click **Font**
   The Font dialog box opens. You use this dialog box to identify font properties.

8. Select **Arial**, select **Bold**, type **18** in the Size text box, point to the color chip next to Color, hold down the mouse, click the color **red** (#FF0000 should appear in the title bar of the color palette) when the color palette appears, click **OK**, then click outside the text box to deselect the text
   The heading appears as red text in a white box at the top of the Stage window.

QuickTip

Click the text box to select it. Use the sizing handles to resize or move the text box. Double-click the text box to be able to edit the text.

9. Click **Modify** on the menu bar, click **Sprite**, click **Properties**, then in the Property Inspector window click the **list arrow** next to the word Copy, click **Background Transparent**, click the **Member tab** [🖼], type **heading** in the Name box, then close the Property Inspector

10. Save the movie

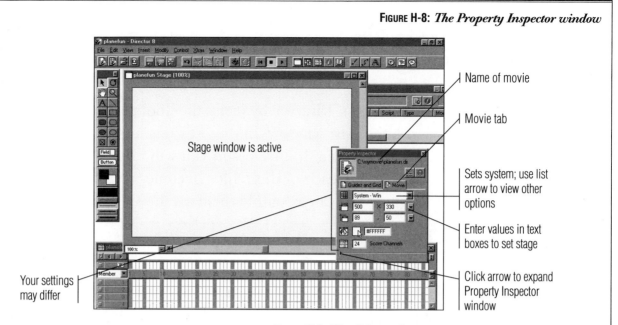

Name of movie

Movie tab

Sets system; use list arrow to view other options

Enter values in text boxes to set stage

Click arrow to expand Property Inspector window

Your settings may differ

FIGURE H-9: *The Color palette in the Property Inspector window*

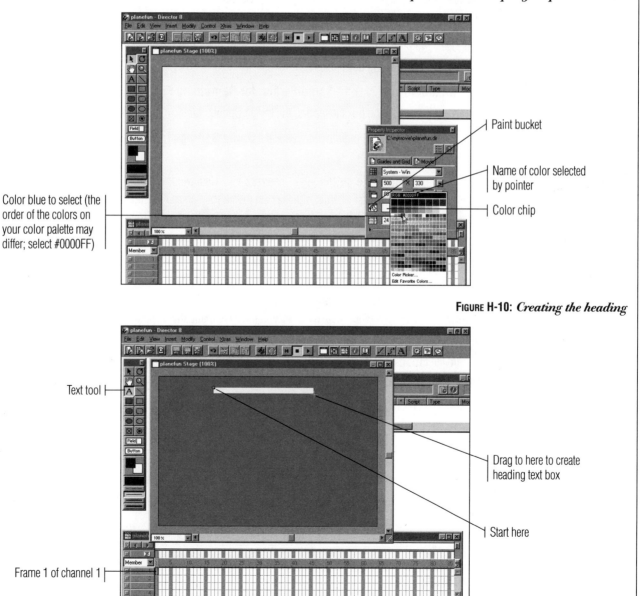

Paint bucket

Name of color selected by pointer

Color chip

Color blue to select (the order of the colors on your color palette may differ; select #0000FF)

FIGURE H-10: *Creating the heading*

Text tool

Drag to here to create heading text box

Start here

Frame 1 of channel 1

Assembling the cast

Cast members can be created within Director by using the Tool palette and Paint window, or they can be imported into the Cast window. In the previous lesson you created a cast member when you created the heading. In this lesson you will import four graphic files and two audio files. Once imported, each of these files becomes a cast member. Once the files appear in the Cast window, you can assemble them on the stage as sprites.

STEPS

1. Click the Cast window title bar to make it active

   Notice that one cast member is present in the Cast window—the heading you created in Lesson 4.

2. Click **File** on the menu bar, click **Import,** use the Look in list arrow to navigate to the **mymovie[your name]** folder if necessary, click **cloud1**, then click **Add**

   The Import Files into "Internal" dialog box appears as shown in Figure H-11.

QuickTip

You should add a total of six files to be imported. The order of your files may differ. Your filenames might include the extension.

3. Continue to add the files **cloud2**, **hotair**, **hotair-snd**, **plane**, and **plane-snd**, then click **Import**

   The Select Format dialog box appears.

4. Click **Bitmap Image**, click the **Same Format for Remaining Files** check box, then click **OK**

   The Select Format dialog box closes and the Image Options for … dialog box appears.

5. Click the **Stage(16 bits)** radio button, click the **Same Settings for Remaining Images** check box, then click **OK**

QuickTip

The order of your cast member matches the order in which the files were imported.

6. Click the **Cast View Style button** , then resize the Cast window until all cast members are visible

   Figure H-12 shows the Cast window with the cast members. You can use the Cast View Style button to toggle between showing the cast members in list form and showing them as thumbnails.

7. Click the **Score window** to make it active, click **frame 1 in channel 2**, then drag cloud1 from the Cast window to the Stage window as shown in Figure H-13

   Cloud1 is a sprite on the stage. The blue bar in the Score window indicates that this sprite occupies frames 1 to 28 in channel 2. When you drag a cast member to the stage, Director inserts a sprite into both the selected frame and the next 27 frames. It also allows you to select manually those frames and channels in which sprites appear. Notice that cloud1 has a white background.

8. Be sure the **cloud1 sprite** on the stage is selected (if necessary click cloud1 so 8 handles appear), click **Modify** on the menu bar, click **Sprite**, click **Properties**, click the list arrow in the Property Inspector dialog box next to the word Copy, then click **Background Transparent**

   The background for the cloud1 sprite becomes transparent, which allows the sprite to blend in with the stage background.

9. Click **frame 1 in channel 3**, drag the plane to the position on the Stage window shown in Figure H-14, use the Property Inspector dialog box (see Step 8) to make the background transparent, click **frame 1 in channel 4**, drag cloud2 to the position on the Stage window as shown in Figure H-14, then use the Property Inspector dialog box (see Step 8) to make the background transparent

   The order in which you place cast members on the stage is important. The last cast member placed on the stage will appear on top of the previous ones, because the previous cast members are placed in a higher channel.

10. Save the file

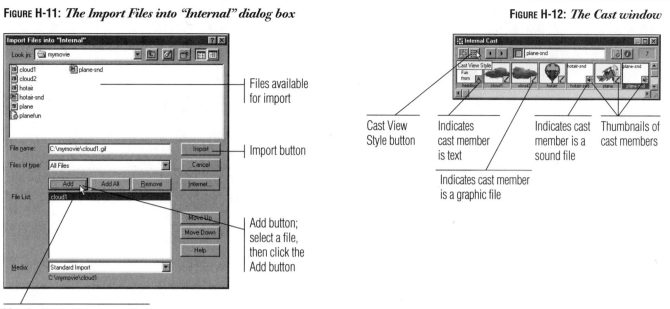

Files available for import

Import button

Add button; select a file, then click the Add button

Lists the files that have been added to be imported into the Cast window

Cast View Style button

Indicates cast member is text

Indicates cast member is a graphic file

Indicates cast member is a sound file

Thumbnails of cast members

FIGURE H-13: *Placing a cast member on the stage*

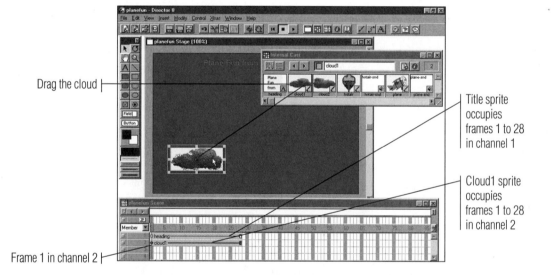

Drag the cloud

Title sprite occupies frames 1 to 28 in channel 1

Cloud1 sprite occupies frames 1 to 28 in channel 2

Frame 1 in channel 2

FIGURE H-14: *The plane and cloud cast members placed on the stage*

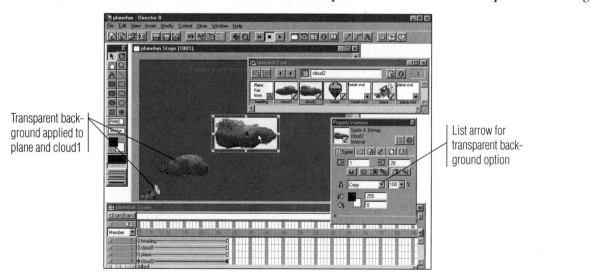

Transparent background applied to plane and cloud1

List arrow for transparent background option

Playing the movie

As you create a Director movie, it is important to play it to make sure that the movie is progressing as expected. You should play the movie frequently so that you can make changes as needed along the way rather than having to make lots of changes at the end of the development process. The control buttons appear on the taskbar. You use them to rewind, stop, and play the movie. When you click the Play button, the playback head moves from frame to frame through all of the channels. As the playback head moves, the cast members in the frames and channels over which it passes are displayed on the stage. The movie will continue to loop until you click the Stop button.

STEPS

1. Close the Property Inspector and Cast windows

   You have finished adding the cast members to your stage, so you no longer need the Cast window. If you wanted to add more cast members, you could open the Cast window by using the Window menu.

2. Click the **Play button** ▶ on the taskbar

   Figure H-15 shows the movie controls available in Director. While the movie plays, notice that the playback head moves across all channels from frame 1 to 28. None of the cast members moves, however, because all of them are in the same positions in frames 1 to 28. Notice that the playback head continues to loop through frames 1 to 28.

3. Click the **Stop button** ■ on the taskbar

4. Point to the **circle** next to the word *plane* in frame 1 of channel 3 of the score, hold down the mouse button, then drag the circle to frame 2 as shown in Figure H-16

5. Click the **Rewind button** ◄ on the taskbar

   The playback head moves back to frame 1, but the plane does not appear on the stage. Because the playback head is positioned over frame 1, only the cast members in frame 1 appear on the stage. Because the plane is found in frame 2, it will not appear on the stage until the playback head reaches frame 2. You can move manually the playback head frame by frame to see the changes on the stage.

6. Point to the **playback head**, drag it to **frame 2**, then drag it to **frame 1**

7. Click ▶, watch the movie loop a few times, then click ■

8. Save the movie

Trouble?

If the playback head does not continue to loop, click Control on the menu bar, then click Loop Playback.

Trouble?

The Stop button on the taskbar must be selected.

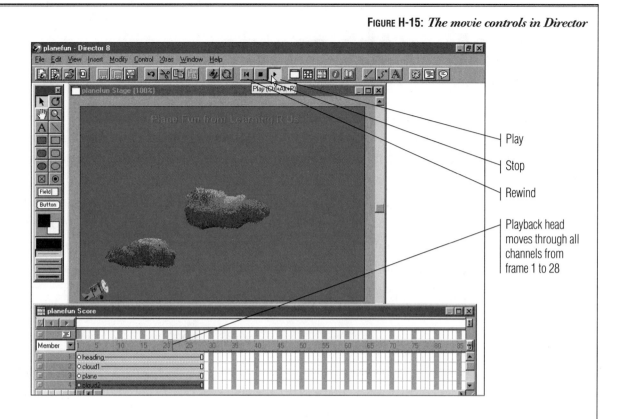

Play

Stop

Rewind

Playback head moves through all channels from frame 1 to 28

FIGURE H-16: *Adjusting the score by moving the plane sprite out of frame 1*

Frame 1 of channel 3

Drag the circle from frame 1 to frame 2

Animating the movie

To create animation in a movie, you change a sprite's position or appearance from one frame to another. Several techniques can be used to create an animation, including dragging a sprite around the stage and recording its movement (path animation), creating a series of sprites that display one at a time (cell animation), and using Director's tweening function. In **tweening**, you specify keyframes in the score that mark the positions of sprites on the stage. Director determines the path of the sprite from one keyframe (position) to another and fills in the score between the keyframes. In this lesson you will use the tweening function to create an animation that moves the plane across the stage diagonally.

STEPS

1. Click **File** on the menu bar, click **Preferences**, click **Sprite**, then make sure that a check mark appears in the **Tweening** check box

   The Sprite Preferences dialog box appears as shown in Figure H-17. A check mark in the Tweening check box toggles the Tweening feature on or off.

2. Click **OK**

   The Sprite Preferences dialog box closes.

3. Click the **circle** in frame 2 of channel 3 (the plane channel) in the score, then click **Insert** on the menu bar

   The insert menu appears as shown in Figure H-18.

4. Click **Keyframe**

   The selected frame (frame 2 in channel 3) is set as a keyframe. A **keyframe** is a frame that indicates to Director that a sprite is changing a property, such as moving on the screen in an animation.

5. Click the **plane** on the stage

   The sprite handles appear on the plane frame to indicate that the plane is selected. Notice the blue circle in the middle of the plane.

6. Point to the **blue circle** in the middle of the plane, hold down the mouse button, drag the plane off the stage as shown in Figure H-19, then release the mouse button

   When you use the blue circle to drag the plane to another location, Director creates an animation path as indicated by the dotted yellow line.

7. Click the **circle** in frame 28 of channel 3, click **Insert** on the menu bar, then click **Keyframe**

   Frame 28 in channel 3 is set as a keyframe.

8. Click **Modify** on the menu bar, click **Sprite**, click **Tweening**, then make sure that a check mark appears in the **Path** check box

   The Sprite Tweening dialog box appears as shown in Figure H-20. It allows you to specify which changes to the sprite you would like to tween.

9. Click **OK**, click the **Rewind** button ⏮ on the taskbar, click the **Play button** ▶ on the taskbar, watch the animation several times, then click the **Stop button** ■ on the taskbar

   Notice that the plane goes behind cloud2, which is the cloud in the middle of the stage, because cloud2 is placed in channel 4, and the plane is placed in channel 3. The plane appears to go behind the cloud because it is placed in a lower channel than the cloud.

10. Save the movie

QuickTip

To reposition a sprite, point to the object and drag it to a new location. To resize a sprite, drag one of its handles.

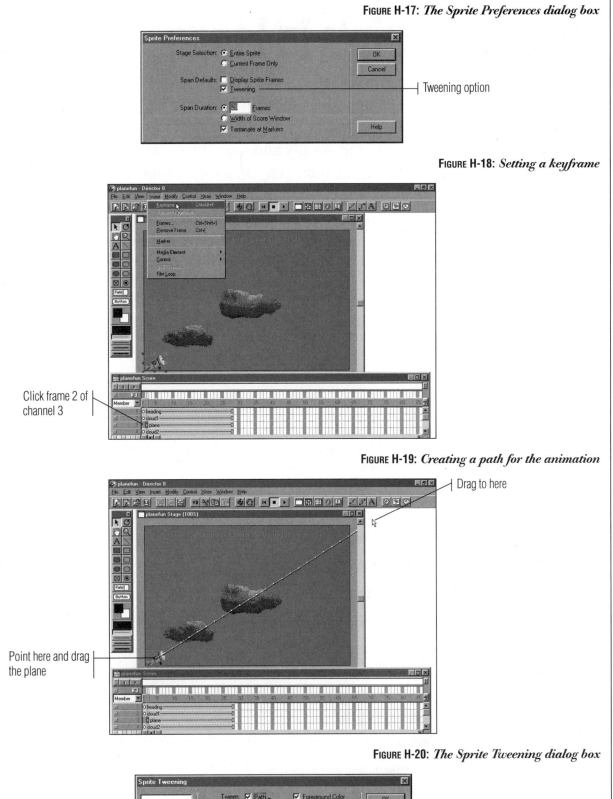

FIGURE H-17: *The Sprite Preferences dialog box*

Tweening option

FIGURE H-18: *Setting a keyframe*

Click frame 2 of channel 3

FIGURE H-19: *Creating a path for the animation*

Drag to here

Point here and drag the plane

FIGURE H-20: *The Sprite Tweening dialog box*

Path check box selected

Creating scripts in Lingo

The controls you have been using to play the movie appear on the menu bar of the Director program. These controls, however, are not available to the user. Without user control, the movie would play automatically and would loop indefinitely. A script instructs Director to carry out a particular function. You can assign scripts to both frames and sprites. Lingo is the name of Director's scripting language. If a script is assigned to a frame, when the playback head reaches the assigned frame, the script executes. For example, to prevent the movie from playing automatically, you can have the playback head pause at frame 1 by creating a script for frame 1. In this lesson you will develop scripts that create user controls for playing movies.

STEPS

1. Double-click **frame 1** in the script channel as shown in Figure H-21, then type **go to the frame** on line 2 in the Behavior Script dialog box

   Figure H-21 shows the completed script in the Behavior Script dialog box. The number in the dialog box refers to the cast number assigned to the script. (Your number may differ.) When you open a script dialog box from the script channel, Director assumes that you will be creating an on exitFrame script because it is such a common script. Consequently, Director displays the beginning and ending parts of the script. You can change these lines to create a different script, if desired.

2. Close the dialog box, click the **Rewind** button ⏮ on the taskbar, then click the **Play button** ▶ on the taskbar

   Notice that the playback head does not move past frame 1.

3. Click the **Stop button** ■ on the taskbar

4. Click **Button** ⬚Button on the Tool palette, draw a button on the stage as shown in Figure H-22, then type **Plane**

5. Click the **Plane button** on the stage to select it, click **Modify** on the menu bar, click **Sprite**, then click **Script**

   The Behavior Script dialog box appears and includes the *on mouseUp* command. The on mouseUp script will be assigned to the button, so when the user clicks the button, the next line of the script will execute.

6. Type **go to frame 2** on line 2 in the Behavior Script dialog box, then close the dialog box

7. Click ⏮, then click ▶

   The movie begins to play but pauses at frame 1, as dictated by the script in the frame 1 script channel.

8. Click the **Plane button** on the stage

   The movie plays and pauses again at frame 1.

9. Click the **Plane button** on the stage

   The movie plays again. In a later lesson you will learn how to create interactivity so that the movie will play more than once.

10. Click ■, then save the movie

QuickTip

When working in Director, you must use the movie control buttons on the taskbar to rewind and start the movie before you use buttons on the stage.

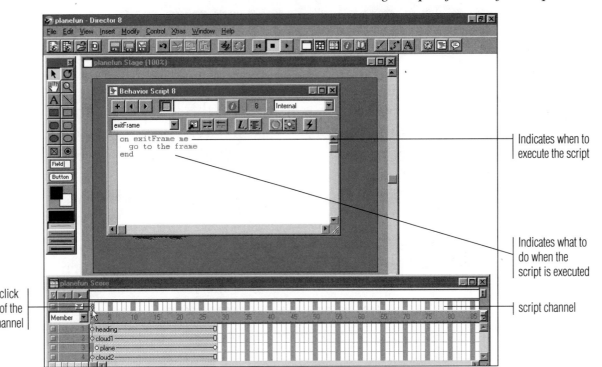

Indicates when to execute the script

Indicates what to do when the script is executed

script channel

Double-click frame 1 of the script channel

Button tool

Drag to here

Start here

Adding a second animation

Currently, the movie is linear. That is, once it begins to play, each frame is played sequentially—frame 1, frame 2, frame 3, and so on. In this lesson, you will create a second animation. You will then set up the score so that the user can jump to a different part of the movie and play frames out of sequence. The second animation will be placed in the same channel as the plane, but in different frames. You will need to change the score so that the other sprites (the heading and the clouds) appear in more frames.

STEPS

1. Click **Window** on the menu bar, click **Cast**, click **Modify** on the menu bar, click **Movie**, then click **Properties**

   The Cast window and the Property Inspector dialog box appear.

Trouble?

Drag the Cast window/Property Inspector dialog box out of the way.

2. Point to the **rectangle** in frame 28 of channel 1 (the heading), drag it to **frame 85** as shown in Figure H-23, then repeat this action for channel 2 (cloud1) and channel 4 (cloud2)

   The sprites in channels 1, 2, and 4 will appear in the movie from frame 1 to frame 85.

Trouble?

Resize the cast window if necessary to see all cast members

3. Click **frame 30 in channel 3** of the score, drag the **plane** from the Cast window to the lower-left corner of the stage as shown in Figure H-24, click the **plane** to select it, then use the Property Inspector dialog box to make the background transparent

4. Click **Insert** on the menu bar, click **Keyframe**, click **frame 57 in channel 3**, click **Insert** on the menu bar, then click **Keyframe**

5. Point to the **small circle** on the plane, hold down the mouse button, drag the plane behind the top cloud so that it disappears, click **Modify** on the menu bar, click **Sprite**, click **Tweening**, be sure that **Path** is checked, then click **OK**

6. Click **frame 58 in channel 3** of the score, then drag the **hot air balloon** from the Cast window to the center of the top cloud

   The balloon will not be visible because it is located in the channel before cloud2. Nevertheless, you can still see the frame and the sizing handles of the balloon.

Trouble?

If you have difficulty selecting the hot air balloon, move the cloud, select the balloon, complete Step 8, then move the cloud back into position.

7. Click a **handle of the hot air balloon** use the Property Inspector to make the background transparent, click **Insert** on the menu bar, click **Keyframe**, click **frame 85 in channel 3**, click **Insert** on the menu bar, then click **Keyframe**

8. Point to the **small circle** on the hot air balloon, hold down the mouse button, drag the circle straight up and off the screen as shown in Figure H-25, click **Modify** on the menu bar, click **Sprite**, click **Tweening**, be sure that **Path** is checked, then click **OK**

9. Close the Cast window, close the Property Inspector dialog box, click ⏮, click ▶, then click the **Plane button** on the stage

10. The movie plays both animations: the plane moving diagonally across the stage and the plane hiding behind cloud 2 as a hot air balloon emerges from behind cloud 2.

11. Click ⏹, then save the movie

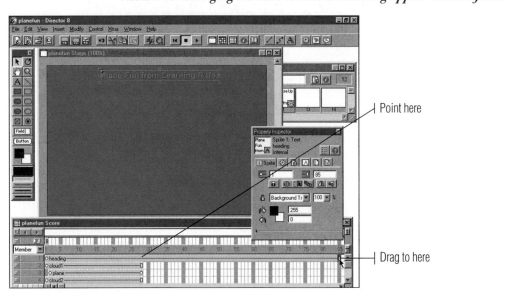

Point here

Drag to here

FIGURE H-24: *Positioning the plane for the second animation*

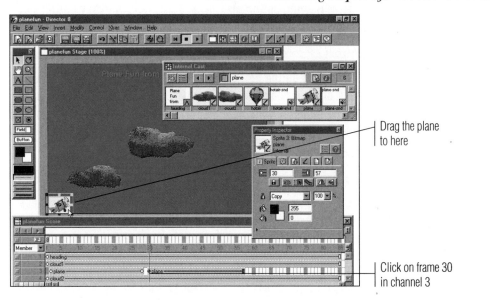

Drag the plane to here

Click on frame 30 in channel 3

FIGURE H-25: *Creating the path for the hot air balloon*

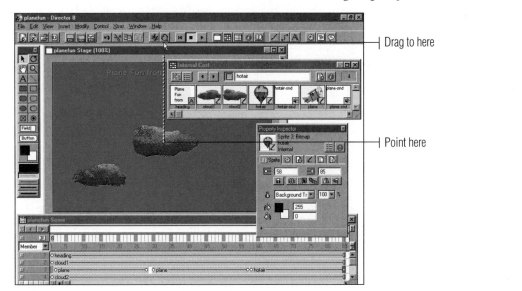

Drag to here

Point here

Creating interactivity with buttons

Your movie is almost finished, but a few more enhancements will make it even better. For example, you want to add buttons to give the user control over the animations and the title. The user should be able to click one button to run the plane animation only and a second button to run the combined plane/hot air balloon animation. The user should also be able to stop an animation that is running so as to make a different selection. Finally, the user should be able to skip these introductory animations and move to the next part of the application. In this lesson, you will create interactivity by adding buttons and scripts.

QuickTip

You may need to move the Score window and the scroll bars to access channels.

STEPS

1. Double-click **frame 28** of the script channel, type **go to frame 2**, then close the Script window

2. Click the **Rewind button** ◄◄ on the taskbar, click the **Play button** ► on the taskbar, then click the **Plane button** on the stage

   Now only the first animation plays.

3. Click the **Stop button** ■ on the taskbar, click **frame 1 of channel 6**, click **Button** `Button` on the Tool palette, draw a button next to the Plane button, type **Fun**, click **Modify** on the menu bar, click **Sprite**, click **Script**, type **go to frame 30**, close the dialog box, double-click **frame 85** of the script channel, type **go to frame 30**, then close the dialog box

   The Fun button is scripted to show frames 30 to 85 continuously.

4. Click ◄◄ , click ► , then click the **Fun button** on the stage

   Now only the second animation, which shows the plane flying into the cloud and then the hot air balloon rising out of the cloud, plays. Notice that the Plane button and the Fun button no longer appear on the stage, as shown in Figure H-26, because the scores for these buttons stop at frame 28 and the script starts at frame 30.

5. Click ■ , click **frame 1 of channel 7**, click `Button` , draw a button next to the Fun button, type **Stop**, click **Modify** on the menu bar, click **Sprite**, click **Script**, type **go to frame 1**, close the dialog box, then drag the rectangle in frame 28 of channel 7 to **frame 85**

   Figure H-27 shows the Stop button and the adjusted score. The score for the Stop sprite extends to frame 85 so that the Stop button appears throughout the movie, regardless of which animation is playing.

6. Click **frame 1 of channel 8**, click `Button` , draw a button next to the Stop button, type **Next**, point to the **rectangle** in frame 28 of channel 8, then drag the rectangle to **frame 85**

   This button will be left inactive for this tutorial.

7. Point to the **rectangle** in frame 28 of channel 5, drag the rectangle to **frame 1**, point to the **rectangle** in frame 28 of channel 6, then drag the rectangle to **frame 1**

   The Plane button and the Fun button will appear only when frame 1 of the movie is played. The Stop button and the Next button will still appear as the entire movie is played.

8. Click ◄◄ , click ► , click the **Plane button** on the stage, watch the animation several times, click the **Stop button** on the stage, click the **Fun button** on the stage, watch the animation, click the **Stop button** on the stage, then click ■

9. Save the movie

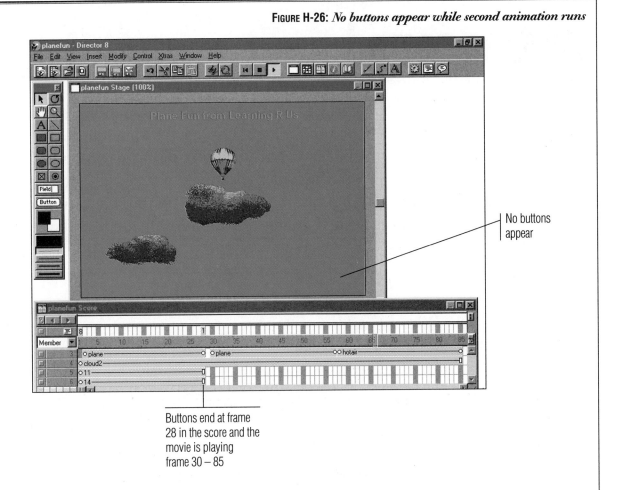

No buttons
appear

Buttons end at frame
28 in the score and the
movie is playing
frame 30 – 85

FIGURE H-27: *Score adjusted so Stop button appears on the screen from frame 1 to 85*

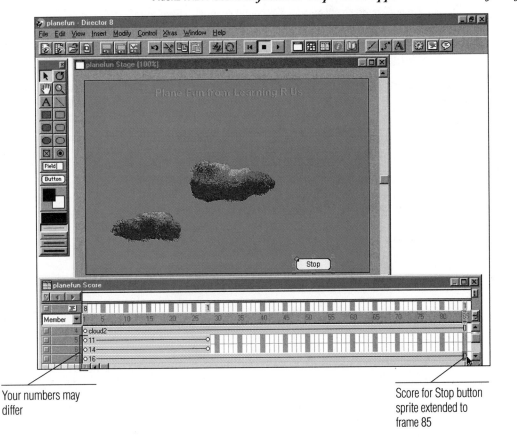

Your numbers may
differ

Score for Stop button
sprite extended to
frame 85

Adding sound

To add more excitement to your movie, you will include two sounds. The first sound, which is the plane-snd file, will play in frames 2 through 57 while the plane is animated. The second sound, which is the hotair-snd file, will play in frames 58 through 85 while the hot air balloon is animated. Director provides two sound channels in the score. To add sound to a movie, you drag a sound cast member to the starting frame in a sound channel and then extend the score as needed. In this lesson, you will add sound cast members to your movie.

STEPS

1. Click **Window**, then click **Cast**

   The Cast window appears as shown in Figure H-28.

2. Click the **Hide/Show Effects Channels button** ⬍ on the Score window as shown in Figure H-29

   The effects channels appear in the Score window. You can use them to insert scripts and sounds, change the playback speed of the movie, and specify palettes and transitions.

3. Drag the **plane-snd** sound file from the Cast window to frame 2 of sound channel 1 as shown in Figure H-30

4. Drag the **rectangle** in frame 29 of sound channel 1 to frame 57

   The airplane sound has been added to sound channel 1. This sound will be heard each time the playback head passes over frames 2 through 57.

5. Drag the **hotair-snd** sound file from the Cast window to frame 58 of sound channel 1

   The hotair-snd sound has been added to sound channel 1. This sound will be heard each time the playback head passes over frames 58 through 85. You are now ready to test your movie with the sounds.

6. Close the Cast window, then click the title bar of the stage to make it active

7. Click **Rewind** ⏮ on the taskbar, click **Play** ▶ on the taskbar, click each button on the stage to test it, then click the **Stop button** on the stage to end each animation

8. Click **Stop** ■ on the taskbar

9. Save the movie

FIGURE H-28: *Updated Cast window*

FIGURE H-29: *The Hide/Show Effects Channels button in the Score window*

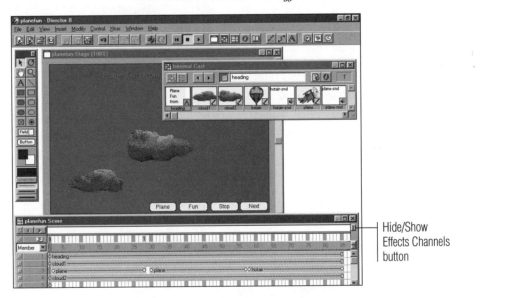

Hide/Show
Effects Channels
button

FIGURE H-30: *Placing the plane-snd cast member in sound channel 1*

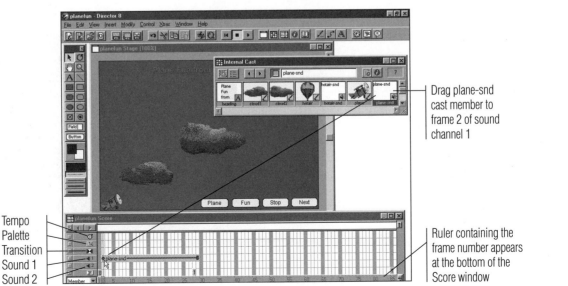

Drag plane-snd
cast member to
frame 2 of sound
channel 1

Tempo
Palette
Transition
Sound 1
Sound 2

Ruler containing the
frame number appears
at the bottom of the
Score window

Distributing the movie

There are three main ways to distribute a Director movie. First, you can save the movie using the Save function; with this function you specify a name for the movie file and the Director appends a .dir extension. You used this process to create the planefun.dir movie. A .dir file can be distributed in the same manner as any other file. To play the movie, however, the user must have the Director program installed on his or her computer. Second, you can use the Create Projector function to create a stand-alone version of the movie. A stand-alone version is a file that can be played without having the Director program installed on the computer. Once a .dir or stand-alone file has been created, it can be distributed on a CD/DVD, on a Zip disk, or even attached to an e-mail.

STEPS

Creating a projector movie:

1. Close all windows except for the Stage window

2. Click **File** on the menu bar, click **Create Projector**, click **Files of type** list arrow, select **Director Movie**, Navigate to the **mymovie[your name]** folder if necessary, click **planefun**, then click **Add**

   Figure H-32 shows the completed Create Projector dialog box.

3. Click **Create**

   The Save projector as dialog box appears.

4. Type **fun-movie** in the File name text box, then click **Save**

   Director creates the projector and saves it in the same folder where the Director movie is located.

5. Minimize the Director window, navigate to the **mymovie[your name]** folder, then double-click **fun-movie**

   A window appears with the first frame of the movie as shown in Figure H-32. The file fun-movie uses an .exe extension. It is an executable file, which means it is self-running.

6. Click a button to run the movie, close the movie window after you have tested all the buttons, then return to Director

FIG H-31: *The Create Projector dialog box*

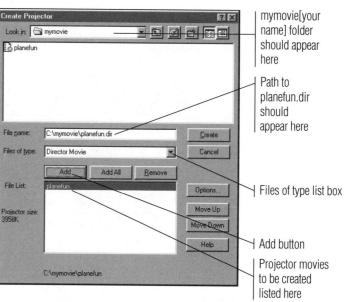

mymovie[your name] folder should appear here

Path to planefun.dir should appear here

Files of type list box

Add button

Projector movies to be created listed here

FIG H-32: *A Projector window*

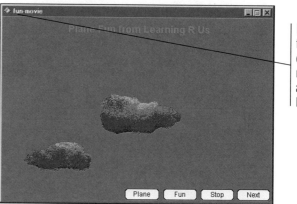

Icon identifies this as an executable movie file created with Director

Third, you can use the Publish function to create a movie that can be displayed in a browser. When you use the Publish function, Director creates a movie in Macromedia's Shockwave format. Then, with the Shockwave player installed on the computer, the movie can be distributed over the Web. The user would not need the Director program to view the movie over the Web. Once a .dir movie has been made into a projector or a Shockwave format, it cannot be edited, even in Director.

STEPS

Creating a Shockwave movie:

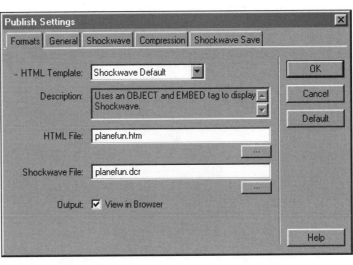

FIG H-33: *The Publish Settings dialog box*

1. Before creating the Shockwave movie, you will use the Publish setting feature to set certain options, including creating an HTML document that will automatically display the movie in your browser. Be sure that the **planefun** movie appears in the Stage window, click **File** on the menu bar, then click **Publish Settings**

   The Publish Settings dialog box appears as shown in Figure H-33. The Formats tab shows that Director will use the Shockwave Default template to create an HTML File named planefun.htm and save the Shockwave file as planefun.dcr. It also shows that the Shockwave movie will be output to the browser for viewing.

2. Your dialog box should resemble Figure H-33; if it does not, make the necessary changes, then click **OK**

3. Click **File** on the menu bar, click **Publish**, then if a message appears asking you to save the movie, click **Yes**

   The Shockwave file (planefun.dcr) and the HTML document (planefun.htm) that plays the movie are created and saved to the mymovie[your name] folder.

   At this point your browser may launch itself, and the movie will start automatically, as shown in Figure H-34. If not, complete Step 4 to view the movie using your browser.

4. Start your Web browser, navigate to the **mymovie[your name]** folder, then open the file **planefun.htm**

   The movie opens in your browser.

5. Click the buttons to play the movie

6. Close your browser, then exit Director

Browser icon   URL of movie

FIG H-34: *The movie playing in a browser*

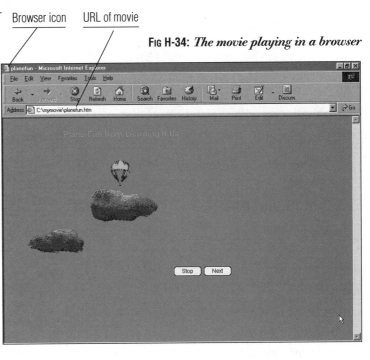

End of Unit Exercises

CONCEPT REVIEW

Label each of the elements shown in Figure H-35.

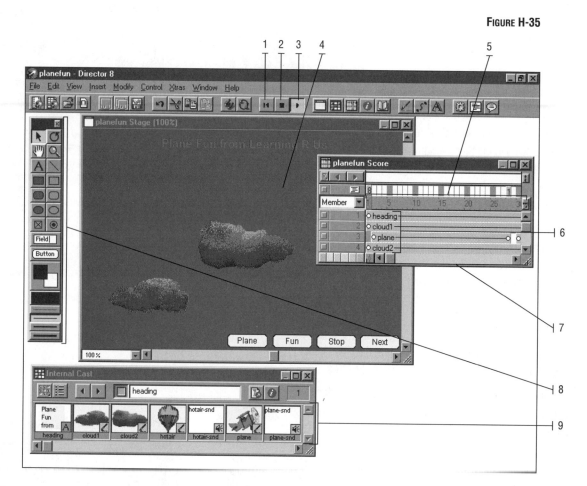

Match the term with the statement that best describes it.

10. Director

11. Sprite

12. Lingo

13. Property Inspector

14. Tweening

a. One instance of a cast member

b. Used to set properties

c. A process to create animations

d. An authoring program

e. A scripting language

Select the best answer from the list of choices.

15. The first step in planning a movie is determining the _____.

    a. Target audience

    b. Treatment

    c. Specifications

    d. Concept

16. **Cast members can include all of the following except** _____.

   a. Buttons

   b. Sounds

   c. Video

   d. All of the above can be cast members.

17. **The Property Inspector could be used to** _____.

   a. Create buttons

   b. Import cast members

   c. Change the background color of a movie

   d. Create an animation

18. **The Button tool is found on the** _____ **palette.**

   a. Tool

   b. Button

   c. Property Inspector

   d. Draw

19. **To place a cast member on the stage, you** _____.

   a. Import it from the Cast window

   b. Copy it from the Cast window

   c. Drag it from the Cast window

   d. Link it from the Cast window

20. **A "go to the frame" script causes the movie to** _____.

   a. Jump ahead one frame

   b. Jump back one frame

   c. Stop the movie

   d. Pause

21. **Which of the following cannot be used by Director to create animations?**

   a. Recording a sprite's movement

   b. Displaying a series of sprites one at a time

   c. Tweening

   d. All of the above can be used to create animations.

22. **The** _____ **command is used to create a Director movie that can be displayed on the Web.**

   a. Publish

   b. Projector

   c. HTML

   d. Convert

23. **The** _____ **command is used to create a stand-alone Director movie.**

   a. Publish

   b. Projector

   c. Shockwave

   d. Convert

24. To play a Shockwave movie you need _____.

    a. A CD

    b. A Shockwave player

    c. The Director program

    d. A projector

25. Which of the following is part of a Director script?

    a. On buttonUp

    b. On MouseUp

    c. When ButtonUp

    d. When MouseUp

SKILLS REVIEW

1. Plan the movie.

    a. Use Figure H-36 to list the goal and target market audience for the movie.

    b. Sketch the storyboard with the navigation options that might have been used to develop the movie.

    c. Create a folder on your destination drive named UHSR[insert your name here].

    d. Copy the files from the drive and folder (UHSR) where your Project Files are located to the UHSR[your name] folder. (*Note:* You should copy six files: airplane.tif, airplane-snd.wav, flower.tif, rain.bmp, raincloud.tif, and rain-snd.wav.)

    e. Refer to Figure H-36 as you create the movie.

2. Set the movie properties and use the Tool palette.

    a. Start Director and open the following windows: Tool palette, Stage, Score, Cast.

    b. Set the movie properties to the following: System palette: Win or Mac as appropriate; Width: 500; Height: 330; Background Color: light blue (#0099FF).

    c. Use the Text tool to create the heading "Plane Rain" with the following specifications: Center top location on the stage; Arial; Bold; 18 pt; green (#336633).

    d. Use the Property Inspector to create a background transparent effect and name the sprite "heading."

FIGURE H-36

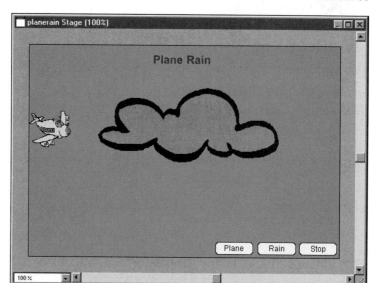

   e. Extend the heading score so that it occupies frames 1–95 in channel 1 of the Score window.

   f. Save the movie with the name planerain in the UHSR[your name] folder.

3. Assemble the cast.

   a. Import the following six files from the UHSR[your name] folder on your destination drive into the movie: airplane, airplane-snd, flower, rain, raincloud, and rain-snd. If requested, set the graphics to bitmap, and the stage to 16 bits.

   b. Show the cast members as thumbnails. Then, starting in frame 2 of channel 2, place the airplane at the left side of the stage as shown in Figure H-36 and make the background transparent.

   c. Starting in frame 1 of channel 4, place the rain cloud near the top center of the stage, as shown in Figure H-36, and make the background transparent. Extend the rain cloud score so that it occupies frames 1–95.

   d. Play and then save the movie.

4. Animate the movie.

   a. Verify that the Tweening check box is selected in the Sprite option of the Preference choice of the File menu.

   b. Insert a keyframe at frame 2 of the airplane score.

   c. Drag the airplane (using the circle) horizontally across the stage so that it passes behind the cloud and off of the right side of the stage.

   d. Insert a keyframe at frame 29 of the airplane score.

   e. Modify the airplane sprite to use tweening.

   f. Rewind and play the movie. The airplane should move from left to right across the stage and behind the cloud.

   g. Make adjustments as necessary and save the movie.

5. Create scripts with Lingo.

   a. Insert a script into frame 1 of the script channel to cause the movie to pause.

   b. Insert a script into frame 95 of the script channel to cause the movie to loop, starting at frame 30.

   c. Select frame 1 of channel 2 and use the Button tool to create the Plane button as shown in Figure H-36. Create a script for the button such that clicking it causes the playback head to go to frame 2.

   d. Rewind and play the movie. Click the Plane button. Stop the movie and save it.

6. Add a second animation.

   a. Create the same animation a second time using a new airplane sprite in frames 30–67 of channel 2.

   b. Select frame 40 of channel 3, drag the rain cast member behind the cloud, and make the background transparent. Make the sprite go from frame 40 to frame 74.

   c. Insert a keyframe at frame 40 of the rain score.

   d. Drag the rain image (using the circle) vertically straight down the stage so that it goes off the bottom of the stage.

   e. Insert a keyframe at frame 74 of the rain score.

   f. Modify the rain sprite to use tweening.

   g. Rewind and play the movie, then click the Plane button. Stop the movie.

   h. Make adjustments as necessary and save the movie.

7. Create interactivity with buttons and add cast members.

   a. Insert a script into frame 29 of the script channel to cause the playback head to go to frame 2.

   b. Using frame 1 of channel 3, create the Rain button, as shown in Figure H-36, and add a script that will cause it to go to frame 30. Reduce the button score to frame 1 only.

c. Using frame 1 of channel 5, create the Stop button, as shown in Figure H-36, and add a script that will cause it to go to frame 1. Increase the button score to occupy frames 1–95.

d. Select frame 68 of channel 2 and place the flower cast member on the stage to create one of the flower sprites shown in Figure H-36. Make the background transparent.

e. Select frame 75 of channel 3 and place the flower cast member on the stage to create another flower sprite. Make the background transparent. Reduce the sprite in the Score window to frames 75–95.

f. Select frame 82 of channel 6 and place the flower cast member on the stage to create another flower sprite. Make the background transparent. Reduce the sprite in the Score window to frames 82–95.

g. Rewind and play the movie, test the buttons and make adjustments as necessary, then stop the movie and save it.

8. Add sound.

a. Place the airplane-snd cast member into frame 2 of sound channel 1 and extend the airplane-snd score so that it occupies frames 2–67.

b. Place the rain-snd cast member into frame 40 of sound channel 2 and extend the rain sound to frame 74.

c. Rewind and play the movie, test the buttons and make adjustments as necessary, then save the movie.

9. Distribute the movie.

a. Create a projector movie and save it to your UHSR[your name] folder with the file name rain-movie.

b. Run the projector movie and test all the buttons.

c. Close the Projector window.

d. Create a Shockwave movie named planerain.

e. Open your browser, run the Shockwave movie, and test all the buttons.

f. Close the browser and exit Director.

INDEPENDENT CHALLENGE 1

You have been asked to create a Director movie that will become part of a series highlighting national landmarks. This movie will include an introductory screen that, when the user clicks the Start button, will be converted to four images. The user can click on each image to enlarge it. Figure H-37 shows the three screens that the user sees.

To complete this independent challenge:

a. Create a folder on your destination drive titled UHIC1[insert your name here]. Copy all files from the drive and folder (UHIC1) where your Project Files are located to UHIC1[your name]. (Note: You will copy six files.)

b. Start Director and open the Stage, Cast, Score, and Tool palette windows.

FIGURE H-37

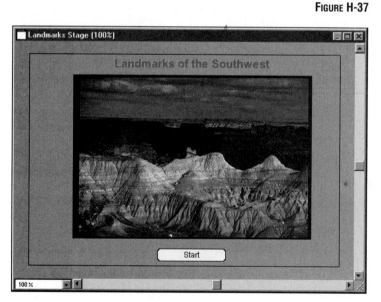

c. Set the following movie properties: System: Win or Mac; Size: 500 × 330; Background: gray (#BBBBB).

d. Import the following files: arches-sm, bryce-sm, canyon-lg, dwelling-sm, monument-lg, and monument-sm. Be sure to set the graphics so they all have the same settings in a 16-bit system.

e. In frame 1 of the script channel, enter a "go to the frame" script.

f. Select frame 1 of channel 1, then use the text tool to create the heading "Landmarks of the Southwest" in Arial, 18 pt, bold, purple; the background should be transparent. Extend the score from frame 1 to frame 82.

g. Select frame 1 of channel 2, then drag the canyon image to the center of the stage. Reduce the score for the image to frame 1 only.

h. Select frame 1 of channel 3, then create the Start button at the bottom of the screen. Create a script for the button to have it go to frame 5. Reduce the score for the button to frame 1 only.

i. Select frame 5 of channel 2, then drag the monument-sm image to the upper-left side of the stage. Extend the score for the image to frame 50. Create a script for the image so that the image goes to frame 55.

j. Continue placing the other three images on the stage as follows:

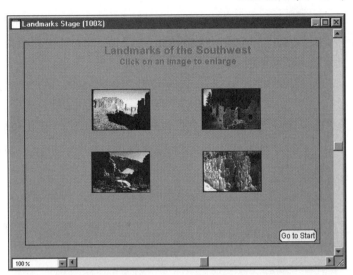

NAME	LOCATION ON SCREEN	CHANNEL	START FRAME	END FRAME
bryce-sm	lower right	3	20	50
arches-sm	lower left	4	35	50
dwelling-sm	upper right	5	50	50

k. Select frame 50 of channel 6 and use the Text tool to create the subheading "Click on an image to enlarge" in Arial, 14 pt, purple; the background should be transparent. Reduce the subheading score to frame 50.

l. Select frame 50 of channel 7, create a button at the right of the stage, type *Go to Start*, add a script that goes to frame 1, then extend the button's score to frame 82.

m. In frame 50 of the script channel, enter a "go to the frame" script.

n. Select frame 55 of channel 2, drag the monument-lg image to the middle of the stage, then extend the score to frame 82.

o. Select frame 55 of channel 3, create the Return button below and to the left of the image, extend the score to frame 82, then enter a "go to frame 50" script.

p. Select frame 55 of channel 8 and create the title "Monument Valley, AZ" below the image in Arial, 14 pt, purple, bold. Make the background transparent, and extend the score to frame 82.

q. Select frame 82 of the script channel and enter a "go to the frame" script.

r. Save the movie with the name Landmarks, then rewind and play it.

s. Click the Start button, then click the monument image.

t. Test all the buttons and make adjustments as necessary.

INDEPENDENT CHALLENGE 2

You have been asked to create a Director movie that will become part of a series of quiz questions. This movie will include an introductory screen that, when the user clicks the Listen button, will play a sound. When the user chooses one of the images on this screen, an appropriate message appears and sound plays. Figure H-38 shows the three screens that the user sees.

FIGURE H-38

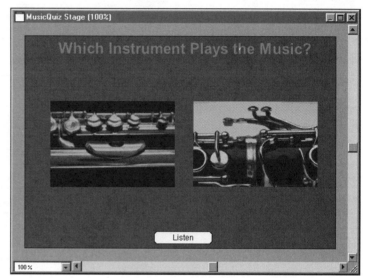

To complete this independent challenge:

a. Create a folder on your destination drive titled UHIC2[insert your name here]. Copy all files from the drive and folder (UHIC2) where your Project Files are located to UHIC2[your name].

b. Start Director and open the Stage, Cast, Score, and Tool palette windows.

c. Set the following movie properties: System: Win or Mac; Size: 500 × 330; Background: maroon (#800000).

d. Import the following files from your UHIC2[your name] folder: applause-snd, clarinet, clarinet-snd, flute, and thud-snd. Be sure that all graphics are set to use the same 16-bit setting.

e. Use the script channel to pause the movie at frame 1 and again at frame 2.

f. Create the heading "Which Instrument Plays the Music?" in Arial, 24 pt, bold, gray; the background should be transparent. Have the heading appear in frames 1 and 2 only.

g. Create the Listen button at the bottom center of the screen, and have the movie jump to frame 2 when the user clicks the button. Have the button appear in frames 1 and 2 only.

h. Have the flute appear on the left of the stage in frames 1 and 2 only. When the user clicks on the flute, have the movie jump to frame 35.

i. Have the clarinet appear on the right of the stage in frames 1 and 2 only. When the user clicks on the clarinet, have the movie jump to frame 5.

j. Have the clarinet-snd sound play in frame 2 only.

k. Have the applause-snd sound play in frames 5–32.

l. Have the thud-snd sound play in frames 35–62. (*Hint:* You can place more than one sound in a sound channel.)

m. Have the following heading appear in frames 5–32 only: "That's Right! It's the Clarinet. You have a good ear for music." It should be in Arial, 24 pt, bold, gray on a transparent background in the center of the stage. (*Hint:* Use Modify, Paragraph, Align Center option.)

n. Have the following heading appear in frames 35–62 only: "Whoops — try again." It should be in Arial, 18 pt, bold, gray on a transparent background in the center of the stage.

o. Have the movie pause at frames 32 and 62.

p. Create a Return button that will appear in frames 32 and 62 that causes the movie to jump to frame 1 when the user clicks the button.

q. Save the movie as MusicQuiz, then rewind and play it.

r. Click the Listen button, then click each image in turn.

s. Make adjustments as necessary.

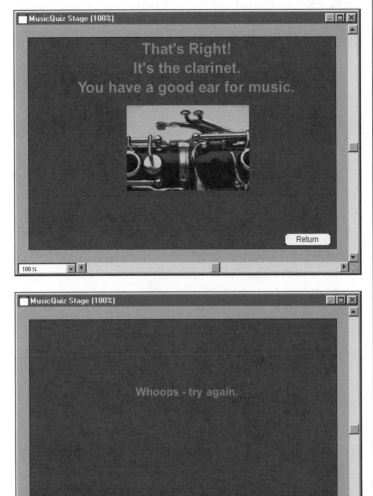

You have been asked to create a Director movie that has an element of surprise. This movie will include an introductory screen that asks the user to find the surprises. The assumption is that the user will start clicking on the screen. When the user clicks on certain parts of the screen, an animation will play. This movie includes two animations: a bird flying from behind trees and a butterfly flying from behind flowers. These "surprises" are created by first placing a background graphic (garden) on the stage, followed by the sprite to be animated (bird, butterfly), followed by a graphic that covers up the sprite (trees, flowers). The trees and flowers sprites have scripts that cause the movie to jump to the appropriate frame to play an animation. Figure H-39 shows the three screens that the user sees.

To complete this independent challenge:

a. Create a folder on your destination drive titled UHIC3[insert your name here]. Copy all files from the drive and folder (UHIC3) where your Project Files are located to UHIC3[your name]. (*Note:* You will copy seven files.)

b. Start Director and open the Stage, Cast, Score, and Tool palette windows.

c. Set the following movie properties: System: Win or Mac; Size: 384 × 256; Background: white.

d. Import the following files: bird, bird-snd, butterfly, flowers, garden, garden-snd, and trees.

e. Use the script channel to pause the movie at frame 1.

f. Use the following table to create the next part of the movie:

FIGURE H-39

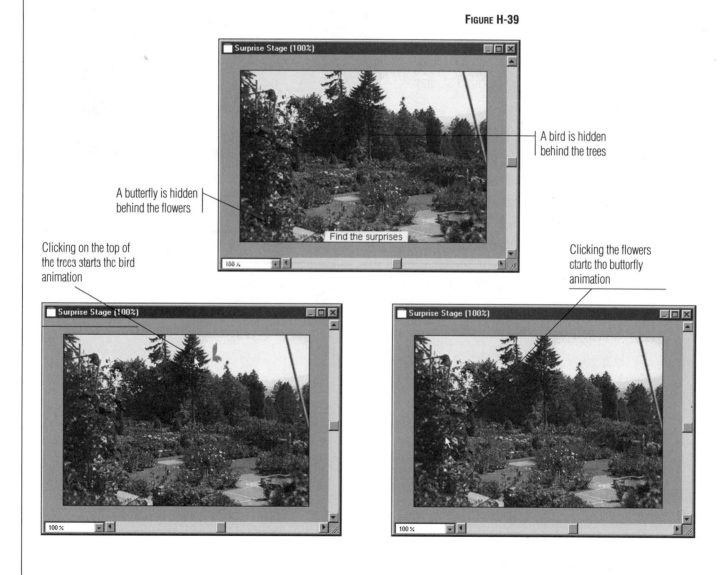

A bird is hidden behind the trees

A butterfly is hidden behind the flowers

Find the surprises

Clicking on the top of the trees starts the bird animation

Clicking the flowers starts the butterfly animation

SPRITE	PURPOSE	PLACEMENT	DISPLAYS OR PLAYS
garden	Used as a background graphic	Covers entire stage	During entire movie
bird	Animation	Starts near top center of stage and moves off the upper-right corner of the stage	When user clicks on trees sprite
butterfly	Animation	Starts near the lower-left corner of the stage and moves off the lower-right corner of the stage	When user clicks on flowers sprite
trees	Used to hide the bird sprite	Aligned with trees in garden background at top center of the stage	During entire movie
flowers	Used to hide the butterfly sprite	Aligned with flowers in garden background at lower-left corner of the stage	During entire movie
bird-snd	Sound to accompany the bird animation	In sound channel	During bird animation
garden-snd	Sound to accompany the butterfly animation	In sound channel	During butterfly animation

g. Create the following heading at the bottom center of the stage: "Find the surprises." It should be in Arial, 14 pt, black. Have the heading appear only in frame 1.

h. Have the movie return to the beginning after each animation has played.

i. Save the movie as Surprise, then rewind and play it.

j. Click on the trees and flowers to view the animations.

k. Make adjustments as necessary.

INDEPENDENT CHALLENGE 4

WEB WORKS

The Web is a rich resource for information about Macromedia Director. In addition to the Macromedia site itself, many other resources are available for creating Director movies. You can use your favorite search engine and the search terms "Macromedia Director movies" to search for information and tutorials on Director. You can also complete the steps in this independent challenge to find resources on Director.

To complete this independent challenge:

1. **Connect to the Internet.**

2. **Go to *http://www.course.com/*, navigate to the Student Online Companion for this book, and then click the link for Unit H.**

3. **The Unit H link contains links to Web sites with information about Director. Click each link to visit the site.**

4. **Write a summary report that answers the following questions:**

   a. Who publishes the Web site?

   b. When was it last updated?

   c. What types of resources are available?

   d. What are the three most useful resources you found and why are they so valuable?

5. **Review two sample movies from the Maricopa site. For each one, include the following information:**

   a. The goal, target audience, and treatment

   b. Features that you liked and why

   c. Features that could be improved and why

   d. New Director features/techniques that you learned from the movie

Create the Director movie shown in Figure H-40, which includes a video clip. First, create a folder named UHVW[your name] on your destination drive. Copy the planet.avi file from the drive and folder (UHVW) where your Project Files are located to your UHVW[your name] folder. Use Director to create a Director movie naming it planetexplore. Be sure to save the movie to the UHVW[your name] folder. Use the callout on Figure H-40 to decide on the other specifications for the movie. *Note:* The opening frame of the movie shows the title and the Play button. When the user clicks the Play button on the stage, the movie plays as seen in Figure H-40. You must have Quicktime installed to run the movie.

FIGURE H-40

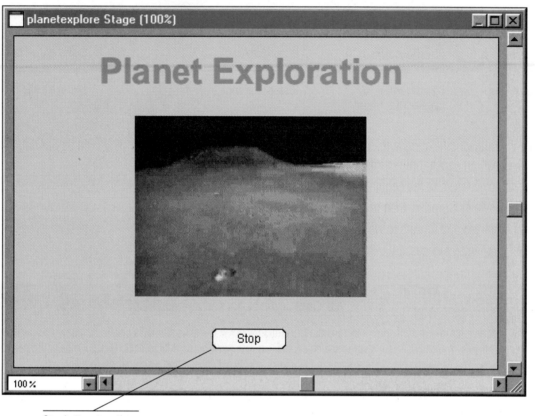

Stop button stops the video clip and returns to the beginning of the Director movie, which shows only the heading Planet Exploration and the Play button

Project Files Listing

UNIT	FILE SUPPLIED ON PROJECT DISK	LOCATION FILE IS USED IN UNIT
G	**Unit G folder:** UGIC1 folder UGIC2 folder UGIC3 folder UGmysite folder UGSR folder UGVW folder	See files listed in each folder below.
	UGIC1 folder: bgtexture.gif resort-lg.jpg roche2-lg.jpg roche-lg.jpg roche-sm.jpg star.gif sunmtn-lg.jpg sunmtn-sm.jpg view.avi warm-lg.jpg warm-sm.jpg warm-sprsnd.wav whale-snd.wav	Independent Challenge 1
	UGIC2 folder: art1.jpg art2.jpg art3.jpg art4.jpg art5.jpg art6.jpg gallery.jpg UGIC2-info.txt	Independent Challenge 2
	UGIC3 folder: balloon.avi balloon.jpg introsnd.wav mail.gif movie-icon.gif UGIC3-info.txt	Independent Challenge 3

UNIT	FILE SUPPLIED ON PROJECT DISK	LOCATION FILE IS USED IN UNIT
	UGmysite: bgtexture.gif resort-lg.jpg roche2-lg.jpg roche-lg.jpg roche-sm.jpg star.gif sunmtn-sm.jpg view.avi warm-sm.jpg whale-snd.wav	Lessons
	UGSR: bluetexture.jpg boom.wav fireworks.avi fireworks.jpg fireworks1.jpg fireworks2.jpg fruits.jpg usflag.gif	Skills Review
	UGVW: Capitol-east.jpg Capitol-west.jpg	Visual Workshop
H	**UHIC1** **UHIC2** **UHIC3** **UHLessons** **UHSR** **UHVW**	See files listed in each folder below.
	UHIC1: arches-sm.tif bryce-sm.tif canyon-lg.tif dwelling-sm.tif monument-lg.tif monument-sm.tif	Independent Challenge 1
	UHIC2: applause-snd.wav clarinet.tif clarinet-snd.wav flute.tif thud-snd.wav	Independent Challenge 2

UNIT	FILE SUPPLIED ON PROJECT DISK	LOCATION FILE IS USED IN UNIT
	UHIC3: bird.tif bird-snd.wav butterfly.tif flowers.tif garden.tif garden-snd.wav trees.tif	Independent Challenge 3
	UHLessons: cloud1.gif cloud2.gif hotair.gif hotair-snd.wav plane.bmp plane-snd.wav	Lessons
	UHSR folder: airplane.tif airplane-snd.wav flower.tif rain.bmp raincloud.tif rain-snd.wav	Skills Review
	UHVW: planet.avi	Visual Workshop

Glossary

ActiveX controls ▶ allows movies, animations, and sounds to be delivered over the Internet

AIFF (Audio Interchange File Format) ▶ and **AIFFC** (Compressed) audio file formats developed by Apple and used as a standard for Macintosh computers

analog wave pattern ▶ recurring pattern of sound waves

animation ▶ a series of still images that when displayed in a sequence gives the illusion of movement. Also, the second step in the process of creating 3-D objects and scenes; the process of defining the object's motion as well as how the lighting and views change during the animation

anti-aliasing ▶ smoothes the edges by blending the colors on the edge of the image with the adjacent colors; because bitmaps are made up of rectangular pixels the outside edge of the image can appear jagged—anti-aliasing adjusts for this problem

applets ▶ small programs that can be shared with other applications and that are developed for a specific purpose, for example, to track stock prices and periodically display them on a Web page

asymmetrical balance ▶ achieved by arranging non-identical elements on both sides of a center line on the screen

audience ▶ a multimedia title's users

authoring program ▶ used to create multimedia applications

balance ▶ refers to the distribution of optical weight in the layout of an image

binary digit (bit) ▶ smallest unit used to represent the coding of data in a computer

binary system ▶ two symbols (1 and 0) used to indicate "on" (1) and "off" (0), as the way the computer represents data and instructions

bitmap graphic ▶ represents the graphic image as an array of dots called pixels

bits ▶ binary digits

BMP ▶ bitmap graphic file format

bold ▶ a font format that is used for emphasis

browser ▶ a visual interface that interprets Web documents and allows for the display of graphics

budget ▶ outlines the costs of multimedia projects

Cascading Style Sheet (CSS) ▶ a template that defines the way a Web page appears, including text fonts

cel animation ▶ based on the changes that occur from one frame to another to give the illusion of movement

child page ▶ a Web page that has a direct link to a parent page as determined by the file structure

clip art ▶ ready to use illustrations

codecs ▶ compression/decompression programs used to reduce the size of files

color depth ▶ color information recorded for each pixel; the range of colors available for pixels

Common Gateway Interface (CGI) ▶ a specification that allows programs to be written that run on a server and provide a way to get information from a user and return information to a user

computer playback system ▶ a computer system capable of delivering multimedia

cookies ▶ small files containing information about a user that are stored on a user's hard drive and made available to specific Web sites

copyright ▶ provides legal protection and grants certain rights to its owner

decorative font ▶ classification of a type of font, such as script-type, that is more stylish and formal

deliverables ▶ the components of a project that will be provided to a client

derivative works ▶ materials based on an original work such as an adaptation or dramatization

digital camera ▶ used to capture still images just like a regular camera, but in a digital form

Director Shockwave Studio ▶ comprehensive authoring package that allows developers to create multimedia applications for CD-ROM, DVD, and Web delivery

drawing programs ▶ used to create draw-type graphics; provides for freehand as well as geometric shapes; useful in creating designs where precise dimensions and relationships are important

drawing tablet ▶ pressure-sensitive tablet used to generate graphics, including fonts based on your handwriting

draw-type graphics ▶ (also called **vector graphics**) represent an image as a geometric shape made up of straight lines, ovals, and arcs

edutainment ▶ the combination of education and entertainment

electronic slide show presentation ▶ similar to presentations using traditional overhead transparencies or slides but superior because of the power of the delivery system—the computer, which allows multimedia elements to be part of the presentation

elements database ▶ used to keep track of multimedia elements used in a title, determine the overall file size, and provide a reference for filenames that might be used in scripting

exploratory navigation scheme ▶ provides little structure or guidance for the user; relies on user interaction such as clicking on objects that appear on the screen

external storage devices ▶ provide additional storage space to relieve the pressure on a computer's hard drive

---

Fair Use ▶ material that can be used without infringing on a copyright

feature creep ▶ when new features are added, which changes the original specifications and therefore changes the development time

file compression ▶ a technique used to reduce a file size of graphics, sounds, videos, and so on; can be used to speed up the transfer of files through the Web.

file format ▶ the type of file created by a program; common graphic file formats include **TIFF** (Tagged Image File Format), **BMP** (Bitmap), **PCX** (Windows Paint), and **PICT** (Macintosh picture format,) which are the standard file formats for multimedia development, and **JPEG** (Joint Photographer Experts Group), **GIF** (Graphics Interchange file format) and **PNG** (Portable Network Graphics), which are the standard file formats for the World Wide Web

font formats ▶ a way to apply emphasis to text such as bold, italic, or underline

fonts ▶ synonymous with typefaces in a print environment; useful in focusing attention on certain text on the screen, enhancing readability, setting a tone (serious, lighthearted), and projecting an image (progressive, conservative)

fontset ▶ used in Web page design to specify which font(s) to try to use and in which order

frames ▶ used in Web pages as a way to divide a Web page into sections

frame rate ▶ speed of an animation

frequency ▶ indicated by the distance between the peaks in a sound wave—the greater the distance, the lower the sound

---

GIF ▶ Graphics Interchange file format

goals ▶ statements that set direction in support of the company vision

graphics tablet ▶ a peripheral device that can be used for freehand drawing

---

hertz (Hz) ▶ unit of measure used to measure frequency in a sound wave

HyperCard ▶ one of the first multimedia authoring programs to use a card metaphor

hyperlinks ▶ text or graphics that are coded to "jump" to another location in their Web pages

HyperText Markup Language (HTML) ▶ the "coding language" for Web documents

HTML tags ▶ used to mark text, for example, the HTML tags <i> and </i> display all text within the tags in italic—*Welcome!* would be coded as <i>Welcome!</i> in HTML

HTTP (HyperText Transfer Protocol) ▶ a standard format that defines how data, such as·video, is transferred from computer to computer on the Internet

---

icon-based program ▶ a multimedia authoring program that uses a flowchart scheme to represent content or a particular event

image editing programs ▶ useful in making changes in images, such as changing the brightness or contrast, or applying textures or patterns

image size ▶ the display size of an image represented in pixels, that is an image size of 640×480 would be 640 pixels wide and 480 pixels high

installed market ▶ the computers in use

interactivity ▶ the ability of the user to interact with an application

interlaced GIFs ▶ graphics files that can load in stages on the Web

interactive titles ▶ intended for use by individuals in a one-on-one situation or, in cases such as Web-based games, by two or more individuals

inter-screen unity ▶ the design that users encounter as they navigate from one screen to another; provides consistency through-out a title

Internet ▶ a vast communications system linking computers around the world

Intranet ▶ an internal computer network set up to facilitate communications among employees, customers, vendors, and selected others

intra-screen unity ▶ how the various screen elements relate on the same screen

---

JAVA ▶ a programming language used to create Web-related applications

JavaScript ▶ scripting language that is specifically designed to add interactivity to Web pages

JPEG ▶ (Joint Photographer Experts Group) a graphics file format

---

Lingo ▶ a scripting language in Director

looping ▶ a technique that sets an animation to play over and over until the user stops the animation or the loop is complete

lossless ▶ a compression process that preserves the exact image throughout the compression and decompression process

lossy ▶ a compression process that eliminates some of the data in the image and therefore, provides greater compression ratios than lossless compression

---

Macromedia Director ▶ time-based authoring program that uses a movie metaphor

Macromedia Flash ▶ an animation program for developing 2-D animations delivered on the Web

masks ▶ used in graphics programs to isolate parts of an image so that you can work on that part

MIDI (Musical Instrument Digital Interface) ▶ a standard format that enables computers and electronic musical instruments to communicate sound information

milestones ▶ significant accomplishments during the development process, such as the development of a prototype for usability testing

modeling ▶ the first step in the process of creating 3-D objects and scenes; the process of drawing various views of an object (top, side, cross-section) by setting points on a grid

morphing ► the process of blending together two images into a series of images

movement ► relates to how the user's eye moves through the elements on the screen

MP3 ► a popular audio file format standard for delivery of music on the Internet because it can compress very large files including complete songs into small file sizes while maintaining CD quality audio

MPEG (Motion Pictures Experts Group) ► a file format that provides frame to frame compression

multimedia ► a computer-based, interactive experience that incorporates text, graphics, sound, animation, video, and virtual reality

multimedia applications ► a broad term that covers all uses of multimedia

multimedia elements ► text, graphics, sound, video, animation, and virtual reality

multimedia presentations ► involve a presenter and an audience of one or more persons

multimedia titles ► refer to specific products, including CD-ROM/DVD-based games like "Flight Simulator," and educational titles such as "Grandma and Me"

nature of an element ► refers to an element's shape, color, brightness, and type

no balance ► a design that has elements arranged on the screen without regard to the weight on both sides of the center line

object layering ► a feature in a graphics program that allows you to include more than one bitmap in an image and edit each bitmap independently of the others

objectives ► statements that are clear, measurable, and obtainable, and that are developed from the company goals

openScript ► a scripting language in Toolbook

OpenType ► a text standard supported by Microsoft and Adobe

optical center ► a point somewhat above the physical center of the screen

optical Character Recognition (OCR) ► a program used to capture text by translating the text into a format that can be used by a word processing program

optical weight ► the ability of an element (such as a graphic, text, headline, or subhead) to attract the user's eye

outsource ► contract a service provider, that is, someone specializing in developing multimedia applications, to produce the title

paint programs ► used to create bitmap images; useful in creating original art because they provide the tools (brushes, pens, and so on) used by artists

parent page ► a Web page that has a direct link to a child page as determined by the file structure

path animation ► moves an object along a predetermined path on the screen; the path could be a straight line or it could include any number of curves; often the object does not change, although it might be resized or reshaped

PCX ► Windows Paint graphics file format

PICT ► Macintosh graphics file format

pixels (picture elements) ► the smallest units a monitor can display

players ► programs that allow users to run multimedia applications on their computers

plug-in ► a program that permits a Web browser to access and execute files that the browser would not normally recognize

PNG ► Portable Network Graphics file format used for graphics that will be displayed on the Web

postscript ► default fonts for the Macintosh; usually installed with the operating system

PowerPoint ► widely used program for creating electronic slide show presentations

processor ► the component that controls the operations of the computer system and performs calculations

programming code ► instructions carried out by the computer

programming languages ► used to create applications and, in multimedia, to produce sophisticated features such as creating animations and searching a database

progressive JPEGs ► files that can load in stages on the Web

project budget ► the financial plan that affects project decisions

public domain ► material that does not have a copyright

random-access memory (RAM) ► temporary computer memory used to store instructions and data that are used while an application is running

Real Audio(.ra) ► a file format developed by RealNetworks specifically for streaming over the Internet; when sounds are saved in this format they are automatically compressed to reduce the file size

references ► examples that prove the service provider's expertise in creating similar projects, or that provide concrete examples of the service provider's skills which are required to complete the project defined in the Request for Proposal

rendering ► the final step in the process of creating 3-D objects and scenes; the process of giving objects attributes such as colors, surface textures, and amounts of transparency

request for proposal (RFP) ► a document that clearly defines a company's needs for a given project; the RFP is made available to vendors who want to bid on the project

right of publicity ► rights of individuals that requires permission and/or payment for using a person's name, image, or persona

rollover ► function performed when an action occurs as the mouse pointer rolls over (points to) an object

RTSP (Real-Time Streaming Protocol) ▶ a continuous playing streaming technology in which the user's computer is in constant contact with the server playing the video

sample rate ▶ the number of times the sample of a sound is taken

sample size ▶ the amount of information stored about the sample of a sound

sampling ▶ the process that changes analog signals (sound waves) to digital signals (digits)

sans serif ▶ a font that does not have a line or curve extension from the end of a letter

schedule ▶ specifies a project's beginning and end dates, as well as milestones along the way

scripts ▶ program code for specific tasks such as a rollover

scripting languages ▶ programming languages used to create scripts

seek time ▶ time required to find a specific piece of data on a CD; measured in milliseconds

serif ▶ a font that has a line or curve extension from the end of a letter

server ▶ a computer with software that responds to other computers and makes data and programs available to them

sequential navigation scheme ▶ takes the user through a more or less controlled, linear process

Shockwave ▶ program that allows an Internet user to play applications created with Macromedia Director

skins ▶ designs for media players with controls such as start, stop and pause

SMIL (Synchronized Multimedia Integration Language) ▶ a program created to enable developers to specify what should be presented, when it should be presented, and to control the use of transitions within a presentation

sound waves ▶ representations of the vibrations created when a sound is made

sprite ▶ one instance of a cast member in a Macromedia Director movie

stock photographs ▶ ready to use photos often sold by companies specializing in providing graphics for multimedia applications

storyboard ▶ representation of what each screen will look like and how the screens are linked

strategic planning ▶ involves determining where a company is in its industry and where it wants to be; reflects the corporate vision

streaming media ▶ a technology that allows audio and video to be played in real-time on the Internet

symmetrical balance ▶ achieved by arranging elements as horizontal or vertical mirrored images on both sides of a center line of a screen

task analysis ▶ identifies the tasks to be done and who is responsible for each task in the project development

telecommuting ▶ working remotely

text box ▶ an area on the screen that holds text that can be scrolled; a useful technique to help minimize text on a page

thumbnail ▶ a small image that is linked to a larger version of the same image

TIFF ▶ Tagged Image File Format; used for graphics

timelines ▶ used to identify dates for the deliverables and key components of the project

Toolbook ▶ an authoring program based on a book metaphor

topical navigation scheme ▶ allows the user to select from an array of choices or even search for specific information

trademark ▶ a name, symbol, or other device identifying a product; it is officially registered with the U.S. government and its use is legally restricted to its owner

transfer rate ▶ amount of time it takes to transfer video from a server on the Internet to the user's computer

transitions ▶ special effects such as fade in and fade out that can be set to occur between frames in an animation

treatment ▶ how the title will be presented to the user, that is the "look and feel" of the title

TrueDoc ▶ a text standard supported by Netscape and Bitstream

TrueType ▶ default fonts such as Arial and Times New Roman on the Windows-based computers, which are usually installed with the operating system

tweening ▶ a process which automatically fills in the in-between frames after you set the beginning position on one frame and its ending position on another frame of an object in a path animation

typeface ▶ a type design such as Arial or Helvetica

unity ▶ *see* inter-screen unity, intra-screen unity

usability testing ▶ a formal testing process in which potential users are filmed as they interact with a title and are asked to verbalize what they are thinking; this type of testing allows the developer to see what users do, why they interact in the way that they do, and what their feelings are as they progress through the title

vector graphics ▶ (also called **draw-type** graphics) represent an image as a geometric shape made up of straight lines, ovals, and arcs

virtual reality (VR) ▶ an environment that surrounds the user so that he or she becomes part of the experience

virtual reality modeling language (VRML) ▶ a computer language used to create 3-D environments on the Web that allow the user to move through a space or explore an object; especially useful in creating games and educational titles; allows the environment to be dynamic and always changing

vision ▶ broad statement of a company's long-term intentions and goals

volume ▶ indicated by the height of each peak in a sound wave—the higher the peak the louder the sound

---

warping ▶ a special effect that results in distortion of an image

wav ▶ an audio file format developed by Microsoft and IBM that has become widely used for audio on the Web

webcast ▶ a broadcast in real time over the Web

World Wide Web ▶ part of the Internet that allows delivery of multimedia and provides for hyperlinking of content

Index